Seven Seasons

Ann Pusey Bloom

Seven Seasons © Copyright Ann P. Bloom 2015
Published in the United States of America
1st Edition

All rights reserved.
This book may not be reproduced in whole or in part or used in any form or by any means to include, but to limited to, printed, audio, or electronic forms without prior permission in writing from the author.

ISBN 978-1-62806-066-9
Library of Congress Control Number 2015956639

Published by Salt Water Media
29 Broad Street, Suite 104
Berlin, Maryland 21811
www.saltwatermedia.com

All photographs, including the cover image, were taken by the author unless otherwise noted in the caption. The places in parentheses that are listed in the captions of certain photos (Adkins Historical Museum and Complex, Inc., Mardela Springs, MD), (Flea Market 13 Antiques & Used Furniture, Pocomoke, MD), and (Mt. Hermon Plow Days, Salisbury, MD. Spring 2012 and 2014) have graciously provided a venue of historical items that have been photographed by the author. All photos are copyrighted by author with the exception of the postcard "Canning Tomatoes at Pocomoke City, MD," which is within public domain, and five family photos. The author does not wish to copyright or limit the use of photos of ancestors that should remain in the public domain and free for family use.
1. "Harvey and Eva Pusey, a snapshot taken about 1940 by unknown person," page xix.
2. Two images - Carey's sawmill and Harvey T. Pusey with crosscut saw, page 43.
3. "Ancestor Mary," page 314.
4. Harvey and Eva Pusey framed family photo taken about 1922, page 332.

Table of Contents

Dedication	vii
Acknowledgements	ix
Foreword	xi
Preface	xv
Introduction	1
Spring Fever	45
Planting	68
Strawberry Time	87
Hoeing	106
Harvesting[1]	121
Corn Husking and Pear Tree Climbing	150
Canning	164
Grandfather's Gift[2]	180
Basket Making	201
Raccoon Hunting	227
Thanksgiving	238
Wreath Making	248
Christmas	266
Hog Rendering	275
Quilts	294
Epilogue	333
Glossary	335
About The Author	336

---

1. Harvesting is a revised version of A Time Forgotten written by the author and originally published in Wor-Wic Community College's *Echoes and Visions* Volume XIII in 2001.
2. Grandfather's Gift is a revised version written by the author and originally published in Wor-Wic Community College's *Echoes and Visions* Volume X in 1998.

Dedication

This book is dedicated to the Ancestors who were born by the early 1900's and experienced the greatest transition in survival methods—a transition due to modernism and the industrial revolution that went into overdrive as the 20th century unfolded.

This book is written for the youngest generation should they choose to, or ever need to, revert back to the methods of their early 20th century Ancestors.

For Elizabeth and Sierra

Acknowledgements

First and foremost I would like to thank my family, my brother, H. Bruce Pusey, for describing our grandfather's chicken house watering system and the mechanics of farm machinery; and my father, W. Brice Pusey, for contributing certain details about my grandparents' formative years, forest history, the planting of crops, and hog rendering sequences; my daughter, Elizabeth Bloom, for identifying errors, searching through hundreds of my oldest negatives, and helping to provoke my memory on additional information to be added; my husband, Bob, for the constant proofreading and encouragement in completing the book; cousin, Linda Parkhill, for her proofreading; and my granddaughter, Sierra Bloom, for painstakingly sketching my Grandfather's watering system for chickens and for posing in Grandmother's bonnet and feedbag dress.

Thank you to the educators, Elinor Cubbage (Doctor of Education) who, from my first days at Wor-Wor Community College, encouraged me to write; and John Wenke Ph.D, (Professor of English, Salisbury University) who stressed the finer points of creating short stories when I attended his writing classes at SU.

To Patricia Dykes Walker Ph.D. for taking the time to read while on vacation and provide descriptive and positive commentary, thanks so much.

Greatly appreciated are the suggestions, proofreading, and concrete statements in the review provided by Jean McKim King, Ed.S.

G. Ray Thompson, Ph.D. (Professor of History, Co-Founder and Director of the Edward H. Nabb Research Center, Salisbury University) is gratefully acknowledged for his proofreading and suggestions. His genuine interest in this project and complementary Foreword have been a great incentive toward publication.

Last but not least, thank you to Salt Water Media for providing the services for feedback and publishing this book.

Foreword

Capturing an accurate picture of any period of time is not an easy task. Yet, in ***Seven Seasons***, Ann Bloom has successfully thrown open a window into a bygone time. She has made her readers feel as if they are viewing, if not participating in, the daily lives of her grandparents, Harvey and Eva Pusey from the Lower Eastern Shore of Maryland, as they move through the seasons of their life in the Pocomoke Forest area.

Bloom has used the concept of "seasons" in a unique way. Rather than examining the world of the Pocomoke Forest through the prism of the four physical seasons of a year, the author has turned the seasons into distinct periods of specialized work characterizing the lives of most rural families in the Pocomoke Forest. The seven seasons—planting, hoeing, harvesting, canning, wreath making, hog rendering, and quilting—are recreated in minute detail and are related in the way in which a storyteller, schooled in recalling the past, describes bygone times.

Although the conversations in the text are not actually word for word as they took place in the various "seasons" of the year 1962, Ann has depicted with stark clarity rural life as it was lived in the post-World War II forest area. 1962 could have been 1952, 1942, or in many instances, even 1862. That rural life went on in the Forest with little variation from one season to the next, from one century to the next. She has not tried to soften or romanticize the lives of her family. Rather, following the method of the French historian and literary figure, Emile Zola, she has sought to "get under the skin" of the survival methods and special events her grandparents' practiced in order to show what their lives were really like. Neither is she maudlin in her depiction, but with a microscopic accuracy she has detailed the lives of those ancestors whom she loved and has memorialized in this fine account.

The seasons represent the endless cycle, the changeless struggle to survive that was done not only by Harvey and Eva Pusey, but by generations of ancestors before them. Day in and day out, back-breaking daily work was the norm, halted only momentarily by sickness or death. Ann's eidetic image-like words bring to life a humbling, more rustic time than today, a time in which life was lived in a very down-to-earth way. She shows how much more in tune with nature her grandparents were than most people are today. Aside from her seven seasons of work interspersed with daily chores, certain recreations such as basket making and raccoon hunting, climbing trees and the pure joy of a walk in the woods were added. Spiritually, the holidays of Thanksgiving and Christmas were greatly valued and the providence of nature is detailed. But within all of these events, the rising and setting of the sun determined their every step. Also demonstrated is just how little free-time actually existed for rural farmers before modernism engulfed the nation.

Seldom have I seen a more thorough or sensitive depiction of a "memoir" of this sort. In her choice of words, Ann reflects on "who" these people were. Their peculiar dialect brings us ever closer to the "true" people they were. We hear their Eastern Shore twang spoken in no-nonsense sentences. Ann's desire to be an accurate historian has led her to create a wonderful image of a past generation. This mindset will resonate not only with Eastern Shore of Maryland descendants, but with thousands of farm families across the US, both those no longer on their farms and others still eking out a living on the lands of their ancestors.

What a debt we owe to these people. They produced what was necessary for their daily lives, for the lives of those around them, and those across the country during wartime. All too often we forget that this country was forged by people such as Harvey and Eva Pusey. Without them we would not have the comfortable lifestyles we lead today. It is on their bowed backs that today's society enjoys the fruits of their labors. Anyone who has an appreciation for the lives which these hard-working, quiet men and women led will appreciate this memoir.

Read it. My guess is you'll enjoy it as much as I did. The account Ann Bloom provides is the best of both literature and local history, yet can be read as a folk story. Readers will read and re-read this account and as they do so, they will feel that they know Ann's forest ancestors and perhaps have a greater grasp of their own past families' lives as well. It may bring you closer to those "seasons" of life that have ceased to exist for many farm families in the last half century.

G. Ray Thompson, PhD.
Professor of History
Co-Founder and Director of the Edward H. Nabb Research Center
Salisbury University
Salisbury, Md

Preface

In writing *Seven Seasons*, the intention is to detail how my grandparents, Harvey T. and Eva Townsend Pusey, contributed to the history of farm families in Maryland during the mid-20th century. Through ingenuity and inventiveness, they performed the daily, monthly, and yearly demands for survival learned and practiced throughout their lives. Harvey and Eva Pusey lived and worked close to the way they had been taught as children by their parents. They continued to perform the tried and true methods that had seen them through two world wars, economic depressions, countless diseases, and epidemics—defying modernism and ignoring most inventions of an accelerating industrial revolution.

Seven Seasons is creative historical literature, a memoir portraying my grandparents' lifetime through a comprehensive introduction (an historical prelude of their lives) and sequential short stories (a memoir told through my eyes at the age of eleven on my grandparent's farm). The tasks of the seven seasons, planting, hoeing, harvesting, canning, wreath making, hog rendering, and quilting, are described the way I remember my grandparents doing each one and are interspersed with details provided by my immediate family.

The conversations within the short stories have been written in an attempt to relate the actual mindset of the person speaking, describe events, or detail historical genres of the era as I saw them. Some of the shorter scenes and conversations within the stories have been included in order to show certain historical events. Most events described happened over a period of years rather than one year, 1962. Examples are my grandparents' seasonal work done throughout their lives and the guineas that the Grandmother kept for many years previous to the 1960s.

Through the eyes of a child, the year began with the first warm day of spring. After enduring the winter riding on cold school buses, and shut inside classrooms all day, and then home at night studying, the first warm day spent out-of-doors in the spring was a gift and eagerly anticipated. During those warming spring months, the elders readied the family garden, repaired machinery, and ordered parts and seed.

From my perspective as a young girl, the working seasons on the farm were divided into separate, but necessary procedures. Within my limited experiences at that age, those working seasons demanded their own order starting with spring and ending in winter. Each progressed as one overlapped the next and, to my mind, numbered seven:

- Planting the family garden and truck-crops began after the disking had been done. The garden was planted in early to mid-spring with peas, onions, greens, and sometimes turnips. In late May, pole beans, sweet corn, cabbage, black-eyed peas, and potatoes were planted: the vegetables varied from year to year. At the same time the planter and transplanter were readied: then the truck-crop planting season began in earnest from late May until mid -June with the crops of tomatoes, watermelons, cucumbers, cantaloupes, and a large field of corn. The fall home garden was planted with turnips, beets, and greens in August and produced well into December.
- Hoeing and cultivating was usually necessary once the first truck-crop of strawberry picking ended. Weeds in the family garden were hoed and pulled by hand. Many of the truck-crops were cultivated: melons and cucumber runners were turned into neat rows with a hoe and weeds weeded.
- Harvesting included strawberries in late May to early June and then the tomato, cucumber, and melon truck-crops once they had ripened in summer. Those truck-crops coincided with picking the garden vegetables

that ripened at the same time. Some of the fruit trees bore fruit during the hot summer and others in the fall. Other harvests included husking and storing corn and robbing bees of honey. The busiest time for harvesting ran through the months of July, August, September, and into October, but the most time consuming and labor intensive crop to harvest was tomatoes, unless firewood could be construed as a crop.

- <u>Canning</u> was sporadic throughout the spring until late fall, but the bulk of food was canned during the busiest months of harvesting. The cooking, filling of jars, and using the canning bath was a hot procedure. October was also a month for cutting and splitting firewood from trees felled in the spring. However, the timing for cutting firewood varied for each family.
- <u>Wreath making</u> in early to mid-December required two to three weeks of work that included scouring the forest for greenery and berries, cutting saplings and making hoops, cleaning the greenery, and finally tying the wreaths for auction. After the wreaths had been sold, the rest of the month was devoted to Christmas and family.
- <u>Hog Rendering</u> usually began during the first weeks of January and was an arduous chore that required several hands. Once started, rendering could not stop until all meat and fat had either been made into lard, scrapple, souse, sausage, hams, bacon or pork shoulders, most of which was salted, hung, and smoked. The hog's feet and ears were pickled and canned in large wide-mouth jars.
- <u>Quilting</u> and Sewing were main events for late January, February, and early March, months that were miserably cold, too cold for doing anything else. Catching up on rest, sewing and mending of clothes,

stitching quilts, and reading were also done. Tending to three woodstoves in the house became a demanding, cold-weather event. The term fire-burnt found its origin from being cooped up in the house hugging a woodstove that had no blowers to distribute the heat. During freezing weather, either your front was hot and your back was cold, or vice-versa. Many times we could be found sideling up to the stove.

Chosen events and mindsets within those working seasons deserve a story; <u>Spring Fever</u> (With warm spring weather came preparation for crops and mischief too.), <u>Pear Tree Climbing</u> (The curiosity of children went as far as climbing pine and maple trees, but not the pear tree, yet the urge was always there to ascend that old, faithful-bearing icon.), <u>Grandfather's Gift</u> (Understanding nature was essential to farm families), <u>Basket Making</u> (The quilts and wreaths my Grandmother made were works of art. Basket making was another art she knew how to do, but is described as one I learned later in life.), <u>Raccoon Hunting</u> (Considered men's recreation by women), <u>Thanksgiving</u> and <u>Christmas</u> (Harvest's bounty and celebrating Christ's birth were idyllic events for family). Some of those events, especially time with family, gave relief from the demands for income and curing and canning food for the year.

Daily chores performed year-round were cooking, chopping and carrying wood (constant in winter), cleaning out the stoves of never ending ash, feeding and watering the chickens and hogs, house cleaning, washing and hanging clothes outside on the line, then bringing them in to fold and put away, and the morning chore of dumping portable potties.

For farm families like my grandparents, Harvey and Eva Pusey, there was always something that needed to be done. They fell in bed at night because they were tired and arose early for the demands that meant survival. However one perceives the seven working seasons, daily chores, or chosen events, there was hard work involved whether for survival or pleasure. Although Harvey and Eva Townsend Pusey have passed on, the work and struggles within their lives will be remembered in this book.

Harvey T. and Eva Townsend Pusey
Snapshot taken about 1940 by unknown person

Introduction

The Eastern Shore of Maryland lies along the Mid-Atlantic coast of the United States. The lower shore counties of Wicomico, Worcester, and Somerset are situated between the Chesapeake Bay and Atlantic Ocean. Those counties are known locally as the Tri-County area, and contain many towns. Five of those towns, Pocomoke, Princess Anne, Fruitland, Salisbury, and Snow Hill are easily accessible from the Pocomoke Forest since much of that Forest is centrally located between those towns on Maryland's Lower Eastern Shore. Rural families who grew up and farmed within the Pocomoke Forest in the early to mid 1900s retained a knowledge of basic survival. The mindset, actions, and traditions practiced by individuals across the United States aid in the making of our country's history and that includes the farmers with all that they contribute.

The lifeblood of survival is food and even with the family gardens currently being grown, large farms provide the bulk of food consumed nationwide. But now very few of those farms are owned and worked by families like the farmers of yesteryear who planted, harvested, and took truck-crops to a local auction block or factory, and supplemented their income by selling butter, eggs, cured meats, and handmade goods.

In the early 1900s most families in America knew how to grow their own food. Within city limits, residents had chicken pens and family gardens in their backyards. Rural farm families worked side-by-side to provide food, crops, and meat for themselves and to sell. Merchants in towns and those running country stores supplied certain necessities. Movable sawmills cut trees as the need arose. But as the first half of the century progressed with world wars, economic collapses, and raging epidemics—the need exploded for those sawmills to provide lumber and for family farms to provide food, not only for tables nationwide, but for war torn Europe and our troops overseas.

Within the Pocomoke Forest, creeks and branches of water from the Pocomoke River run throughout the forest. At that time, some of those waterways ran into large ponds where mill wheels ground wheat into flour and corn into cornmeal at rural country stores. Families living on farms could easily find a branch or creek to throw a fishing line in and go home with supper. Throughout the Tri-County area, ditches were being dug through farm fields and timberland to lower the water-table on land throughout the three lower counties.

Old sprawling farmhouses and fields ranging from a few acres to one hundred or more dotted the landscape. Portable sawmills were set up wherever timber was to be cut. Each rural community contained enough people, to sustain a country store, church, and one-room school within a six mile radius. Also, a voting house and post office often served two or more of those communities. Most of the residents living in those areas were farmers and their helpers, sawmill workers, and the occasional wandering musician who might stay for a while. Most families stayed within their own small community frequenting the closest church, store, and school. Peddlers selling all kinds of wares traversed through the forest communities with some items that the country store did not offer, things such as spices not found locally, fish, ice, and used items such as pots and pans.

For rural families during that era, the local country store purchased some fundamental necessities for the farmers and sawmill workers—items such as coffee, tobacco, sugar, salt and pepper, flour and cornmeal that had been ground on the premises, wood burning stoves, a minimum amount of clothes such as overalls for the men, and material known to the wives as 'yard goods.' Each store was a place where men gathered and women traded dressed chickens, eggs, homemade butter and cheese, and treadle-sewn clothing for items they needed. Farmers ran a tally at the store, a bill to be paid when their crop was sold, or goods were brought in for trade. A current Sears, Roebuck Catalog was placed on the counter of each country store so that items not available in the store could be purchased through mail order. Usually in the center of each store was a potbellied stove and a checkerboard surrounded by chairs or rockers where men sat hurling their chaw of tobacco at the many spittoons placed in strategic places. Many evenings men sat around a potbellied stove tellin' yarns and spittin'. (See page 237.)

As the industrial revolution picked up pace, one-room schools in the Pocomoke Forest had been boarded up and abandoned by the early 1940s. Even most of the two-room schools had closed: children were being bussed into towns. That transition of rural residents frequenting town began to accelerate during the 1950s and early 1960s. During that time, several family farms produced truck-crops that were taken to local auction blocks. Those families still grew and rendered their own meat and bought only a minimal amount of food from grocery stores in town. Although rural schools had closed, several rural stores, churches, and one or two election houses still remained open.

Most rural roads were still unpaved and chains were required on the school bus tires during heavy snowfall. Up and down the paved and dirt roads alike, one could fully expect to see children on bicycles going from one family farm to another, yet staying within a couple miles of home. Farm dogs ran loose, but usually stayed within the confines of the family farm. Packs of wild dogs, unwanted dogs dropped off in rural areas by townspeople, roamed the woods and became a problem for many rural families.

From the 1960s to the 70s some rural businesses were still open, yet abandoned buildings could be found dotting the landscape within the heavily-wooded Pocomoke Forest. The small rural election houses were defensively held open by forest residents. The rural post offices had closed and several churches were being abandoned and boarded up as well, while others struggled to stay open. And as attempts were made to save the church structures, several of those country stores became overrun by vines and left to ruin. Portable sawmill use declined as well.

For the rural residents of the Pocomoke Forest, the mid to latter 1900s saw the demise of their convenient places of worship and doing business—all due to an industrial revolution that had begun to accelerate. Rural life on the Lower Shore changed immensely. Rural roads were being paved, tar and chipped, as vehicles and equipment improved in performance and speed. At the same time, electricity and telephones became increasingly available out into remote areas. As a result of electricity, household appliances were drastically improved enabling women's laborious tasks to be completed at the flick of a wrist.

Over the span of just a couple decades, people could easily access the local towns. The country stores closed because advancements in roads and vehicles enabled residents to quickly travel to one of the surrounding towns and back. Also, rural shoppers could get a better selection and better prices from the larger stores in town that were able to buy in bulk and sell for less than the smaller stores. The Sears, Roebuck Catalog that had been provided by the local country store was replaced by the Sears Catalog which was ordered by residents and mailed to homes by the end of WWII.

The sawmills that had been set up wherever trees were being felled became fewer and fewer. The mules, oxen, and carts were replaced by skidders, cutters, and logging trucks. The population in rural areas began to dwindle—workers found employment in the surrounding towns.

Caught in this revolution were many people born in the late 1800s and early 1900s. Well into the 1960s, they were still following their ancestor's way of surviving—a knowledge of how to subsist off the land requiring little from the outside world. Maryland's Lower Eastern Shore Farmers were primary examples of this work ethic.

Many children born in the 40s and 50s grew up listening to their parents and grandparents talk about how life used to be; about how the rural stores and schools closed; about the illnesses and wars their grandparents had witnessed; and about their wagons, mules, and horses. The nostalgia of losing a way of life grandparents had lived for so many years has been remembered by their children and grandchildren who listened and have not forgotten.

My grandparents, Harvey T. and Eva Townsend Pusey, lived and worked within that setting and largely ignored modernistic changes during the industrial revolution. They were born on rural farms just a few miles apart located in and near Eden, MD, a rural community in northwestern Worcester County. He was born in 1889 and she in 1891: they both passed away in 1973, just months apart. As youngsters, horse and buggies were used, not cars. They both attended a one-room school, church, and frequented a country store, all within the Pocomoke Forest of Maryland. When they were older, they cast their ballot at the rural election house and used the rural post office. All amenities were located within five miles of their home.

They were children during the dawn of the 20th Century and married in April, 1916 as war raged overseas. America entered The Great War in April of 1917 and in January of 1918 they had their first son, Orville. Later that year an influenza epidemic swept the world as The Great War was ending: millions of people died. A slight economic depression followed. After 1920, Grandmother Eva Pusey exercised a woman's right to vote for the first time.

They had witnessed many sicknesses; influenza, typhoid fever, scarlet fever, measles, and chicken pox, some at epidemic proportions. They endured the Great Depression of the 30s while living in the Pocomoke Forest on a farm they called 'The Home Place' where Harvey's parents had lived, located on Greenbriar Swamp Road in northwestern Worcester County. At that time, they were able to feed not only their six children (Orville, Welton, Willard, Howard, Brice, and Doris) but other families as well, simply because they continued the same lifestyle of raising their own food.

My grandfather began logging, using crosscut saws to fell the trees and used oxen, horses, and mules to pull the log wagon. (See page 32, 43.) My grandparents began farming with mules pulling the plows, transplanters and planters. They planted their own food and canned as much as possible: they grew their own meat and rendered lard, while trading within the neighborhood. Rarely buying food, they only bought items such as coffee, tobacco, extra condiments, and once in a while, extra canned food was bought such as corned beef or spam. Some items were purchased from the occasional wandering peddler.

Grandfather trapped muskrats along Dividing Creek and sold them to a man named B. Levin. At that time, the meat and hides from muskrats were a popular income; hides that were stretched and dried. The muskrat was also an additional meat to the hogs and chickens they raised, extra food on the table. Grandmother made Christmas wreaths from forest greenery while grandfather logged. Both grandparents farmed for necessary income and survival. That self-sufficient income was needed to keep the farms up and running and give them the ability to maintain their independent lifestyle.

Neither of them worked at traditional jobs. They used wood for heat and cooking, and occasionally bought coal. Their electricity was used for lights and a refrigerator. They hand-pumped well water their entire lives, yet finally accepted a water pump with running water, but in the kitchen only. They used portable potties and never had a flushable toilet or modern bathroom of any kind, not even an outhouse. They witnessed and experienced the epidemic of 1918 and many illnesses for which they relied on home remedies, rarely on doctors or prescription medications. Although they bought much of their clothing, my grandmother repaired her sons and husband's trousers and shirts, made her own dresses, and saved every scrap of material for quilts. All these events happened during a nonstop industrial revolution that had moved into high gear—a revolution that they largely ignored. Even during the post-World War I economic depression and the 1930s Great Depression—they made do with what they had.

My grandfather dug what were later known as tax ditches, ditches that would help drain waterlogged farmland and woodland in Worcester County. Teams of horses and mules were used to drag the wide scoops to begin digging the Pusey Branch that would later become a part of Dividing Creek watershed. The properties along those ditches were taxed in order to fund the ongoing maintenance of the watershed.

During World War II, 1941-1945, my grandparents and their sons grew crops for the war effort at 'The Home Place' and on their recently bought farms on Fleming Mill Road near Pocomoke. At that time, one son, Orville, entered the army and served in the Pacific Theatre during WWII. During those war years, the number of chickens raised and crops planted by them incorporated all the farms they owned. Food and gas were rationed, and their vehicles inspected. A Certificate of War Necessity was issued with allowable miles to be traveled and quarterly fuel allotments. (See pages 37-41.) Also, signed on February 27, 1945, was their 1945 Farm Plan for 110 acres of cropland. That plan showed the following:

- 16 tons of liming materials; 15 acres of winter legumes, S Clover; 25 acres of small grain, Rye.
- Intended increased crop production from the previous year—field corn from 40 acres to 60 acres; Irish potatoes from 3 to 7 acres; Sweet potatoes from 5 to 10 acres; Tomatoes for processing from 12 to 15 acres; All tame hay from 7 to 9 acres.
- Livestock and poultry production stayed the same for the following year—2 cows and heifers for milk; 200 Hens and pullets for laying; 24,000 broiler chickens; 5 sows.[1]

My grandparents had moved to their farm on Fleming Mill Road shortly before World War II. That farm was located six miles north of Pocomoke in southern Worcester County and contained roughly 240 acres, of which 60 acres were farm land and the balance timberland. Approximately half of the cleared land was used for truck-crops. Adjacent to that farm, they bought a 40-acre parcel in the woods that belonged to an ancestor, John Frank Pusey who passed away in 1887. It was the farm where his 'cow tree' stood—an old hickory that he had used to hang his cows for rendering. (See page 36.) They still owned

---

1. Information from Harvey Pusey's copy of the 1945 Farm Plan from the Agricultural Conservation Program of the War Food Administration. (See page 42.)

'The Home Place' complete with house and barn. They also obtained some woodland tracts within the Pocomoke Forest near 'The Home Place.'

The farm on Fleming Mill Road was situated on the east side of Burk's Mill Branch and Dividing Creek which flowed to the Pocomoke River. That county road ran through their farm splitting a small section of farmland on one side and a larger section on the other. The woods near that branch and creek contained what the older folks called—a virgin cypress—a cypress tree that had not been cut when the surrounding forest, including cypress, had been harvested time after time. It stood as a relic, centuries old.

Across Burk's Mill Branch stood an old millhouse in the 1950s. That millhouse had previously been located on my grandparents' farm on the smaller section of farmland across the road from their house. The old millstone survives today as do some of the nails that had been used in that old cypress timbered house. The millstone, dated 1860 on the back, contains initials which appear to be L.F.H. and O.E.H. (See page 66-67.)

When my grandparents moved to the Pocomoke Forest, some of their older sons stayed at 'The Home Place' and worked back and forth between the Pocomoke and Eden farms. Shortly after moving to the Pocomoke Farm, Grandfather raised milk cows at his Aunt Amelia Butler's farm just a mile away, but a few years later he turned to mainly truck-cropping in the 1950s—a decade for both grandparents that could be seen as the hay-day of family truck-cropping. Farms with old barns and silos can be seen today, along with big two-story farmhouses. As well, farm ponds can be found dotting the landscape. (See page 19.)

Beginning in the late 1940s through to the 60s their family grew as they gained 15 grandchildren. Just four years before they both passed away, one grandson, Bruce, entered the army and was sent to Vietnam.

During the 1950s and 60s, my grandparents' farm on Fleming Mill Road contained a large farmhouse, cypress barn with attached shed and pig pen across the back, chicken house, smokehouse with attached chicken pen, two-bay shed, surviving fruit trees, and WWII era farm machinery. The animals were chickens, pigs, and dogs, and cats, all of which came and went. Grandfather harvested timber off the land that they bought. On their farmland, they produced their fair share of truck-crops throughout those years. (See page 20-21.)

That farm had orchards when they bought it, but not the traditional orchards we see today. The fruit trees, pear, peach, apple, and cherry had lined the fields around the edge of the woods. Those fruit trees were old, so they cut them down to make the fields larger. They left two pear trees standing several yards from the woods in two separate fields, two crabapple trees beside the lane on the north side of the house, and two peach trees near the chicken house. Also, persimmon trees had been dotted along the edge of the woods across the road from the home, but they took out many of those as well.

The large farmhouse had three bedrooms upstairs with a huge attic above them. Grandmother's bedroom was at the bottom of the stairs on one side of the landing, opposite was the living room which led to the dining room and straight through to her kitchen. That kitchen had three exterior walls, an addition to the house that faced the backyard and outbuildings. (See page 62.) The dining room had an adjacent narrow room grandmother called the sewing room, although it was never used for sewing since it was unheated and located on the north side of the house. It was used for storage, especially items that needed to stay cool. A small door in the dining room led underneath the stairs revealing a pantry with long shelves storing home-canned goods. Another dining room door led to a screened porch. One kitchen door led to the same porch. On the other side of the kitchen, a door led directly outside to a flower garden that ran the length of the house. (See page 22-24.)

That garden was a colorful pageant of lilac and snowball bushes, forsythia, daffodils, and bridal wreath, all dotted here and there along the north side of the house. As well, daffodils surrounded the front porch appearing to form a short fence. The foundation was not closed in, so chickens would settle in the cool dirt beyond the brick piers during hot summer days. (See page 85.)

The porch held her wringer washer, a load of stacked firewood, and numerous nails that held coats and hats, a washtub, and pails. Just a few feet from the wringer washer, outside the porch, stood a hand-dug well lined with a 30 inch wide glazed tile that continued several feet below the ground. A wooden platform had been placed atop the tile. The pitcher top hand-pump sat atop that wooden platform and needed to be primed with every use. The last person using the pump would fill a coffee can with water that would be used to prime the pump again. Offset from the well were two huge maples; the roots from each tree had formed large circles above the ground, making areas of play for children. (See page 24, 64, 162.)

A yard-bell stood at the corner of the porch. The bell was used to signal the person in the field for whatever reason, whether for an emergency or lunch.

Outbuildings were numerous and each had a specific purpose. The smokehouse, where hog rendered meats were cured, stood directly in back of the kitchen and had a chicken coop attached which was actually a wire pen with a few stacked wooden nests attached to the backside. Outside that pen were some old grapevines that had originally consumed the back of the smokehouse. Sometimes, Grandmother would pen some of her hens at night to keep them safe from predators. Beside the smokehouse was a corn-sheller that would be used in the mornings to scatter corn for the chickens or for hulling black walnuts that fell from a walnut tree nearby. (See page 30.) Grandmother's clothesline was strung in the back yard close to the house, a place that was just a few yards from the wringer washer on the porch. (See page 30, 64.)

Beyond the smokehouse stood a large building, a barn made from Bald Cypress grandfather had logged from the nearby Pocomoke swamp and milled by Will Pusey's mill. The wide, grayed boards had been erected vertically and painted red. My Uncles and father helped to build that barn. After several decades, very little red remained, but the cypress stayed nearly the same as when it had been milled, showing the rough blade cuts. Even the two doors, which were about two to three feet off the ground, were cypress and led to separate rooms. (See page 26-27.)

The left room of that barn served as a corncrib and had a high cutout open hole for a conveyor elevator to feed the corn into the building. When the corn was piled high, children climbed up to the hole to look out over the farm and throw corn to the hogs. The right side of the barn was a large room for storing half-bushel and bushel baskets with lids, burlap bags, feed and seed, old yokes, and harnesses that were no longer used. Those wooden yokes for oxen and mule harnesses hanging on the walls were left over from the years my grandfather had logged in the Pocomoke Forest. During World War II that room held Irish potatoes and sweet potatoes that were fed through an opening in the back of the barn. As spring neared, Pop-pop and his sons sat in the barn and quartered the leftover Irish potatoes for planting. Attached to the right side of that peaked barn was a sloped, tin-roofed shed with one or another piece of farm machinery parked there. The pigpen ran the entire length of the back of the barn and sloped shed. (See page 189.)

Within the wooden rail fence were wooden troughs and an old abandon bathtub on four feet that had been used to hold water for teams of oxen and mules years ago. When feeding his pigs, Grandfather would shake feed and slop into the troughs and then hand-pump water into a hollowed out cypress tree. Wherever he needed a pitcher-top pump outside, such as the pigpen, he drove a well. In spots, a pump simply sat atop a pipe.

Over to the right of the barn-shed stood a large open-front shed full of farm machinery where hens and roosters roosted on the beams at night and left droppings on the equipment stored there. Half-bushel baskets for the hens had been strategically settled here and there inside both open sheds in order to easily gather eggs. However, a broody hen was a force to be reckoned with.

Beyond the machinery shed stood a chicken house where my

grandparents raised 5,000 chickens to sell, a small amount to the number raised during World War II when they had used the chicken houses on all their farms. Grandmother took care of the 5,000 capacity chicken house most of the time. In 1942 the chicken house was filled with 5,000 Rock Chicks from R.C. Cobb, Massachusetts @ 9 ½ cents apiece = $475.00. The 1954 contract payment for her chickens shows what good care she had taken of those birds. She had been paid what was a very good price for raising 5,000 chickens at that time. Those chickens, not free ranged, had to be fed and watered every day. (See page 25.)

Grandfather had a great system for watering those chickens. In the middle of that long one-story, chicken house was a two-story feed-room which held bags of feed and his custom, gravity fed, watering system. The middle section of the chicken house was two-story in the back and sloped to one-story in the front. The two-story back, had a door below with two windows above. The one-story front of that feed and water room had only a door. The entire chicken house had German lap siding. From the back, the entire length of both sides of the chicken house had doors but no windows. The front of both sides had a series of openings to cool the chickens in summer. Windows similar to the house windows that could be raised and lowered had been installed, but heated the chicken house in summer. So many of them had been boarded up while the house was in use. Long one-board flaps that let heat out during the hot summer days ran the length of the house on each side of the feed and water room.

The chicken house watering system was powered by a gas-driven, kick-start, Maytag, washing-machine motor that was attached to a bicycle wheel by a rubber belt. With the bicycle tire having been removed, the belt then fit the groove rounding the wheel. There was a petal type mechanism in the middle of the wheel attached to a four foot long, one by four inch board. The other end of the board was attached to a wire that was attached to the plunger inside the pitcher-top water-pump. The top of that water-pump had been removed. The pipe supplying water to the pump had been driven several feet below ground level until water was reached; then pipe had been added several feet above ground and the water-pump sat atop the pipe. The bicycle wheel had been mounted above that pump, held in place by short boards extending from a tall 4x4 driven in the ground. Both wheel and water-pump had been raised several feet in the air with the spout of the pump holding a trough that ran to the first huge water barrel. That one barrel fed water to two more barrels through water pipes attached at the bottom of each barrel. The last barrel had a water pipe extending out and down. That pipe had been T'ed at the bottom and ran to troughs on each side of the chicken house. The barrels and pump rested on a heavily fortified wooden cross-member platform raised four feet in the air. (See page 28-29.)

Most of the farm machinery and vehicles used on my Grandparents farm in the 1960s had been bought during WWII when Grandfather had joined the war effort. The hay-rake, planter, and transplanter had originally been fit for mule or oxen and converted to a wooden oak tongue bar hitch so each could be towed by a tractor or truck. There was no 3 point hitch. The following is a list of machinery and vehicles they owned:

- C-model Allis-Chalmers Tractor on rubber tires bought 6/14/1943 for $710.00 from Pilchard Brothers, Pocomoke City, MD. Paid cash. Allis-Chalmers sent a letter of encouragement and offered help to their customers during WWII. (See page 31.)
- Dump Rake 19 X 30 bought 3/17/1944 for $57.60 from Farmer's Supply Co. Oliver Implements, Snow Hill, MD. Paid cash. Also available were Parts, Harnesses, Hardware, Lime, Feed, Seed and Fertilizer. (See page 31.)
- Tiger Transplanter bought 3/8/1944 for $115.00 from Harry E. White, Makemie Park, Virginia. (See page 31.)
- A horse drawn two row Planter, origin unknown.
- 1941 Ford, 1 ½ Ton, Stake body truck used during World War II. Grandfather was given Certificates of

War Necessity and gasoline rations for this truck.
- A 1954 Dodge Car, flat head V8—The first automatic transmission—two speeds in low and two speeds in high and the clutch was only used between the highest low speed and the lowest high speed. To change between the two lowest speeds, you let off on the gas a little and it shifted to the next speed. The two high speeds were similar, fluid driven. This car is believed to be the car Eva bought with her income from making wreaths.
- A 1946 Dodge Truck with a flat head six cylinder, green body with black fenders was used for taking truck-crops to auction. It had a floor shift, eight speeds forward and two speed reverse, standard. That Dodge broke an axle nearly every time it carried a heavy load. (See page 147.)
- A 1961 Allis Chalmers Tractor, origin unknown.
- An Old model Oliver tractor, origin unknown.
- Corn-sheller. (See page 30.)

The one row transplanter (used to plants seedlings) had two seats in the back, one on each side within a few inches of the ground. A barrel holding water sat forward of the seats. The lid to the barrel had another seat which had been used when the transplanter had been mule drawn. The person handling the reins would sit on top of the barrel. But in the 1960s, that seat was empty. Instead of guiding mules, grandfather drove the tractor pulling the converted transplanter via a drawbar. The two people on the seats low to the ground carried plants (mostly tomato seedlings) in their laps and took turns placing plants into an open furrow in the ground made by a V shaped plow on the front of the transplanter. In the center of the V (spade or shoe as it was called) a hose dripped water in the furrow, then tomato plants were dropped in by the two riders, followed by small angled wheels in the back which closed the furrow around the plants. (See page 34-35.)

As well, the mule drawn planter had been converted to being pulled by a tractor. The newer planters planted four rows, but his planter, bought around the end of World War II, planted only two. Mainly used as a corn planter, it had one high seat (no water barrel) that had been used by the person leading the mule team. When pulled by a tractor, someone still sat in that seat to work the lever which raised the planting gears (shoes) at the end of each row and lowered it at the beginning of the next. That lever had not been changed to operate from the tractor. Seeds were planted by rolled teeth. After the seeds were dropped into the furrow, wheels directly behind the shoes closed the dirt over those seeds. (See page 33.)

Also, the markers on each side of the planter were connected by a single chain and had no lever. When one marker was lowered to the ground, it cut a line in the field to mark the outside of a row. The other marker automatically stayed raised in the air by that chain. When the tractor turned down the next row, the marker in the air was then lowered and the other marker was automatically raised off the field by the chain again. The seesaw effect of lowering one side and then the other was either done by the driver using a lever or by someone on the planter raising and lowering the chain by hand. A new line was always marked outside of the last row planted. My grandfather, as well as many farmers in the forest, was slow to convert to tractors and newer equipment—'if it ain't broke, don't replace it,' seemed to be their motto. The markers on his planter still had to be raised and lowered by hand. The markers cut a line in the ground that one tractor tire followed on the way back to keep rows straight and evenly spaced.

We grandchildren growing up in the 1950s and 60s did not know we were witnessing the end of an era. Family truck-cropping as we knew it was coming to an end. A mindset for and the knowledge of how to live a self-sufficient lifestyle on the farm was passing. A wealth of survival methods was slowly being left behind, leaving with each road that was paved, with each new piece of machinery invented, and with each grocery store that was being erected.

After my grandparents, Harvey and Eva Pusey passed away in 1973, their farm showed remnants of the early 1900s—the bygone era of logging the Pocomoke Swamp, WWII era truck-crop equipment, pigpen, and smokehouse with attached wire pen and nests, and a long chicken house, clothesline, double-bay shed, barn, and last but not least, their home—all grown up in weeds. If we could stand in their yard and rewind time, a busy and laborious yet functioning lifestyle of survival would emerge before our eyes. And if we would listen and pay close attention to them, we could learn how to become self-sufficient. (See page 22-36.)

We can reminisce about what has changed, but unfortunately for us returning would be difficult. Yet we can know what hardships and joy their seasons entailed and which of those have been lost.

Spring and early summer brought planting followed by hoeing and disking, but the seeds and seedlings ordered at that time are rarely the ones that we can order today. Our seeds have been and continue to be genetically modified. And now, it is not often that we see tractor and disk sending dust clouds across a field, no-till farming has become standard. The present day farm equipment and vehicles have become so advanced, that the tractors and cars of the World War II era can be seen in museums as relics of the past; however, it seems that the hoe has stayed the same, but is largely unused today except by the family gardener.

Although many people grow gardens today, the variety of truck-crops as a livelihood on the family farm is hard to find. We might see one huge field of tomatoes or one of strawberries. Somewhere else we see one of watermelons or string-beans. Large companies have taken over much of the truck-crop industry, crops that had been handpicked on family farms and carried to a local auction block or canning factory by the man who worked his own land.

Grandfather logged with mules, oxen, and timber cart, rather than tractors, cutters, and logging trucks now seen regularly. Mules and horses dragging scoops to create ditches will not be seen today.

Rather, mowers keep trees and grasses from growing and clogging those ditches and backhoes or excavators are used for cleanout. The number of men needed to log timber and cleanout ditches is far fewer today—a revolution in itself of machines taking the place of manual labor.

The country store stocked with the necessities of yesteryear, a store as it existed in rural areas decades ago, is now hard to find. And where are the storytellers? Where is the homemade cheese? Where are the *real* free ranged chickens and eggs—chickens that wandered the farm eating seeds and leftover crops and laid eggs with deep orange yolks? The majority of food consumed in America today comes from grocery stores that have now become an essential place to purchase food. Yet, increasingly, much of that food is not grown in the United States.

Today, dogs are still dropped in the Pocomoke Forest. Occasionally one of those dogs will be taken as a family pet, but when a stray is seen, the local dog pound or animal rescue is sometimes called. And where is the corncrib and corn-sheller, the clothesline, the featherbeds, handpicked goose and duck down pillows, 'out and out' biscuits, the coal-oil can to fill the coal-oil (kerosene) lamps, the foot-pump organ, and the hand pump and well? Some of those items can still be ordered but most are found in specialty and antique shops and now cost plenty.

There are also remembrances that hold little nostalgia like emptying potties, taking niter and caster-oil, stepping in chicken poop, the spurring rooster, passing out in a hot tomato field, falling from a tree and losing our breath, and tobacco hurled between our toes—but they are things that give us plenty to laugh about now.

Barely surviving are the raccoon hunts and the occasional hog rendering, as well, only a few backyard chicken coops are seen. Canning of vegetables is now done on a much smaller scale since the grocery store provides a variety of meats and vegetables year-round. Hand husking of corn endures, but mainly for fun or competition since combines husk and shuck ears of corn and blow the kernels into farm dump trucks thus enabling many acres of corn to be harvested and transported to the nearest granary in a single day.

Basket making, hand done from tree to basket, is nearly a lost skill. The crowsfoot wreath is rarely seen, even at fairs, and only one or two are made by those who know where to find the greenery and have practiced the art of making wreaths. Over the years, the patches of crowsfoot and running cedar, along with the many types of berries, have been greatly diminished by logging and most likely by herbicides used on crops for weed control.

Not only wreaths, but hand-stitched quilts are a rarity. High tech sewing machines stitch intricate designs on quilts, quilts that are no longer completely hand-stitched with thimble and needle. The black, heavy-handled, rotary-dial telephone sitting on a stand is not seen anymore: having just one phone in the house is simply not acceptable today since nearly everyone has their own phone and carries it everywhere they go. Also, where are the drugstore and street corner telephone booths that held rotary telephones: phones that took quarters, dimes, and nickels to get three more minutes of long distance? Where is the wild turkey retrieved from the woods for Thanksgiving dinner or the Christmas tree standing in the window lit only by the moon shining on tinsel?

If we could ask the Old Ones what happened to force such a drastic change in the way of life they practiced, no doubt they would not use the term 'Industrial Revolution,' but simply say that electricity and larger, faster, improved farm equipment and vehicles killed our country stores, our churches, our post offices, one-room schools, and our voting houses, but surely they would also say, "It was pavin' them roads that done it."

The rural residents of the early 1900s have grandchildren who have not forgotten some of their grandparents' survival methods. After participating in several seasons of farm labor, a grandchild could better understand those unchangeable methods their grandparents clung to. Also understood is the quiet fortitude with which the Old Ones worked and survived through world wars, epidemics and disease, and economic depressions. They had seen enough to know that due to those catastrophes, hard times could be right around the corner and strike without warning. They remained prepared. If a self-sustaining lifestyle should become necessary today, the learning curve for most people would be monumental.

This farm is a common sight on the Eastern Shore of Maryland in years past, as well as now—a large farmhouse, sheds and barns with old silo, and farm ponds with geese having migrated to Eastern Shore farms in winter. Throughout the winter in the Pocomoke Forest, maple, oak, and gum trees lose their leaves. Pine trees hold onto green needles (shats or shatters), and the cypress and cedar trees keep their needle-leaves as well. The cedar produces small blue berries and the cypress grows cones—cones of a much different shape than pine cones. Holly boasts its red berries and shiny green leaves.

Layout of Harvey and Eva Pusey's Fleming Mill Road, Pocomoke, MD Farm in summer. (Sketch by author.)

Views of Harvey T. and Eva Townsend Pusey's family home on Fleming Mill Road in Pocomoke, MD, standing vacant a decade after their passing.

This is a partial view of the south side of the house. On the left is the washroom and on the right is the screened-in porch, both had doors that opened into the kitchen. The right side of the porch had another door that opened into the dining room. The well stood just in front of the porch. The porch screen door is where everyone exited the house and where the out-of-doors daily activity began. Dog was always waiting for someone to come out and cats could usually be seen peeking out from under the house. Snow and rain created such a mess that keeping floors clean was nearly impossible. Also, during a dry summer, the sand carried into the kitchen would nearly fill a dustpan daily.

Eva Pusey's 1954 broiler chicken contract and payment for 5,000 chicks grown for nine weeks.

The cypress barn and attached shed just before it was torn down, with chicken house to the right.

Their cypress barn, chicken house, smokehouse, and family home with maple trees in front of the porch. The walnut tree is growing near smokehouse with corn growing in the back field.

Barn with slope shed, truck, and Allis Chalmers tractor with chisel plow.

Close-up of Allis Chalmers tractor and chisel plow, Brice Pusey driving.

This back view of the middle section of Harvey and Eva Pusey's 5,000 capacity chicken house shows where the chicken feed was stored and where the massive watering system stood.

Harvey Pusey's chicken house watering system drawn by Sierra Bloom from a description by Bruce Pusey.

An old Maytag washing machine with a gasoline, one-cylinder, kick-start motor similar to the one used for Harvey Pusey's chicken house watering system. (Flea Market 13 Antiques & Used Furniture, Pocomoke, MD)

Every farm yard had a solar powered clothes dryer similar to this abandoned wooden T with clothesline and attached clothespins.

Views of a free-standing, manual corn-sheller similar to the one that stood near the smokehouse and clothesline.

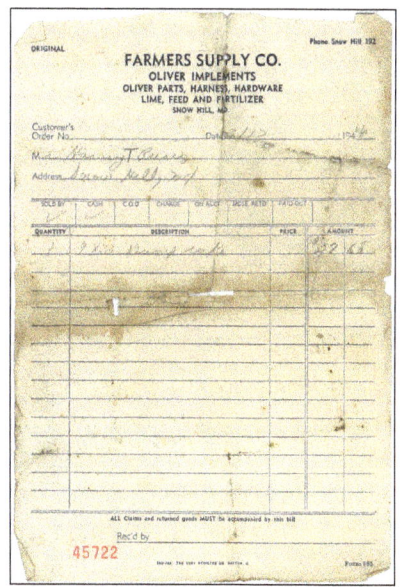
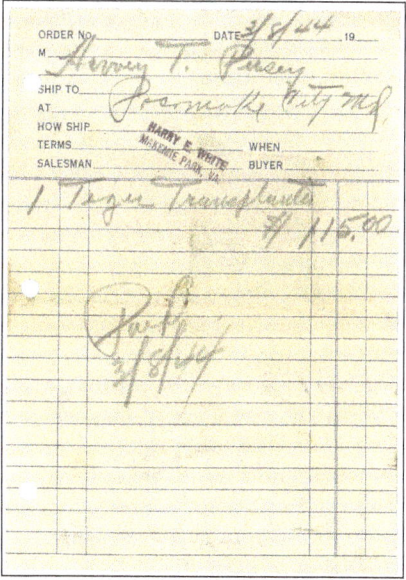

Receipts to Harvey T. Pusey for the Allis Chalmers C Tractor, Dump Rake, and Tiger Transplanter dating 1943-1944, paid in cash.

Logging Cart.
(Taken during Mt. Hermon Plow Days, Salisbury, MD. Spring 2012)

Hay Rake.
(Taken during Mt. Hermon Plow Days, Salisbury, MD. Spring 2012.)

Corn and soybean planter.
(Taken during Mt. Hermon Plow Days, Salisbury, MD. Spring 2014.)

Front view of transplanter.
(Taken during Mt. Hermon Plow Days, Salisbury, MD. Spring 2014.)

Back view of transplanter with the seats low to the ground. The water barrel with seat had been used when drawn by mules, but no longer used when drawn by a tractor. (Taken during Mt. Hermon Plow Days, Salisbury, MD. Spring 2014.)

Until the 1980s, a hickory tree called "The Cow Tree" still stood in the woods near the old abandoned farm of John Frank Pusey. The picture on the left is that hickory and on the right is Walter Brice Pusey pointing to the branch of that tree where the cows were hung. The pictures were taken in the early 1980s.

One-room school of the early 1900s. (Adkins Historical & Museum Complex, Inc., Mardela Springs, MD)

WWII government forms and correspondence, Certificates of Necessity, application for ration cards, ration books, and rules and regulations as to canning food and using ration books.

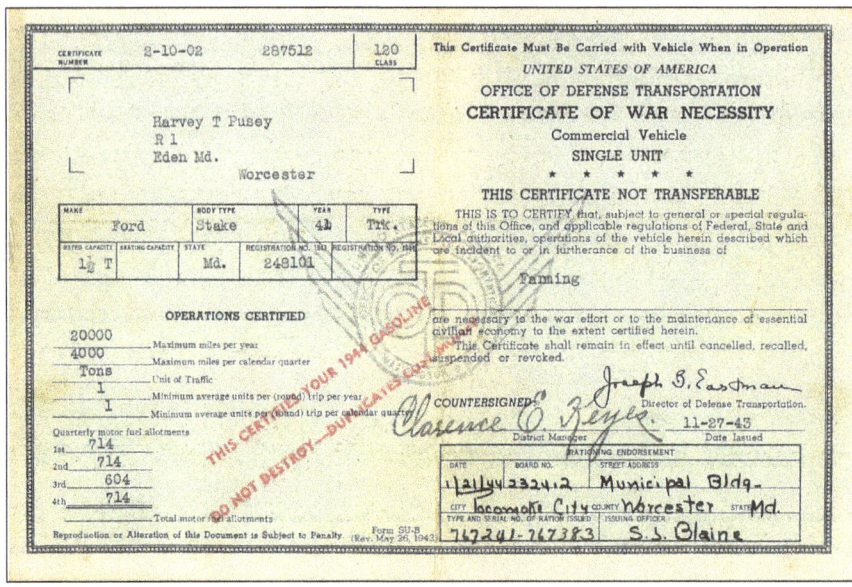

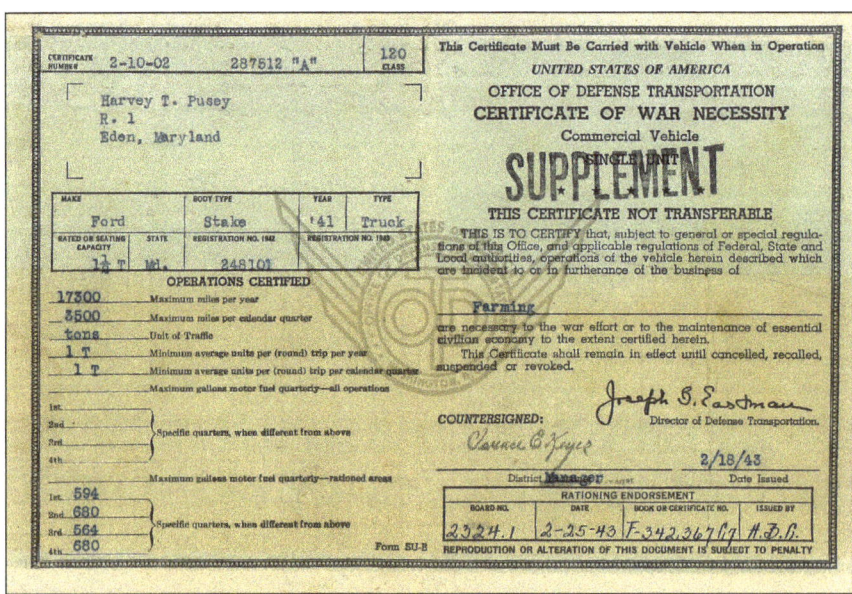

MR. AMERICAN FARMER

You, Mr. Farmer, play a very important part in the entire rationing program. THIS PROGRAM IS WORKING. To keep it working your Government needs your help. You can help strengthen this program by living up to the following pledge:

THIS IS MY WARTIME PLEDGE

1. I WILL DESTROY ALL STAMPS IN MY FAMILY'S RATION BOOKS THAT MY HOUSEHOLD DOES NOT NEED.

   My farm produces a share of the foods we eat.

2. I WILL COLLECT THE REQUIRED RATION POINTS FOR ALL FOOD I SELL OR TRANSFER.

   The food my farm produces is part of the Nation's food supply.

3. I WILL TURN IN TO MY LOCAL RATION BOARD ALL RATION CURRENCY I COLLECT.

   All ration points collected must be returned to OPA.

4. I WILL ENCOURAGE MY NEIGHBORS TO COOPERATE WITH THE FOOD RATIONING PROGRAM.

   A successful food rationing program will help win the war.

(See other side)

OPA Form R-1618
(F-1680)

DEAR SIR:

The wartime rationing laws of our country require that persons who sell or transfer rationed foods must collect ration stamps or other ration currency. Rationing means fair sharing of scarce foods. Retailers, wholesalers, farmers, and all others who sell or transfer rationed foods must collect points so that all consumers shall share fairly regardless of from whom they buy.

The enclosed Report of Farmers (R-1609) must be filled out if you have sold or transferred any meat, lard, butter, or cheese in any reporting period (usually a month). See instructions on form.

For your convenience, six copies of the form and three envelopes addressed to this War Price and Rationing Board are enclosed. When you have completed and signed the form, put it in one of the envelopes and enclose the red or brown stamps or other ration currency you have collected from your sales or transfers of meat, lard, butter, and cheese. You may also enclose blue stamps or other ration currency collected from any sales of home-canned fruits and vegetables. Keep the additional copies and envelopes for future reports. Points must be collected for foods in the amounts shown on the Official Tables of Point Values. Be sure the envelope is tightly sealed, then affix postage and mail.

Additional forms and envelopes may be obtained from this Board. Official Tables of Point Values are issued monthly and copies may be obtained from this Board.

Office of Price Administration.

(See other side)

Form No. R-129   Form Approved. Budget Bureau No. 08-R417

United States of America—Office of Price Administration
APPLICATION FOR WAR RATION BOOK NO. 3

One application must be made for each group of persons who are related by blood, marriage, or adoption and who regularly live at the same address. Persons temporarily away from home (for a period of 60 days or less), such as students, travelers, hospital patients, etc., must be included in the family application. Persons living at the same address BUT NOT RELATED by blood, marriage, or adoption must file SEPARATE applications. If additional applications are needed, you can get them at your post office.

A person may be included in only one application for War Ration Book No. 3.

The following may *not* apply or be included in any application for War Ration Book No. 3: Persons in the armed services, whether or not eating in organized messes, including Army, Navy, Marines, Coast Guard, and all Women's Auxiliaries; and inmates of institutions of involuntary confinement such as prisons and insane asylums.

Print below full name and complete mailing address of the person to whom books are to be mailed. Books will be delivered by July 21, 1943, to address given below. Books will NOT be forwarded. If you are not reasonably sure of address between June 15 and July 21, 1943, do not submit application. Such applications will be accepted later.

Print in Ink or Type

Name: Harvey T Pusey
Mailing address: Route 1
  (Number)   (Street, R. F. D., or General Delivery)
City or post office and State: Eden, Maryland

702601 AJ

This application must be mailed between June 1 and June 10, 1943. After June 10th, applications will not be accepted before August 1. Affix postage before mailing.

Print in the spaces provided below the name of the head of the family, the county in which persons included in this application live, and their complete mailing address. If you are not a member of a family group, print your own name and address.

Print in Ink or type   Do Not Fold or Tear Off

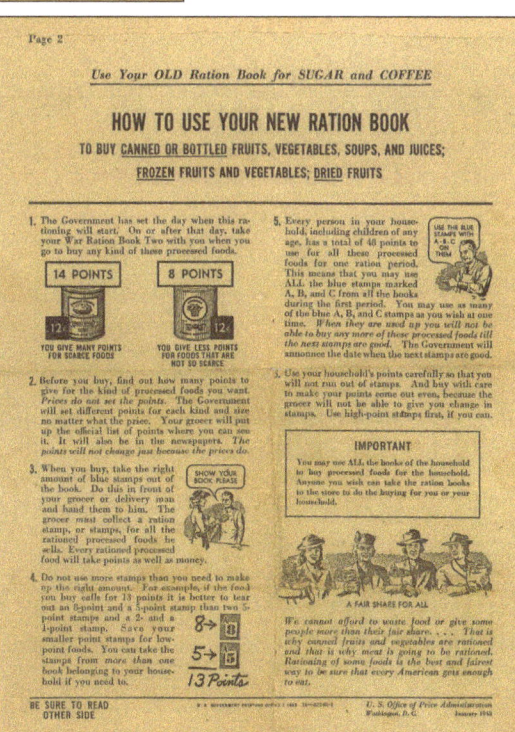

Harvey T. Pusey's 1945 Maryland Farm Plan from the War Food Administration

Carey's sawmill with lead mule, oxen, and logging cart.

Harvey Pusey on right, John Stout on left, using crosscut saw with Carey brothers in the background. Pictures were taken by a traveling photographer who would stop at certain places and take pictures families could buy, per Brice Pusey. (Photos taken about 1920.)

Spring Fever

The wind blew hard on my back helping to propel my blue bicycle toward Mom-mom and Pop-pop's house. Sand slapped upward inside the fenders. Some sandy sections of the road between home and my Grandparents' farm were difficult to wield a bicycle through, but I remained undeterred, pushing the pedals for all I was worth while taking in the woods and homes belonging to relatives. I was energized by the first warm sunny Saturday in April. Even though there had been a few warm days in March, they had fallen on school days. Free from school for the weekend and wearing new pink gingham pants, I had hurriedly fixed my ponytail which now fell sideways. I felt free as a bird, ready to take on whatever adventure came my way.

When passing each house, I waved even though no one was outside and heartily waved to one Aunt who was surveying the winter damage to her rose garden. A bluebird whizzed in front of me just as both sides of the road opened into Pop-pop and Mom-mom's farmland, land that would soon be planted with summer truck-crops and corn for the animals.

My brother, Bruce, had gone fishing and I had asked to go, but wasn't allowed. He had called some school buddies over to net the herring that were flipping up Dividing Creek. Water from spring rains gushed through ditches emptying into the branches and creeks where the herring were running. I had little patience for fishing unless the fish were plentiful, which they were right now, but I had never attempted to catch fish with a net. I would have to be satisfied with trying to hook catfish during the summer, that is, with someone older around. Turning eleven years old in a few days would bring no changes in what I was, and was not, allowed to do—in part, because I was a girl. One of those unchanged rules was, 'no fishing alone.' My wanting to fish today had been somewhat half-hearted. The real joy was simply being outside and wandering where I willed. Life began when bicycling was possible, so getting outside was the goal.

Wheeling in the driveway, I saw Mom-mom in her garden and that was proof enough that the day was fit for nearly anything. Probably, she had checked to see if the peas she had planted a few days ago had poked above the ground. But now, she was pulling and hoeing weeds. Come late May and early June, it would be time to plant truck-crops and the family summer garden.

The guineas created such a ruckus when I entered the lane that she looked up to see what was happening. Those fowl were her sentinels, signaling the arrival of any type of animal or disturbance to the farm. She liked having them around for eating bugs too. I waved to her and lowered the kickstand on my bicycle. Thirsty, I ran to the well standing in front of the side porch, and poured the coffee can of water in the top of the pump while pumping the handle. Water spewed from the spout. I drank, taking big gulps from the cascade of cold water and then filled the coffee can again so the next person could prime the pump.

Pop-pop caught my attention as he stepped down from the corn crib onto a wooden block used for a step and, with little effort, down to the ground. He was better than six feet tall and long legged. One of the straps on his overalls had sprung loose and flapped as he shut the cypress door and turned the wooden knob. *No doubt*, I thought, *he has been checking how much corn is left to feed the animals from now until fall and has counted his number of baskets and sacks of hog feed too.* Now was the time for him to make sure that he had ordered enough fertilizer, seeds and plants for truck-crops, and seeds for the corn crop too. He was always checking and double-checking his orders.

He walked over to the pigpen and primed the pitcher-top pump overhanging the fence. While he pumped, water fell into an old hollowed-out cypress log, one he had hand-hewn years ago. He didn't stop pumping until that homemade water trough overflowed. When he turned away from the pen, that's when I saw them—baby pigs.

"Pop-pop, you got baby pigs," I yelled, running toward the fence.

"Best if you stay away from the barn altogether," he ordered. "Was gonna tell you when I come to the house—that sow has done had her pigs, a couple weeks ago now, so don't go nowhere's near that pen. She'll go after you if she takes the notion, and too, might eat her own pigs. And, don't name um!" He knew that if I named a chicken or pig, that made it a pet and I would plead for it not to be eaten. 'Don't name your food' was a rule. I was disappointed but knew he was right. I scooted back to the house.

The planter and transplanter had been converted from mule drawn to being pulled by a tractor. Pop-pop had removed both pieces of machinery from the double shed and walked over to inspect for any broken or worn parts that might need to be ordered. The transplanter looked like fun, riding the seats just barely above the ground, and plugging tomato plants in the fresh furrow the shoe had dug, but the younger grandchildren were not allowed. So I would have to be content watching Mom-mom and Bruce placing the plants while Pop-pop maneuvered the tractor pulling the transplanter from row to row.

Pop-pop absorbed satisfaction by just walking across the land. When weather permitted, he rarely missed spending the day working outside. He hoed his many acres of corn and took a break by leaning on his hoe. He would remain in that same position while appearing to have been transported elsewhere. During those moments, he could look right through you as if you weren't there and then go back to work. *What is he thinking about so hard that when he stands stone-still his surroundings disappear?* I wondered and nearly shouted the question out loud. The farm seemed to be his entire life—his energy—his church. His cash, with the exception of occasionally betting on horseraces, went into his land when others' cash went into the latest equipment, new vehicles, or modern home furnishings. The land gave him strength. He was in tune with the earth, growing various crops, and yet he brooded a great deal. But, if sweating is a cleanser, he was cleansed many times over.

The two of them working in the garden and in the fields was a comforting sight from spring to fall, and today, I had fully expected to see them outside doing something. *I'm tired of winter, I'm tired of riding a cold school bus, and I'm tired of being cooped up at home and in classrooms, but most of all, I'm tired from studying book after book. There has to be more to learn about life that isn't found in a book.*

With springtime at my fingertips, I was ready to get busy out-of-doors where the most freedom could be found. I retrieved a dipper off a nail in the porch and took Mom-mom some water, which she downed quickly. Her bonnet nearly slipped off her head revealing a row of bobby-pinned finger curls, she called spit-curls.

"Mom-mom, did you plant turnip greens and kale this spring?" I asked.

"Yes, a few for pickin' but not cannin', they's tastier with cooler weather in the fall and last longer in the garden too. But, I like peas better when planted in the spring, so I got my peas and onions in the ground. Them peas is up good."

I went to investigate. Plopping down on the ground I could look up and down the rows and see the lines of tiny green. A mound of dirt had been placed off to the side since last fall and I began to make a tunnel into one side. I placed the dirt neatly outside in a row, making a road. The dirt was still cold and moist. The next clump of dirt I pulled out was moving. I dropped it quickly and a toad lay on its back attempting to move. "Look," I said. "A toad, and it can't hardly move." I held it between my fingers to show her.

"That toad's too cold. You got it out from hibernatin'. Set it in the sun and it'll move along directly."

"I want to play with him."

"If he pees on you, he'll give you warts. Besides, he don't want to play with you."

"He's got some warts of his own, on his feet and a whole bunch on his back."

"See," she said.

It must be true, I thought. *I've heard that so many times.* So, I put him down on the ground. Within a few minutes the toad began to hop and when I reached out for him he hopped quickly across the garden and was gone from sight. I shoved the dirt back in the hole figuring there might be more toads inside and went back to looking at her rows of spring plants.

"Which rows are the greens?"

She pointed to the outside rows, so I went to inspect.

"They've sprouted good and grown some too," I said.

"Be ready in a couple weeks or so. In May, I expect," she said.

"Next week is Easter, and Mom got me a brand new Easter outfit. I got a round hat, wrist gloves, laced socks, and new shiny shoes with a strap and buckle—all of them are white for spring. And she got me a pale green dress with white lace collar. We're going to the Presbyterian Church in Pocomoke for Easter services." I said excitedly.

"That all sounds very nice," she agreed.

"Are you going to Olivet Church for Easter services?"

"May be, don't know yet. We live a ways away from there now." And then looking at me, she asked, "What's that you got on the side'a your mouth? Looks like egg yolk." Grabbing the bottom corner of her apron, she rubbed my mouth hard with the edge. "Clean," she said triumphantly.

Oh phooey! What difference does it make if I have a dirty face? It stays that way in the tomato field, I fumed. To keep from having my face rubbed again, I turned toward the house looking for something to investigate when a call came from the road, "You-who," causing us both to turn. Stella Facejew, a neighbor from the next farm over, had appeared and hanging from each hand was a duck, fully plucked and ready for cooking. Stella had killed them by cutting off the head, letting them bleed, and then dipping them in hot water in order to pluck the large outer feathers. I thought, *She has probably saved the clean dry down next to the duck's skin for pillows, much the same as with a goose.* She and Mom-mom ordered ticking from the Sears catalog, not only for making pillows, but for recovering their feather mattresses and older pillows. Mom-mom had even used that heavy twill material to cover the seat of a chair. I could see it all, the whole process from duck to pillow just by way of those two ducks dangling from Stella's hands.

Mom-Mom waved her into the lane and we headed toward the house to greet a most welcome neighbor. Stella and her husband Filip were from the Ukraine and the only people living on the road who were not related to our family. She was a hefty, sturdy looking woman with a tight bun on the top of her head and wore a dull flowered dress with hem nearly touching the ground. Her broken English sounded a bit harsh, but she was as kind and gentle a person as anyone could have possibly been—and sing! She sang so beautifully, even though most words were sung in her native language.

I said, "Hello, Miss Stella," and she smiled and nodded. The children, as a form of respect, addressed the older ones as 'Mister' or 'Miss' and then their first name, even if the woman was married.

Mom-mom went into the kitchen and came back outside with a large enameled pot and asked me to fill it with water. While I hand-pumped water from the well, she and Stella went into the kitchen—their words drifting outside.

Their conversation consisted of only certain words, not sentences. Mom-Mom broke her English down to words Stella understood and Stella spoke broken English, but they communicated well. When Stella came down the porch steps, she had one of Mom-mom's new bonnets on her head and carried a slab of bacon. Trading was a simple task for them. Mom-mom's sewing and certain hog meats could be swapped for ducks, cow meat, and cheese from Stella and Filip. It was more like neighbor helping neighbor, trading what they each could spare, especially since little money was to be had in the spring and canned foods had been depleted throughout the winter. If Stella had something Mom-Mom needed and Mom-Mom had something Stella needed, they figured that the sensible thing to do was to swap.

I finished pumping water for soaking the ducks and wandered into the backyard, but stayed a good distance from the pigpen. The sow had her dirt covered nose pressed between the fence boards while I looked for the babies. Suddenly, a voice boomed, "I told you to git away from that fence! She'll eat whatever falls into the pen, even you!" Pop-Pop was passing between the sheds when he saw me, but he disappeared before I could come to my own defense. *I'm a long ways back from the fence*, I thought. *Guess I can't even look at them.* We grandchildren had been warned that when the sow had her babies, she could be pretty nasty and any hog could suddenly turn mean, especially a boar. The message was, the pigpen was off limits, as were the bee hives. Those hives were settled near Burk's Mill Branch in a section where we children never went anyhow.

 I turned back toward the house once again and saw Stella going out the lane. She walked down the road and crossed the small bridge. Her house had been a millhouse decades ago and had been moved to the other side of the branch. She and her husband Filip, had a small farm with cows and their house was within yards of Burk's Mill Branch.

 The Facejew's had many ducks that wandered the yard and swam in that branch of water running between the two farms. That branch joined Dividing Creek and that creek bordered the back of Pop-Pop and Mom-Mom's farm. Filip's cows kept breaking out of his fence and he could be seen up and down the road herding them back home. He spoke very little English and was suspicious of nearly everyone. It seemed that he and Stella had not been treated too kindly in their home country. He had been wounded on one side near his ribs and the skin was so thin it was only membrane that moved in and out when he breathed. A large gauze was kept over the wound to save him from further damage.

 With butcher knife in hand, Mom-mom took the ducks to a stump in the yard and whacked their feet off. That was all that she needed to do as the fowl had not only been plucked, but gutted. She then dropped the ducks in the pot I'd left under the hand-pump. When we entered the kitchen, she sprinkled a good amount of salt into the water to let them soak for a few hours. She placed that pot on the Hoosier's white enamel countertop in the kitchen and went back outside to pull weeds. In winter, I could hardly set foot inside her kitchen without wishing for the warm winds of spring and summer that would blow in one door and out the other. Today was the beginning of that long awaited vision. I flung open the back kitchen door and breathed deeply.

On the table, a bowl of her morning biscuits got my attention. I grabbed one, now nearly as hard as a brick. The lazy-susan in the middle of the table held the salt, pepper, sugar, butter, and syrup all covered by a cloth. I pulled the squared piece of feedbag material off the condiments for the butter. After putting a thick slice in the middle of my biscuit, I thought the better of it and licked the butter off. Filling a saucer with King Syrup, I sopped the biscuit around in that thick gooey molasses. My biscuit wasn't hard anymore. Stuffing the last of the crumbs in my mouth, I bounded down the porch steps to resume my investigation.

Chickens pecked in front of the house, around the front porch, and near the road—scattered far and wide from one another. Even they seemed delighted with the warmth of the sun now in full force. They scratched, kicked leaves, and hardly moved out of my way as I wandered, looking for anything that might be sprouting. The guineas ran together in a group looking like a cloud of silver flowing across the yard with their heads poked above that cloud like little black and white dots jerking back and forth.

Mom-mom had various kinds of daffodils spread about the front yard in no particular pattern, except surrounding the porch. There were small white daffodils with orange centers that had not yet bloomed but had stems and leaves protruding from the ground. And crocus had bloomed and gone leaving small green leaves. Both plants formed a fence-like structure which seemed to accent the porch. From all the daffodil stems, I found two that had flowered.

There was a ditch dividing the front yard from the road. The slope of that ditch was covered with creeping phlox. At one end of the ditch, beside the lane, stood a small glazed clay tile about a foot wide and cut to three feet tall. That piece of tile had originally been used for drainage, but now held a wandering pink rosebush that would flourish in late spring. Soon, tiny pink roses would dot the stems making archways of cascading roses circling the tile.

Standing in the yard was another clay drainage tile that measured about three feet across the top and three feet tall with the wider bell end up. Mom-mom had filled it with dirt and planted pink creeping phlox that would cascade down and around the tile's wide top in summer. In a straight row on the north side of the house, the perennials were budding. Even the lilac bush and the stems of the snowball bushes had produced green buds. But the forsythia bush took the prize. It was in full bloom. The little yellow flowers had bloomed up and down every long stem that protruded from the ground and those stems gracefully arched over, nearly touching the ground. Upon seeing the forsythia, spring fever really took over.

Skipping my way into the backyard, I lifted the clothesline that had been strung with laundry, parted two of Mom-mom's dresses, and walked between them. I gazed toward the creek and yearned for the road that went back to two landings, one called Figs' Boat Landing and the other called Pusey's Boat Landing, where high land sloped to water's edge—slight cove's where small boats pulled into years ago.

Further north, near those landings were the remains of an ancestor's farm covered over with briars and vines, and a tree called, 'The cow tree.' It was an old hickory with huge limbs and one giant limb that had grown parallel to the ground. On that limb, our ancestor, John Frank Pusey, hung his cows when butchering. I had only seen the tree once while walking with my father. Timeworn chains still hung from that huge limb, but it was the old farm I loved. There was something about the abandoned homestead of my ancestors that made me yearn for it and since that time I had only attempted to find it once while alone.

I had snuck there while everyone had been in the fields. Grapevines hung long and low from high branches and I'd latched onto them and swung until my hands hurt from holding on. Pop-pop said it was a dangerous place for those who did not know where the old well was, or where the caved in root-cellar had been dug. I had not gone near the house, and coming back through the woods I had become afraid of every noise, sounds my imagination related to wild dogs. Just the same, there was something comfortable about the old place. I knew that each month would become warmer and warmer now, so I would have many days to explore. *But I must wait. Maybe someone will take me there this summer*, I thought hopefully.

Looking one way and then the other, I wondered where Pop-pop had gone. My attention turned to the grayed barn with only specks of red paint remaining on the outside, and the inside that held the balance of last year's corn. *This time of year, the corn pile is too low for me climb up to the high window and look out over the fields*, I decided. *So I can't do that.* The window could not be gazed through again until early fall when corn would be dumped by a conveyor elevator through that opening once again. We grandchildren were warned about sitting in that window since it was so high off the ground, but we did anyhow. If anyone of us fell out of the opening an arm or leg would surely be broken and too, the pigpen surrounded the back of the barn and if anyone should fall the sow would be close enough to reach her snout through the wooden rails.

Well, Pop-pop's not in the barn. Both doors are closed and knobs in place. Puzzled, I turned to look at the long, open-front shed to my right, now empty of equipment. He wasn't there either. It seemed he must have taken off for the long chicken house that angled toward the woods. Running past the pair of peach trees, I stuck my head in the feed-room door.

There stood the monstrous platform holding barrels of water. The kick-start motor hummed as it turned, spinning the belt attached to the bicycle wheel which pulled the plunger on the pitcher-top pump up and down. Water flowed from the spout, ran through each barrel, and then down through a pipe that was T'ed at the bottom running water to both sides of the chicken house. Pop-pop's watering system was huge and very different from Dad's chicken house where the feed-room was small and an electric water pump sat in the corner.

The only time watering the chickens was done by hand was when they were baby chicks. Watering-jars had to be filled, lids screwed on, and jars turned up-side-down.

Yet pouring feed into the troughs was done by hand daily. Feed had to be carried from the feed-room to each side of the house, a strenuous chore. I thought of the wooden carriers that slid on a ceiling rail that could be pushed by hand through each side of the chicken house. That carrier could haul all the feed sacks needed for each side of the chicken house, stopping beside each trough so feed could be dumped from the sack into the trough.

Standing in the feed-room, I looked down each side of the chicken house where the nearly grown chickens seemed to do nothing but eat. Pop-pop was nowhere to be seen. *He can't be far away, after all, he had to have started the motor.*

Back in the yard, I noticed a single guinea was perched up on the shed roof surveying everything. Since he was used to me now, he paid no attention to my wanderings. Mom-mom said that one had to be a male and she called him 'The Watcher.' If he began to squawk, the whole flock would begin such a racket that their screeches hurt our ears. Once, after he squawked, I saw a Red-tail Hawk flying low over the farm forcing all the guineas to run under the lilac bush. Even 'The Watcher' had flown from his perch to take cover.

Nests in the long empty shed caught my eye. I went inside looking for eggs the hens had laid in baskets that had been stuck here and there. I entered, inching my way forward, making sure no snakes were near or in the nests. I only found three eggs. I grabbed them quickly and ran into the house, putting them in a bowl on the Hoosier countertop. My mother didn't have a Hoosier at our house: she had lots of cabinets and not just a single metal one like Mom-mom's over her kitchen sink. Sticking my hand out, no heat seemed to radiate from her Home Comfort woodstove. My mother didn't have one of those either: she had a gas range. To me, the difference in their kitchens seemed as big as night and day. Wood had to be chopped and stacked for the Home Comfort woodstove, but the gas range could provide heat for cooking by the turn of a wrist. Yet Mom-mom preferred her woodstove, not even using the convenience of the electric cook stove in the corner. The wood and coal stoves required constant filling and cleaning of ash. An oil stove heated our entire house. Also, we could simply flush a toilet at home, another flick of the wrist. Here, potties had to be dumped and cleaned. The daily work for Pop-pop and Mom-mom was so much harder, but they seemed to want it that way. *Maybe someday she will warm up to that electric stove. Oh well, nothing for me to do in here*, I thought, and returned to the backyard.

Suddenly my wanderlust and Pop-pop were forgotten when I spied baby chicks just outside the sloped shed attached to the barn. They were wandering alone. How unusual for a hen to hatch baby chicks this early in the spring, and leaving them alone was stranger yet. From what I had seen, chicks always followed their mother wherever she went. Too, mother hens were fussy about keeping their babies close. Since Pop-pop had disappeared, I didn't know what to do. Mom-mom was busy too, so I found a shallow tin pan and filled it with water. I gathered the chicks to give them a drink, but when I got up to leave they followed me all the way to the house. They followed me everywhere, so I slowly trekked out to the garden.

"Mom-mom! Look at this!"

She looked at the chicks, then looked at me, "You best git them biddies back where you found um. That mother hen'll claw your eyes out when she comes back to look for her babies."

"Well, where's their nest? They weren't in it."

"They weren'ent in it cause she took um out to scratch and eat. Hens'll leave their biddies sometimes, but she won't be gone long. The nest is inside the sloped shed off'a the storage side'a the barn, but don't go in there. Just put um on the ground where you found um and run away. They cain't trail you that fast."

When I reached the shed I looked around for the mother hen and not seeing her, I spied the basket and decided that I should put them back. I gently placed all six in the nest one by one. That is when the mother hen appeared behind me. She attacked my back with her claws. She was mad. I screamed. Trying to get away I fell over the wheel of the cultivator and onto a cultivator tine, cutting my leg. Blood was running into my oxford shoe, turning the white shoestring red. Tears rolled down my cheeks.

Pop-pop appeared out of nowhere, bellowing, "What in tarnation is happenin' in' here?"

"Those babies were following me around the yard. I'd just put them back in their nest when that mother hen clawed my back," I said between sniffles, pointing to the hen now settled with her babies and glaring at me.

"Don't s'pose you done nothin' to cause um to follow you?" He said and added, "Let me take a look at that leg."

"Well, I gave them some water: they looked thirsty," I angrily brushed the tears away trying to show how tough I was. "Well, I didn't name them," I said in defense, wanting him to know that I had followed at least one rule.

After pulling my leg out straight, making sure there were no broken bones, he spoke in a tone that left no room for an excuse, "You got more sense than that!"

"No I don't." I said defiantly, and sniffed, "Where'd you come from anyway? You were lost!"

He just shook his head, and yelled, "Evie," the booming sound was so loud it probably carried across the farm and back to the creek. "This young'un has hurt herself."

It seemed that Mom-mom was there before I could blink, she must have heard me scream. "What's all the commotion?" She asked.

While she inspected me, Pop-pop stood behind her and pointed his finger at me, "You ain't s'posed to frolic around no farm machinery and you knowed it. You knowed it when you done it."

"Wasn't playing," I said sullenly. He shook his head again and left Mom-mom to fix my wound.

"Alright now, let's git to the house and tend to that cut. It needs cleaned and Iodine put on it. That is a rusty old tine you cut yourself on." She paused in thought, "You is gonna need a tetanus shot."

"Don't want one!" It sounded horrible. "What is it?"

"Never you mind; come on, let's git into the house. It's quit bleedin'."

All I could answer was, "Sounds like a needle, don't want it."

She retrieved a basin off the washstand and a short stool from the little washroom, a room that had been part of the porch and walled to make private bathroom. Then she went through the dining room and I could hear her rummaging in the sewing room for bandages. I had not seen her sew in that room. It was hard to heat in winter and was on the north side of the house with an outside eve hanging over the windows and door. That eve hung so far over that no sun entered the room at any time of the year, not even in the summer when the sun rose further east. Windows and a door also made up most of the wall between the dining room and sewing room with windows on the outside wall too. The long narrow room had become more of a storage room, especially for some canning jars, large cooking pans, and for her hard-wrought Christmas wreaths to stay cool until they were sold. Somewhere in her organized storage, she found gauze.

She sat on the stool while I fought her all the way through cleaning the gash. But no amount of pleading or white knuckled gripping of the table stopped her. When the Iodine touched my wound it felt like she had put a lit match on my raw meat. All done, she placed my leg up on the stool. She pulled my blouse up to take a look at my back and saw no broken skin. "You is gonna have some brusin' there," she said, and went into the dining room. She rested one hand on the telephone stand and picked up the long black receiver with the other. It was a party line and someone was talking. She politely asked if she could use the telephone, telling the person that she had an emergency. She replaced the phone in its cradle and picked it up again in a few seconds, put her finger in the hole, O, and spun the rotary dial. When the operator came on she said, "141M please."

While she made the call, I gazed past the small refrigerator, an ice box that Pop-pop had unwillingly consented to buying, and through the bathroom that held items passing for bathroom fixtures to the large window covered with a muslin curtain. That room was used to bathe, shave, and do what came naturally in the metal pot with a lid and swing handle. The pot was the potty; a slop-jar that looked like a large enameled cooking pot. It sat in the right corner of that little room. In the left corner stood a small one-door corner cupboard. An aged mirror hung above the washstand that had just held the basin. On that stand sat Pop-pop's double-edge razor, shaving mug with brush, and a man's wide hairbrush. He had been nearly bald as far back as I could remember and I'd never seen him sport a beard. Having pondered the square bristled monstrosity as part of his toiletry many times, I wondered once again, *What could he possibly use it for?*

That room was so small we could hardly turn around. When shaving, he usually left the door open for more light. So on a couple occasions I had sat at the kitchen table and watched him shave. He began by producing a desired amount of lather, swishing his shaving brush around in a cup containing a splash of water with tidbits of soap. After steaming his face with a cloth from the basin of hot water, he swabbed his cheeks and his chin with the lathered soap, next he dipped his double edged razor into the steaming basin and made rasping sounds across his face.

Looking at his basin that was now on the kitchen table and full of bloody water, I wanted to start the whole day over again and knew it was not possible. Feeling sorry for myself, I dreaded going home, *Oh Lord, my father is going to be mad as that hen and Bruce is going to tease me.* Then I immediately felt guilty, *I've ruined Mom-mom's day in the garden.*

After she had called Dad, she came in the kitchen and gave me the once over. She said, "Stop that poutin'. It's gonna be alright, but you sure ruined them pretty pants."

She was letting me know that the only long term problem was the pants. Looking at the torn material, I agreed with her. Just a few hours ago I had been so proud of the pink gingham, an early birthday present from my mother. *Oh, what a mess.* Resting my chin on the top of the chair back, I gazed out the kitchen window at the buildings with all hopes for a grand adventure squashed.

"A dog," I yelled jumping from my seat! "A dog with a mop that's ugly as a post just ran across the backyard."

Mom-mom came to the window and looked in all directions as far as she could see, "Don't see no dog. May be you was mistaken."

"No, I saw one alright."

"Well, we is gotta wait to see if it comes back is all. Most likely, they's no pack if it was just one dog. Now, set down and prop that leg back up. I got to git the clothes in from the line."

Once I settled back in the kitchen chair, with injured leg propped, I stared out of the window hoping to see the dog again. My eyes scanned each building in turn. The smokehouse with its attached wired chicken coop loomed directly in back of my window, so I could only see the part of the Cypress barn. To the right of the barn I could see the front of the chicken house. Closer to the house there was a clear view of the front of the open double-bay implement shed where the chickens roosted on beams at night, but there weren't even chickens to be seen. The only real color was the little bit of red paint that clung to each building. I, as well as all who entered the kitchen, had gained the habit of glancing out at the buildings at the back of the house where something always seemed to be happening, but there was nothing to see, no chickens, no smoke from the smokehouse, and from where I sat, not even the hogs could be seen in the pen—nothing to entertain. No dog. Just Mom-mom taking each piece of clothing from the line, folding one after the other, and carefully placing each one in her basket.

Coming inside, she put the basket of clothes in the dining room and came back into the kitchen. She began to bake the ducks. So, halfheartedly, I watched her get out a roasting pan and rekindle the fire in her woodstove, a huge Home Comfort. She did not touch the electric stove in the corner. The thermometer on the oven door of the woodstove had ceased to work years ago, but she knew how to build and maintain her fire for each food she baked, just like she knew how to dress a chicken and season each dish.

She poured the salt water from the ducks down the sink, a sink that had been piped outside for drainage. Water from the sink ran into a shoveled out gully sending water away from the house. No electric water pump had been bought so the spigot pipes had not been run. She retrieved another pot of water from the well outside, came back into the kitchen, and rinsed the ducks thoroughly. Placing them in the roasting pan, she stuffed the empty cavities with onions and scattered additional chunks on top, peppered the fowl heavily, added a quart of water, and put the lid on the pan. The ducks were smaller than Mom-mom's chickens and greasier when cooked. Too, they always seemed to retain more of a wild taste than the chickens, yet really good eating when smothered with onions. The marvel of watching her cook was how fast she could whip up a meal and put it on the table, at times, before you could even come from the field, wash up, and sit down.

But, I wasn't allowed to stay or spend the night. I was whisked off to Dr. Sartorius's office in Pocomoke for a tetanus shot, which wasn't nearly as bad as the searing pain of the Iodine. At home, no one except little sister Lyn asked about my mishap. There was no fussing from Dad or Mom and no teasing from Bruce. So as I had visions of Stella's ducks fresh from Mom-mom's Home Comfort, I sat at our kitchen table eating Bruce's bone-filled herring.

Harvey and Eva Pusey's kitchen was attached to the back of the house, and the flow of air moved nicely through the two exterior walls and porch side of the kitchen in the summer. The porch is on the right. Through that back kitchen window most of the buildings and fields could be viewed by anyone sitting at the kitchen table.

A sink with drain board very similar to the one in Eva Pusey's kitchen. (Adkins Historical and Museum Complex, Inc.) On right: An electric coffeepot somewhat similar to the non-electric coffeepots used on woodstoves with a glass dome at the top. When the water boiled, it would perk up to the bubble and fall in the strainer holding coffee grounds. As the coffee got darker, one could judge when the coffee was done to their satisfaction. There was no such thing as a paper strainer at that time. (Adkins Historical and Museum Complex, Inc., Mardela Springs, MD)

On left: In the kitchen, Eva Pusey's Home Comfort woodstove sat in the center of the wall that had a chimney. The electric stove sat in the corner.

On right: The dining room coal-woodstove was on the opposite side of the wall from the kitchen Home Comfort and both stoves were piped into the same chimney. The living room stove was similar to the dining room stove pictured and both burned coal or wood.

An electric clothes washing machine like the one used by Eva Pusey. It only washed the clothes. Each piece of clothing must be taken out and run through the wringer by hand. (Adkins Historical and Museum Complex, Inc., Mardela Springs, MD)

Eva Pusey's feather pillow with a variety of feathers, most likely goose, duck, and chicken.

A toad unearthed from its hibernation a little too early.

Filip and Stella Facejew's home on Fleming Mill Road showing the wooden rail fence, Burk's Mill Branch is on the right. Filip had put up the fence rails that fronted the farm, but the fencing in front of the branch had been constructed by Harvey Pusey. At that time, the county guardrail was not there.

Blacksmith made nails from the millhouse that stood at Burk's Mill Branch.

Millstone from the millhouse that stood at Burk's Mill Branch, Fleming Mill Road, Pocomoke, MD, that contain the initials who were apparently the importers and retailers of Millstones that came from England.

Initials on Millstone, O.E.H. and L. F. H.

Planting

The farm exploded with life that had begun during the first warm days of March and continued well into May. Warm days and spring rains had nurtured flowers that bloomed in sequence; hardwood trees that budded and then leafed, except the walnut tree in the backyard which produced leaves a couple weeks later; fruit trees that blossomed and now bore small nodules soon to become peaches, pears, apples, or persimmons. Insects, birds, and animals of other species seemed to appear suddenly, making their presence known. After Mid-May, the chance of frost had passed, frost that might kill tender young plants. The time had come to plant more than just the late winter and early spring vegetables of peas, greens, and onions in the home garden: the air and ground temperatures were warm enough for pole beans, sweet corn, potatoes, black-eyed peas, squash, and string-beans to be planted. But, that warming also brought other time-consuming demands—disking the fields and planting truck-crops and corn.

Plenty of rain had fallen in early spring, but in the last two weeks it had rained only once and I watched as Pop-Pop disked dry fields. He disappeared into clouds of dust stirred by the disk being drug by his 1943 Allis-Chalmers tractor. A large flock of seagulls had arrived and followed the disk up and down the field. At times they were so thick, I couldn't see the disk. I wondered if the gulls had flown inland from the Chesapeake Bay or the Atlantic Ocean. *How did they know disking was happening so many miles away?* They flew down picking at the disked ground and up again and down. Today was the last disking he would do before first planting tomatoes and then planting his other crops. When he came in from the field, his leathery face and hands appeared powder coated. He blinked and that fine silt fell down his cheeks. I trailed him while patting his back and watching as dust flew. My presence went unheeded as he plodded toward the house. Trotting beside us, Dog sneezed.

Dog was the same scruffy, matted-hair vagrant I had seen after my mishap. People from town were always dropping their unwanted dogs out on the back roads: dogs they thought they had wanted, but changed their minds when the dog became too much trouble. This one was not the first to be left on our road and probably would not be the last. Dog had come closer and closer to the house. Since he had been deemed a male by Pop-pop, Dog had been allowed to stay. After that, Mom-mom began to feed him. He had been accepted as a part of our lives and he had learned quickly the dos and don'ts on the farm, not that he followed all the rules. I was tickled pink with him and could not wait for summer vacation. *Those hot months will arrive in the next few weeks so Dog will be my wandering partner*, I decided.

Pop-pop ignored Dog. Once we were in front of the porch, Pop-pop pulled his hat from his head and slapped it on his leg. He quickly pumped water and stuck his head under the spout, scrubbing his face and hands, and then he drank thirstily. I jumped ahead of him and held the screened porch door while making a sweeping motion for him to enter. Still paying no attention to me, he shook like a bear while beating the dust from his clothes. He even snapped his suspenders, overalls having been discarded due to warmer weather. When entering the porch, he turned to spit tobacco on the ground. I was still holding the screen door and ducked behind it fearing Beechnut juice between my toes as he had done before. He grinned and hurled the juice out into the yard. When his aim was perfect, whether a spot in the yard or between kid's toes, he had an absolute gleam in his pale blue eyes; we knew he had been satisfied with that shot.

"Feelin' your oats this mornin', I can see that." he said entering the porch, dashing his hat against the woodpile for extra measure, and then placing it on a nail.

"Yep," I answered, yet glancing back at the puddle of brown slimy mixture, my stomach turned queasy, but I wasn't about to say so. *I might have a spoonful of some nasty stuff shoved in my mouth. I have nightmares about seeing small brown bottles coming my way.*

There was little peace in being sick around Mom-mom, but there was no lack of concern and attention. When I had been sick just after warm weather had come, she had fussed and stewed over me like I was on death's bed even though it had only been a 24-hour upchucking event. She was convinced that I had the flu. She had me sip on blackberry juice and spoon fed me chicken broth, both of which seemed to be administered for a variety of ailments. But she was convinced that I needed cleansed and that castor oil had cleaned my system out slick as greased lightning.

During the 1918 Influenza she had nursed two elderly, distantly related, family members who lived across the road. Despite all her care, both had died. At that time, Mom-mom and Pop-pop had lived at the original home of his parents, 'The Home Place' in the forest. Pop-pop went to Snow Hill for caskets and had doctors sign the necessary papers. He buried both people on 'The Home Place' behind the barn on a rise across the ditch. *Her worrying every time one of us grandchildren sneezed must come from the loss of those two people*, I thought, *she's seen firsthand that flu kills*.

Later, in 1924 another flu made her sisters very ill. Her memory of those illnesses had her hovering over me, spooning the unwanted chicken broth into my mouth, and laying cold cloths on my forehead. Each time she had helped someone over a sickness, she stayed close until they began to mend.

Earlier this morning, I had dressed just as Mom-mom was cutting thick slices off a slab of meaty bacon and fried what seemed to me to be chucks of meat instead of slender slices of bacon. We ate her hastily fixed biscuits stuffed with those fat chunks and went out into the garden, a garden ready for planting. She carried packets of seeds and talked as we walked. "I finished stringin' poles for beans and hoein' this week," she offered.

One day, I had ridden my bicycle down as far as Miss Stella's and on the way back saw Mom-mom working in the garden, stretching her hands as high as she could to reach to the top of the poles. Her barely five-foot height forced her to struggle for that top nail. I had simply waved to her and headed back home.

"You need to get Pop-pop to pound the poles into the ground a little further so you can reach the top," I'd said.

"They weren't too much of a problem," she had said and entered the garden turning to look at the fading greens and turnips. "Going to miss the spring greens, they is goin' to seed now and the spring turnips is nearly past eatin' too, gettin' pithy. Oh well, I'll plant more in the fall."

She had carefully placed all her packets of seeds on the ground, except one and began planting. As she finished one packet, she picked up another packet, and then another. Watching her plant lima beans that would later run up the poles and strings, I had joked about Jack's Beanstalk. I joked about how the sweet corn would have silky blond hair that would turn brown as it got older, and about the black-eyed peas watching the first dark-haired man come in the house on New Year's Day, and about the funny shaped potatoes we had seen in years past. She smiled at my child's play once in a while, but kept up a steady pace fingering seeds in small holes made with the corner of her hoe.

Watching her plant the different seeds, I told her how I had noticed that some seeds were the food itself, like the corn, lima beans, and black-eyed peas. Other seeds were inside the food that was eaten, like the squash, watermelon, and cantaloupe. Some foods were seeds like the onions and potatoes.

Bent over at the waist, and still moving down a row, she had seemed interested in what I was saying and turned her head, "Some of your ancestors' growed tobacco. Those tiny seeds came out of a flower at the top of the plant that stands three to four feet tall."

"Really? How tiny are tobacco seeds?"

"So tiny that you can't hardly see one in your hand."

"Wow! And one seed grew a plant that big?"

"Yes, indeedy."

As I walked around the garden I had marveled about other plants, like the flowers, some had bulbs like the daffodils and others a cutting could be taken and rooted, while some spread roots underground growing new plants that popped up here and there, like the crowsfoot for wreaths. Finally, I had wandered over to the other side of the house to watch Pop-pop disk and lost sight of Mom-mom, thinking I knew where she was.

But now Mom-Mom was nowhere to be seen as Pop-pop and I entered the kitchen, but food was on the table and a nice breeze moved through the two open doors. Cold fried ham, the daily load of morning's biscuits, canned apples from last fall, and a bowl of peas had been put on the table along with our place settings. She had placed the pan on the stove shelf to cool. I ignored the table and roamed through the house and back into the kitchen looking for her. She was nowhere to be found.

So now, I was flustered, "The spider and the ham are cold. She must have left a while ago."

Pop-Pop simply said, "Eat! She'll be along directly."

"But where is she?"

"Eat," he said again.

"I want to know where she is," I insisted, but I could not explain that no matter where I was on the farm, not knowing where she was worried me. The thing was, I needed to picture her somewhere. I could be out in the field knowing she was in the kitchen and I was fine. It was an odd worry, but it was one I had felt as long as I could remember, and one I could not cure.

He didn't answer. *He doesn't know where she is*, I thought, *but I can't roam the farm over looking for her.* I sat down and began to eat, but usually when we were eating, she was in the kitchen puttering or eating. I picked at my ham and peas.

Suddenly, the back screen door opened and she stepped into the kitchen. Curiosity got the better of me.

"Where'd you go, Mom-Mom?"

"Took a walk."

"Where to?"

"Stella's place."

"Never saw you go out. Would have gone with you. Did you see any animals on your way? I saw a fox the other day. It ran along the woods line. The red and white showed up real pretty. I like foxes. They're fun to watch, pouncing in the field. Did you ever watch one pounce and pounce? They really are pretty. Bet we could make a pet out of one, huh." I couldn't stop jabbering.

She just patted me on the head and said, "They's gray foxes too."

Pop-Pop said, "Fox eat chickens."

"So do we," I replied.

He just threw me a look, downed the rest of his lemonade, raked his chair backwards, snatched his hat from the nail, and headed outside.

"You like eggs and the fried chicken you had the other day, don't you? If foxes get um, we wouldn't have no eggs and not much meat 'cept hogs," Mom-Mom said, as she sat down to eat.

"And the ducks Miss Stella brings!"

"And them ducks."

"A little cow meat and cheese too."

"Yes, that too."

"Well, in year's past we've seen fox come up near the house and even snatch a chicken, but we haven't this spring. How come?"

"Cause now Dog keeps um away, them and snakes. I'm kind'a glad he come."

"What do fox eat then?"

"Mice and moles mostly."

"Oh. Well, they could have fed their whole family in our house this winter. We had mice running everywhere, but I don't like the mousetraps 'cause sometimes those traps don't kill them so quick. Nothing worse than a squirming mouse in a trap."

"I expect."

"Well, we could feed the fox scraps from the kitchen."

"No, that would draw um too the house and anyway, most scrap goes to Dog. The rest'a the leftovers goes to hogs, and chickens."

"Oh."

"Foxes is pretty, I'll give you that. You know what a fox den looks like. It looks like a dug out hole, usually in a bank of dirt. It slopes down, but not straight down like a snake hole. Don't never go near a fox den. The female might come after you protectin' her babies. And, don't never try to feed no wild animal. You can get bit. They's just about no need to worry about foxes. They's right smart and keep away from people, but if you see a sickly looking one, especially if it is near the house, tell your Pop-Pop. Same, if you see a mangy lookin' raccoon in the daytime."

"What'll he do about it?"

"They might'a got rabies and bite us or our animals, and then we could get it, so, he'll shoot a sick wild animal in the yard."

"Far as I'm concerned, you can give those fox that castor oil. That's bound to cure them or half kill them. If they have rabies, it'll sail right out their other end." I said. But, then feeling bad about sounding ungrateful, I added, "The broth was good though." *Truth is, I hadn't wanted the broth since I felt it would just come back up again—which it had.*

As if she read my thoughts she added, "Some stayed down, I reckon."

It was unusual for a conversation with either Grandparent to last so long, but rabies must have been important enough for her to be sure I understood. Just then, Bruce came in.

"Where have you been?" I asked.

He ignored me and asked Mom-Mom when they were going to plant tomatoes. She said, "Tomorrow."

Unexpectedly, the mailman blew his horn. A package had come that had been ordered from the Sears catalog, which Mom-Mom promptly took into the privacy of her bedroom. *Could be a new dress or some personals,* I thought, *or maybe it's extra material for making a quilt during the winter. She has piles of fabric, but she might want to add a certain color.* My imagination covered what I considered was every conceivable possibility, but she kept that to herself.

The next morning, Pop-pop hooked the old Oliver tractor to the transplanter. Even though he had two Allis-Chalmers tractors, one bought during World War II and another just last year, he was determined to keep that old Oliver running in tip-top shape. The sun had not risen above the pines when work began. The kick-start pump ran steadily and the hose running to both ends of the chicken house had been disconnected, another hose attached, and that hose was run outside the feed-room door of the chicken house into the transplanter's metal barrel.

As Pop-pop drove the tractor pulling the transplanter, Dog and I trotted along behind Mom-mom and Bruce as they followed that planter. It rolled from beside the chicken house, through the backyard, and on past the house. When they crossed the road to begin their first long row, Dog and I stopped beside the mailbox. Before she sat on the planter, Mom-mom had asked me to either stay in the house or out in the yard where they could see me from the tractor. She then ordered, "Stay away from the planter and disk over yonder," while pointing directly to each one, "and don't go in any'a them sheds or near them shoats, or sow, or boar in the back pen." I knew that the baby pigs had been weaned, and as shoats they could eat just about anything now. Pop-pop had said over and over, "A hog'll eat anything, even you, if you was to fall in." That vision was pounded into our minds lest we forget the dangers of hogs. She didn't mention my hen and chicks incident from April, but I was pretty sure that was the reason for such detailed instructions.

Pop-Pop slowly drove the tractor pulling the transplanter. Mom-Mom and Bruce were seated low near the ground and lightly bounced over the disked ground while setting tomato plants. Facing the ground, their heads bobbled occasionally. They only looked up as the tractor turned to begin another row or when they called for Pop-pop to stop for more plants, wetted plants that he had covered with wet burlap bags and placed beside the road. Once the small spade located in the front of the transplanter had made a cut in the dirt and water had steadily dripped into it, they plugged plants in that wet furrow. Small wheels in the back of the planter folded dirt in around the plants and filled the furrow.

As the procession came and went, I could only watch as plants were set in the ground by family members who were older and experienced. The cloudy, overcast day was a plus since the best time to plant would have been near evening. Due to the clouds, the plants would not have the sun beating down on them and would have the coolness of night to perk upright.

Tired of standing, yet not seeing anything to sit on, I went in search of something that would pass for a seat. Three half-bushel baskets had been left outside the barn door, so I tugged until one separated from the others and carried it near the edge of the road, beside the tall rosebush. The lined pink branches sprang out of the tile and draped nearly to the ground. Glorious buds of deep pink yet to awaken blended with the paler pink roses already open. Not to be outdone, Mom-mom's nearby daylilies boasted bright orange blooms and shiny green leaves in a sharp contrast of color. I flipped the basket and sat beside the rose arbor. Dog came over and stuck his head in my lap. Right now, he looked as forlorn as I felt with nothing to do. "We're bored aren't we, Dog?" I said.

He brought me a fallen twig from under the walnut tree and fetched each time I threw it, scattering pecking chickens and forcing one hen from a nest under the front porch. That hen was not amused and seemed to squawk at us for far too long. We both grew tired of the game so he began to play in the road. Not that cars were a problem; there had not been a single vehicle pass all morning. Wondering what I could do to entertain myself, the old deserted farm near the creek crossed my mind, but orders were orders. Besides, I reasoned, I wasn't sure I wanted to make that trip alone again.

Dog began to pant and plopped in a hole he had dug near the front porch, upsetting the hen for a second time. She warily circled him, but did not get back on her nest. The slow movement of the procession up and down the rows forced a yawn, so I wandered into the backyard. The vines that produced the orange flowers that fit upside-down on my fingers were claiming one side of the open-front shed, but those flowers had not yet bloomed. We grandkids called them witch's fingers and would play chase wiggling claw-like hands at one-another. I surprised myself by suddenly seeing the witch's fingers as child's play. Gazing at the vine, I wondered if that had medicine too. The various shades of green from Mom-mom's flower bearing plants caught my eye and made a sharp contrast against the house's faded white.

Wandering back to the front porch, I sat leaning against the house with one hand petting Dog's fur. A robin with grass dangling from its beak flew back and forth in front of us, back and forth building a nest in the lower branch of a maple. My attention was drawn to what looked like one large knot of black that moved across the woods where the beehives stood. *Better remember to tell Pop-pop about that*, I decided, as I began to doze.

Occasionally, sounds from the tractor caught my attention and I roused to watch as the procession turned again, moving down the field and around the end of rows, slowly dragging the transplanter. The scene was similar to the dusty disking of yesterday, but the tractor moved much slower today not stirring such thick clouds of dust. Suddenly, the memory of how parched Pop-pop had been yesterday sent me running into the house.

I found three quart mason jars, pumped water filling them to the brim, and screwed the lids down tight. Hugging the filled jars to my chest, I carried them to my seat. When the planter began to turn a row near the house, I held up one jar. Pop-Pop slowed the tractor and waved me across the road. When they were finished drinking, they tucked the jars in my circled arms. I held them to my chest and backed away from the equipment. Just as the tractor began to move, Mom-mom asked me to sweep the kitchen floor.

"Sure," I called back.

Sweeping was not a favorite chore of mine, yet glad to have something to do, I went inside and grabbed the broom, even sweeping behind the Home Comfort and around the wood-box, getting the small pieces of wood and dirt. I swept the pile out onto the porch and cleaned around the woodpile there. Kicking open the porch screen-door, I swept it all down the steps and out into the yard. Finished with that chore, I perched myself on the up-side-down basket once again. It did not take long for my eyes to droop. The coolness of the ground lured me to sit beside Dog, and this time I fell sound asleep. I awoke to Mom-Mom shaking my shoulder and then feeling my forehead. That temperature checking was a natural act for her. After having six children of her own, no doubt she had been used to checking one or the other of the children for some malady or another.

After a cold lunch, hastily fixed, Mom-mom asked, "Can you put them dishes in that basin'a water in the zinc?" She had always called the sink—zinc, and when I asked Pop-Pop why, he said that sinks used to be made of zinc. But we rarely questioned the Grandparents' way of talking, what we considered their misuse and mispronunciation of words. At home, Mom always corrected Bruce's and my less than correct English, especially when we strayed too far from speaking properly. But the Old Ones had their own way of getting their point across and were never corrected by Bruce or me. Our mother wouldn't allow that disrespect.

The afternoon wore on much the same as the morning. They drank the water I carried to them in midafternoon. They finally stopped work for the day at suppertime, each shaking and beating the dust from their clothes and dousing their faces in water spilling from the spout of the hand-pump, except Mom-mom. She took the bonnet off her head and shook it. A ring of dust could been seen across her forehead. She went in the house to wash her face in the basin.

But as tired as Pop-Pop was, he still took time to look over his leaflet from Ocean Downs Raceway. He liked to go to Berlin, a town north of Snow Hill, and bet on the horses. He could be found pouring over even the old papers, studying names and dates, then penciling in the margins of some pages. Nobody disturbed him as he studied the horse's names, while attempting to project the winner.

It had been a late supper. At the table, I told Pop-pop about how the bees had seemed to move in one giant ball. He said he hoped they had not swarmed, and added, "I need them bees to stay put for to get enough honey. If some swarm and set up camp in tree-holes som'mers, I'll never find them hives." Mom-mom nodded at his statement and since darkness had begun to descend, she cleared the table and then retrieved her coal-oil can from the porch. Filling wall hung lamps, she moved from room to room topping off one after the other, even the handheld ones. I watched as the dining room took on a soft glow and then the living room flickered to life. She had to refill her can only once from the larger monstrosity on the porch.

Pop-pop went back into the living room to look over his racing papers and turned on an electric lamp. He blew out the coal-oil lamp. I guessed he wanted a clear view of his racing books.

Mom-mom retrieved her Bible from the bedroom and came back to the kitchen table. She seemed to be looking for a certain verse. She fingered through the Old Testament and finishing, she turned to Matthew. A hen's sudden shriek, caused her head to raise and she asked, "Will you go pitch some corn into the chicken pen? When you do, the hens'll go in there and then close the gate. I should pen um more often to keep from losin' some'a my good layin' hens. Foxes is still hungry just after winter."

Most of the hens would perch in the beams of the double open front shed, but I guessed that right now she didn't want to lose even one good hen. The hens did just as she predicted. I had to fiddle with the latch on the wire door before it finally closed.

Dusk showed orange hues beyond the trees next to the creek. The settling of evening brought sounds of whippoorwills, toads and frogs, and a pair of angrily squawking ducks flew low across the back field. As I stood near the chicken pen looking at the sunset change colors, Dog came and sat beside me, looking in the same direction as if he knew what I was doing. I turned back to the house and through the back kitchen window, I watched Mom-mom turn on the electric overhead light and go back to flipping pages in her Bible.

Two whole days were spent inserting tomato plants into long rows and the exhaustion could be seen on each of their faces. We ate cold meals of fried chicken, ham, some canned fruit, cheese, and peas, all washed down with hot coffee. I drank water. To me, the coffee tasted too close to some kind of tonic and how they could drink it on such a warm day baffled me.

Pop-Pop and Bruce were still tired after the tomato planting, but they unhitched the transplanter from the Oliver tractor, hitched the planter to that tractor, and poured sacks of corn seed in the planter bins. While Pop-Pop drove the tractor, Bruce sat on the high seat raising and lowering the planting shoe. Tractor and planter became one single blob at the far end of the field, but slowly reappeared as separate pieces of equipment when coming back toward the barn and pig pen. Row after long row, they rode over the field behind the barn that he had disked for corn, corn that Pop-pop wished he had gotten in the ground a little earlier.

After a day's break, he cultivated the last field in order to throw up elevated rows using cultivator teeth normally used to pile dirt around the roots of young corn plants, teeth that now produced raised rows for cucumbers, cantaloupes, and watermelons. He moved straight up and down the field. How he kept those rows so straight was a mystery to me. The result was one long, narrow raised hill, parallel to the next, and the next. He preferred to plant the watermelons and cantaloupes in raised beds since too much rain could rot the melons if the water did not drain.

Out in the field again the next morning, I watched as they all planted the watermelon seeds. Pop-pop had placed manure in the row, slightly flattening the hill. Bent over at the waist, Mom-mom came along behind him fingering four to five seeds in one spot three to four feet apart. Pop-pop came along behind her, closing and tamping each hill of seeds. Once the seeds sprouted, they would be thinned, the smallest plants weeded out.

In the following days, Bruce stayed home from school while they planted the cucumbers and cantaloupes by hand as well. Pop-pop had decided to grow a few cantaloupes, even though he had never favored them as a truck-crop, believing that they ripened and rotted faster than watermelons. I had said to him that if he wanted just a few to eat he could go buy cantaloupes in town and not fool with the planting, but he had only frowned at me, almost seeming puzzled at such a suggestion. The mere mention of buying something that they could grow was totally unacceptable to either of them. Why buy something when you can grow it yourself was the mindset. After all, the only things that needed to be bought were items you could not grow or make.

From one day to the next, dad let me off the bus to watch the planting. Dog and I were partners. While watching the planting, we wandered out to the field and back, and looked for eggs in the sheds. We wove in and out of the flowering lilacs and small bushes seeing if we could flush any rabbits from around the house. But since Dog had come, I guessed that he had already run the rabbits off. I watched everyone drag in from the field, tired, and freshen up as best anyone could from a hand pump. Each day, they ate cold suppers without talking.

The following Saturday, Pop-pop sent word for Roger to come. He was a local black man our family hired to help when help was needed who I had guessed was around thirty. Roger would announce himself by whistling. He lived on the other side of the tomato field through the woods and there was a path through that woods from his place to the field. I could not pick up the tune he whistled and figured it was one that he made up as he went along according to his mood, which was always jovial. He also announced a loud hello that resounded through the trees. Dog took offence, but settled once Pop-pop called back in greeting.

Just the day before, Mom-mom had sliced corned beef and baked cornbread, so I grabbed a chunk of that cornbread and ran outside waving to Roger as he passed through the yard to the shed. He waved back, hollering, "Hey, baby girl!"

While the men worked on some of the equipment and reorganized the feed-room in the chicken house, I sat on the porch until they finished. Sounds of Mom-mom busy in the kitchen rang out onto the porch as did clanging sounds from the men's work. The warmer days had an effect on me, so I decided to stretch out on the featherbed. Just to be on the safe side, on my way through the kitchen I announced to Mom-mom, "I'm alright! I'm not sick!"

When I awoke, Roger was saying his goodbyes to Bruce and Pop-pop and he headed down the lane to the path through the woods whistling like he always did, coming and going. A profound happy tune filled the air and I listened until the last sounds faded away.

Through the days of disking and planting, Pop-pop had not shaved. At dinner, I reached over and ran my hand over the stubble on his face. "Feels like my hand's caught in a blackberry vine," I said, "Just like the ones that run up our lane at home." There might have been a glimmer of amusement in his look, but he was weary. He was 73 and Mom-Mom was 71. Planting fields of crops for so many years had taken its toll on them. Although they had help from some of their children and grandchildren over the years, they had also hired more pickers and the occasional helping hand around the farm. Even though they had planted less acreage in the last couple of years, they still looked drawn, careworn by decades of too much sun and hard work.

The sudden realization that they were now old and tired held a dread that I couldn't explain and didn't want to explore. I started to babble in order to break the silence. "I saw a squirrel today, high up in that old walnut tree. It wasn't a black squirrel neither."

"That's good," Mom-Mom said.

There was a superstition that the lesser populated and rarely seen black squirrel was bad luck. Pleased just to get a response, I continued,

"And it ran up and down like it didn't know which way to go. Then another one chased that one round and round the tree. Dog barked his fool head off and then they ran back up the tree. What's Dog's name anyway?"

"He has no name as we know of," Mom-mom said, and added, "Why folks in town think all farmers would love to own their city dogs is beyond me."

"May I give him a name, after all, he's not an animal we're going to eat." I reasoned.

"Suit yourself. He looks a sight better than when he first come."

She almost sounded fond of him, I thought, *but that might be wishful thinking on my part.* "Mom named our dog Plato, after the philosopher, but I'll name this one Fred, Fred the dog."

That brought a chuckle from both Grandparents and a cross-eyed stare from Bruce with admonishment for me naming every animal, Fred.

In reply to my brother's stare and accusation, I replied, "Well, I don't know any people named Fred, can't get mixed up about that."

"Except, which animal you're talking about," Bruce said. "Suppose you said, 'Fred barked.' Who would know if you were talking about the dog or the multitude of squirrels you've named Fred?"

"Don't use those fancy words with me and squirrels can't bark! Can they Pop-Pop?"

But for an answer, he gave his usual grunt.

I took that as a no and stuck my tongue out at Bruce. He just shook his head at my ignorance and the half-hearted razzing was over.

They had been so all-fired serious when they had come in, looking as if they might fall down from exhaustion, but the mood had lightened considerably. So I slipped a small piece of ham off the platter and, before anyone could object, flew out the door to tell Dog that he was now officially—Fred. But, he didn't seem to care what his name was, as long as he got that piece of ham.

The seats on the transplanter where family members would sit and place plants in a furrow (cropped from page 35).

Shown here are the old rose bushes with small pink flowers like Eva Pusey grew in front of her house. The vines would wander and cling to anything nearby that was standing upright. She had planted hers inside a large tile and the vines would fall in a nearly circular pattern around the tile.

Trumpet Vine, the flowers called Witches Fingers, worn by children as they chased one another.

Trumpet Vine in full bloom.

Strawberry Time

When Dad reached my Grandparents' house, he stopped the school bus and let Bruce and me off at the lane. Dad had started driving the bus by substituting for Brian Denston, a distant relative who drove a 1953 Chevy school bus. So this year Dad bought a brand new 1962 International and began his own bus route. Pop-pop was just leaving the garden and raised his head to watch the bus move down the road and into the trees. When Pop-pop had lived near the crossroads in the forest, he had driven a school bus too, a wagon in which the seats were lined on the sides and the children faced each other. Looking at him, I wondered, *Has he ever thought about how his life might be the same as his son's?*

Dad was driving a bus just as Pop-pop had done, and they both farm. Pop-pop had driven rural children to one-room schools in the Pocomoke Forest. Since one and two-room schools had closed in the forest, Dad drove rural children as well as a few town's children to schools within Pocomoke town limits. Their lives paralleled one another, but the machines they used now were different. Dad didn't farm quite as much acreage as Pop-pop, but Dad had updated equipment. Pop-pop and Mom-mom's house had not been redone with running water: change was not easy for them to accept. Yet, our house had most of the modern conveniences. Most of my parent's generation had quickly accepted the mechanical advances that made life easier.

When Dad and his brothers were young, two of them had lit the stoves in Atkinson's two-room school near those crossroads in the forest and got paid for doing that chore. But those country schools had closed more than twenty years ago. The year Pop-pop was born seemed so long ago, 1889, and Mom-mom in 1891. I could hardly imagine just horse and buggies on the road, no vehicles. He and Mom-mom were raised that way, bouncing over rutted dirt roads, legs covered with blankets in the winter, parents cooking over fireplaces that were later replaced by woodstoves for cooking and warmth. Too, they had endured the manual labor of planting and harvesting, scrubbing clothes, chopping wood, and rendering their own meats.

Walking up the lane, I looked over at Mom-mom working in the garden with Fred at her side. No doubt she had readied and planted her garden the same way her parents had done. She cooked with wood and made her biscuits the same way as her mother. The same methods of working, cooking, and basic living had probably gone on for many generations, but now it seemed broken by the fast pace of new equipment and vehicles, and better roads that made the towns seem closer. The grocery store in town was only minutes away.

When we went to get groceries, we came back with three or four paper bags, but Mom-mom and Pop-pop grew their staples and came back from the store with a half bag containing coffee, sugar, flour, salt and pepper, spices, and some chewing tobacco; Beech-nut was his favorite. They rarely bought canned food, but corned beef was a treat. Fred broke my concentration. He left Mom-mom's side and ran to greet us in the lane as if it was the most natural thing for him to do.

Soon, Fred and I could take off together since there were only a couple days of school left before that summer vacation. I wouldn't miss the studying, but I would miss some of my friends and the monkey bars at the middle school. The bars were such fun to swing from one to the other. I had just hung by my hands from them today, legs swinging helping me to maneuver as the plaid skirt I had gotten for Christmas jerked back and forth.

But I had to get playtime off my mind. It was strawberry time. Bruce and I were going to spend the night with Mom-mom and Pop-pop so we could get up early to pick. Mom-mom looked up from her hoeing when we got off the bus, but went back to whacking at the ground. Weeds were a constant problem.

"You were yacking up a storm on the bus, squirt. Guess you haven't had any more episodes of upchucking like you did in early spring?" Bruce asked me.

"No, but the blasted cure is worse than being stopped up."

"The castor oil was so you don't try to get out of going to school by faking sick."

"I couldn't go to school after taking that stuff, couldn't get off the pot," I replied, "and what's worse, I had to clean out that pot when I was done."

I stopped my defense short as Mom-mom appeared with hoe in hand. "You young'uns hungry?"

"Sure am. Forgot my lunch money this morning and I didn't get any lunch," I replied.

She stopped in her tracks. "You mean to tell me that they will not feed you unless you got the money?"

"I guess they would have, but I was embarrassed—I had a nickel for milk." I said defensively, suddenly knowing that I had made a mistake in saying anything about having had no lunch. If there was one thing Mom-mom couldn't tolerate, it was for anyone to be hungry.

She waved her hand toward the house, "Git yourself to the table and I'll fix you a nice plate. You need to speak up for yourself. Lord knows you got gumption enough to do it here. Anyway, they should keep an eye on you young'uns to see you is taken care of, and, you just over being sick and no lunch today. That's a disgrace!" She grumbled all the way to the house with at least five words for every step she took.

"Your lunch money was on the table and you were supposed to get it," Bruce said.

"I forgot, okay!"

"Jeez," he said, and went off in search of Pop-pop.

Seated at the table, I gave the lazy-susan a spin and lifted the cloth for some butter. *I was over being sick weeks ago*, I thought, *but there is no need to remind her.* I ate all the food she heaped onto my plate and asked her what she had been doing today in an attempt to change the mood.

"Gettin' weeds from around them bean poles. Don't take weeds long to come." she said, opening the back kitchen door to let air inside.

Immediately, I saw the towering pear tree far across the field, standing alone. It's trunk seemed to reach the sky. The full white blooms were beginning to fade. Then the scent of her lilacs filled the kitchen and I turned my head to see the huge purple blooms covering her decades old Lilac bush. "Oh, that smell! It's heavenly," I said.

"The carnival glass vase on the buffet is filled with um," she said proudly.

I ran into the dining room and stuck my face into the flowers, nearly tipping the tall slender vase over. *Once you smell lilacs*, I thought, *you will always remember the joy of the smell.*

"Miss Stella's got a lilac bush doesn't she?

"Yes."

"I smelled it when I went down to the ditch that's off the side of the branch to look for tadpoles."

"I remember. You brought some tadpoles up here."

"You made me put them back."

"Back where they belong."

"Well, I'll be able to catch some of the frogs and toads this summer."

"Long as you let um go. You like um more'n they like you. Tadpoles don't belong cooped up here in a bowl on the table. They'd probably die. And, frogs and toads don't belong in your pocket neither."

"I know," I said. Mom-mom knew I liked to go looking for frogs clinging to the sides of trees and buildings and to chase toads. Just by walking through the yard or the garden, I could flush toads from their hiding places and then the chase was on.

"Next thing, you'll be catchin' some of them little green snakes and takin' um to bed with you!"

I shivered, "You don't have that to worry about. A harmless little snake puts fear in my heart."

Nothing else came to mind to talk about, so I cleaned off my plate with half a biscuit, and after changing out of my skirt into knee pants, I followed her to the garden. She decided to quit hoeing and just pull weeds here and there around the plants. While she worked, I sat drawing figures in the sandy soil; Fred watched first one of us and then the other. She was done within an hour and we went inside to fix the evening meal, but as much as she coaxed, I couldn't eat a bite.

The next morning, Bruce and I entered the kitchen smelling sausages cooking in what Mom-mom called her 'spider.' She had always called her frying pans 'spiders' since she was young when her mother's frying pans had short iron legs and had been named spiders. While those sausages sizzled in her legless, long-handled frying-pan, Mom-mom was in the little washroom dabbing her fingers in a white agate basin of water and wetting small sections of her short hair. She wrapped that wet hair around a finger and jammed the small bobby-pins in her mouth in order to separate the ends before sliding one over each dampened curl. She did this in preparation for any unexpected company. Adept at snatching pins from her hair and running a hairbrush through what had been poker straight strands, she produced wavy hair within seconds, ready for any visitor. It crossed my mind that maybe she used the wide hairbrush, instead of Pop-pop.

When she finished setting her hair, Mom-mom told us to wash our face and hands and added, "Use plenty of baking-sodie on them toothbrushes, then set down here to breakfast." Bruce and I fairly inhaled our breakfast of runny eggs, sausages dribbled with molasses, and jellied biscuits. With our bellies full, he picked up a straw hat and we stepped out onto the porch yawning and stretching, faking weariness—prelude to a game we played. Suddenly, we raced to be the first one outside. Mom-mom quickly snatched a bonnet from a porch nail and slapped it on my head as Bruce and I bounded down the porch steps like hounds were after us. After rounding the house we stopped short, nearly flipping the basket bench and then practically running into Pop-Pop. He was carrying a bucket of slop for the hogs. That slop contained hog feed, water, and any leftovers, whether from scraps of food to rotten garden vegetables of which there were none right now, to any dead chicken or animal found in the yard. We didn't care to look at or wear the smelly concoction. Years ago, Pop-pop had turned his hogs loose into Dividing Creek Swamp to forage for the winter, but now, he fed them year round or until they were sold or butchered. Every time we even glanced at the pigpen, we remembered the never ending warnings about the dangers of hogs.

Our excitement for the moment was that summer freedom was nearly here. The early June sky was a clean bright blue with brilliant sunshine that had dried most of the dew from the leaves as we headed toward our chore for the day, picking berries. No great pressure was ever put on us to do farm work, but the necessities that must be completed during the truck-cropping months were many and varied as spring waned to fall. Fred followed us into the patch and promptly took off running after some unseen thing.

The strawberry patch was next to the yard on the north side of the house, so we didn't have far to go. At first, we separated the wooden quart baskets in packs of ten and dropped those packs up and down several rows. We each started a row while holding a group of ten neatly fitted inside each other and began to fill the top one. We left each filled basket in the row, and filled the next basket, and then the next, until the last one. Then we found the closest ten pack and started the same routine all over again. We continued that way for a couple hours, me with a bonnet I didn't want, and Bruce with a hat he didn't' want either, but both coverings were good shade in the bright sunlight and wearing them pleased Mom-mom. While we worked, we ate strawberries to quench our thirst, but finally, a thirst berries couldn't relieve sent us to the well for water. Fred suddenly appeared and followed along beside us.

After priming the hand-pump, Bruce and I pumped water, one for the other as we each drank from the flood running from the spout. We could have gotten a glass to drink water from, but it didn't matter to us. We splashed water over our faces, cooling our cheeks. I filled the old pail used for Fred's water bowl. He lapped quickly and long as if he had been working in the hot sun with us and when finished, he crawled under the porch to lay down. When I asked Bruce what Fred had been chasing in the patch, Bruce just shrugged his shoulders. But, we had not resumed our picking more than a few minutes when I spied a snake.

"Bruce, there's a snake! Oh, my God, there's a snake!"

"Well, leave him alone and he'll probably go away. And, quit cussing."

"I'm not."

"Baloney."

"You're my brother! Get rid of it!"

"And you're such a sissy."

"Uh-oh, it's crawling this way, jeez, it is right in front of me crawling down the row! Look, between you and me coming my way."

"That snake is not interested in you; black snakes love strawberries; he's just eating. Stand still. We won't scare it toward either of us. Just be still."

"Yikes!"

"There. There it goes across to the next row."

"It might come back!"

"Not likely."

"It might be a she like me, not a he like you, and she might have babies nearby. We've been told a snake is more likely to strike in the springtime when she's got babies."

"Not if you leave them alone. Now, leave me alone!"

"You don't have to be so bossy!"

"Look, we've got at least half of this patch to pick today. Not that anybody makes us do it of course, but we make money and besides that we have nothing else to do. Now, we've only got about a fifth done so far and it's only two hours 'till lunch. How about that new thing called a Mohair sweater you want for wearing to the record hops. Think about that while you're being all squeamish about a snake that doesn't even notice you anyhow."

"Okay! No need to get huffy. Anyway, I can't even find one with mohair in the catalog yet, just heard about them," I said getting flustered and yanking the bonnet from my head, "Too blasted warm for this thing."

"Well, it beats the weather we have in August while picking tomatoes; that sweltering sun bakes our brains."

Our bantering waned as we bent over the long mounded rows holding ripened strawberries, berries that needed to go to market as soon as possible. I knew he was right since the chore of picking strawberries was light work compared to harvesting tomatoes. Tomato picking involved half-bushel baskets that weighed more and more as we pulled them down the row while battling the occasional round of biting flies and mosquitoes. So who could really complain about picking plump strawberries that quickly filled the quart basket and no biting pests to slow us down? A vision of the soon to come tomato harvest and enduring heat and pests settled me into a steady rhythm.

Once several quarts had been filled, we placed them in the wooden handled hand-carrier and toted it to the beginning of the rows where crates had been placed by Pop-pop. We used the carrier over and over making several trips to fill the crates with our quarts and then resumed picking. After reaching the end of a row at the woods, Bruce stopped and looked out over the fields of truck-crops that had been planted. Looking around as well, I saw Pop-Pop begin to pick near the crates, so I shouted, "Hey," and waved to him. Pop-Pop looked down the rows directly at me, which was all the acknowledgment he usually showed. He never waved and might grunt a hello, but we all understood his ways and did not think one way or the other about it.

"There's a snake in the patch," I yelled to him.

Pop-Pop raised up, spit a stream of tobacco, and hollered back, "They's most likely a dozen," then he began picking again.

I froze.

Bruce groaned.

Staring hard at my brother, I was ready to open my mouth when he said, "Snakes can hear you and they move out of your way. That one just got caught between us. You can bet it heard us, especially with you yelling. You probably scared it to death." Then looking at my frown, Bruce added, "You're getting on my last nerve." Having finished one row, he began picking another, working his way out of the shade and away from me.

Bending back over my baskets, I rattled them, wondering where the ears were on a snake's narrow wiggly head. I grabbed a new pile of ten, shook them, and kept clearing my throat. *That's what Fred was after, snakes,* I decided. So, I yelled for Fred and then I tried to whistle, which to my frustration came out as spit no matter how hard I tried. "Bruce, you whistle for him," I insisted. Without turning around, Bruce shook his head and kept on picking. My mouth had gone dry.

Thirst overtook my fear for the moment. I plopped some berries in my mouth and watched as Bruce did the same. The sweet liquid satisfied us and the closer it got to noon the more we ate. The sun moved directly overhead reminding us of summer's sunny days, but a light breeze kept us comfortable. I kept a wary eye out for movement in the plants.

We continued to pick until Mom-Mom called from the house, "ChiLLLL-dreNNNN." She always called us that way. When she called, the L's and N's were high pitched and drawn out. It was a sound that I was sure could be heard a mile down the road and to some, may have had the effect of fingernails down a chalkboard. The screech had no problem reaching us. When we were out in the field and heard it; that meant lunch or supper was ready. Suddenly, we smelled fried chicken. So we put our unfilled berry baskets down, and I retrieved my bonnet from the ground as we hurried toward the house.

The killing of chickens was done freely in front of us grandchildren. The shooting of a hog was a little different. The younger ones were distracted, kept in the house, by someone when a hog was shot, but the rendering was not hidden. The act of killing a chicken was a year round event and done when the need arose. The hog rendering was done only once a year and usually in January when the temperature hovered around the freezing mark. On the farm, those renderings meant either getting through the year with meat, or going without.

Her regular sequence of cooking chicken began with putting a pot of water on the stove to heat and then going outside to shell some corn. When the chickens ran over to eat the corn, she hooked the leg of her desired young rooster for frying and grabbed it by both legs hoping it wouldn't curl and peck her hands. With a block and axe close by, she laid its head across the block and chopped it off. She immediately pitched that chicken out into the yard. While the chicken bled out, she retrieved her pot of boiling water from the house and dipped the chicken inside, only removing it from the water after a good dousing. Then she began plucking feathers until she had removed all, only missing the occasional pinfeather. Finally she gutted the bird, singed the hair, and cut it up into frying pieces of legs, thighs, a halved breast and back. She also saved a length of neck, and the heart, gizzard, and liver. She inspected the skin for feathers and put all the pieces in salted cold water to soak for a few hours. Later she rinsed the meat, floured and fried each piece to a golden brown. An old rooster or old hen was too tough to fry, so she would stew them, which meant gravy and dumplings. She prized her young hens for the eggs they laid daily.

Fried chicken was not all she had been doing this morning. Besides the mound of chicken, the table held a pot of fresh spring peas with dumplings, vinegared greens, and fried potatoes. The kitchen smelled so good it made my mouth water. She had poured some warm water in a basin in the little washroom off the kitchen. We took turns washing our hands in that same water and then we dove into the food. The red strawberry stains had not come off our fingers.

Besides the fried chicken, the peas and dumplings were delicious. The pea plants that had sprouted in the garden in early April had produced an abundance of peas. There was a certain amount of pride in eating those peas since I had helped Mom-mom shell them just a couple days ago. We had settled in the rockers on the porch with basins full of pea pods in our laps. A nice breeze had blown through the screens. Peas were no trouble to shell. I'd just popped open the pod and run my thumbnail down the middle. The peas made a pinging sound as they hit the agate. Lima-beans did not pop out as easily, so I had not minded the peas. There had been little conversation while we shelled. We had let Fred into the porch and he laid down beside the wringer washer and stayed there. He never really chased the chickens, but would run through them and they would scatter, but he never sucked eggs. Before Fred came, it was not unusual for Mom-mom to see a snake with a big lump, an egg in its body. But since Fred had come, she saw fewer and fewer snakes and more eggs. That was one of the reasons why she had let him stay, and had let him onto the porch, but just the porch, not inside the house. After I had managed to shell one pan full, the steady *zzzzzz*'s of Fred, the rocker, and breeze had lulled me to sleep.

Voicing my thoughts, I said to Mom-mom, "Fred helped us shell these peas."

"Fred helped you to nod off; that's what Fred done." She replied, grinning and then wiping her forehead, she said, "Harvey, I had trouble tryin' to heist that window."

Glancing at the closed window by the table, Pop-pop just grunted at Mom-Mom's remark. Bruce reached back and pushed every-which-way on the window, finally loosening it enough to raise it a few inches. Suddenly, a cool breeze came directly from the back of the house and moved over us as we sat eating a lip-smacking lunch. But, just when we had stuffed ourselves with all we could hold, Mom-Mom proudly produced a huge bowl of stemmed and sugared strawberries with sliced biscuits for shortcake. Bruce and I looked at each other. After eating strawberries that morning and then gorging on lunch, we had little want for more berries. Pop-Pop had not overeaten and grunted once again, this time his approval when she handed him a plate.

That afternoon we moved sluggishly down the rows until the

fullness in our bellies finally wore off. We ate very few strawberries while picking, just enough to quench a dire thirst. And there weren't any more snakes or any other excitement to break up the monotony, just a rabbit hopping its way across the field. We would take a break once in a while, stretching our arms. The mild 70 degree day wore on with the sun on our backs, shade from the woods at the end of each row, and no insects to bat away—the best of working conditions. Still, it was a long afternoon.

Bruce and I met halfway, him coming back on a new row and me finishing one. The air had cooled and the sun was beginning its afternoon descent, so we stopped for a moment. I said, "The second season will begin soon."

"What do you mean? Everybody knows it's spring and that summer comes next," Bruce answered while inspecting his khaki pants where his knee had torn through from kneeling.

"Not our weather seasons, I mean our working seasons. Planting season is the first season and that one is done, we've started the early harvesting, which is really the third season, but hoeing is the second season and starts in the next couple of weeks."

"Guess I get where you are going, but I can't see more than three of them."

"Mom-mom's seasons are more and Pop-pop's too."

"I don't follow, but I don't need too. I'm just ready to be done with these strawberries for the day."

Paying no attention to his brush off, I continued, "Look, there's planting, then hoeing, and then harvesting: that picking is the hardest season. Then there's the hot sweaty chore of canning. Mom-mom cans lots of food during the summer and fall when the crops ripen. Then comes tying wreaths and that has its own season for sure. Her fingers get torn up making those wreaths. She works for two to three weeks and Pop-pop helps pick and cut the saplings for hoops. Right? That's five," I said having produced a finger for each one, "And then there's hog killing time which is lots of work as you know. Last is sewing which includes mending clothes, but mostly quilting quilts. Sewing is done when it's too cold to do anything else. So hog killing and quilting make seven! That quilting and sewing being number seven for Mom-mom. I guess chopping and toting wood makes Pop-pop's seventh season." I held up seven fingers, but Bruce was not there. He was just disappearing into the woods. *Boys, there's some things they can do a whole lot easier than girls.*

When he came back, I was further down my row and he called, "Now, what were you saying?"

"Never mind," I yelled. "You would've found the need to correct me anyhow. Go on about your business."

"I had an urgent call. No need to be so cranky," he replied.

Mom-mom had come out to the field with a stack of baskets in hand. She began picking steadily. After she had filled several baskets, she used the carrier to fill the bottom of a crate. Lost in thoughts of mohair sweaters and movies, I did not see her leave the field. A while later she called us to supper with her usual, long, shrill treble, but we were glad to hear it.

Thankfully, we finished the basket we were filling, grabbed a carrier, and filled it one-by-one before we headed for the house. Settling my last few baskets in a crate, I noticed her bonnet pitched on the end of a carrier filled with berries.

Turning to Bruce, "I never saw her leave a carrier full without putting the rest of her filled baskets in a crate and she left her bonnet in the field too?"

"She had a bee in her bonnet," said Bruce.

"What?"

"You heard me!"

I knew she could show her temper, sometimes, but for Bruce to use that saying about Mom-mom made me mad! "Take that back! How can you say such a thing?"

Bruce became irritated, "Because a bee really got in her bonnet and I think she was stung."

"Oh, no!"

Meeting us at the crates, Pop-pop nodded toward the house and said, "Weren't nothin'; she's fine."

Settling down, I took that moment to give Pop-pop my total of quarts picked so I could get tickets. He said, "It's only us in the field. I got your total."

But he didn't understand. I liked to have the little blue tickets and count them out, and then hand them back when it came time to get paid, just like all the other pickers. The transaction felt more like an accomplishment. It felt real to me and I explained that to him, but he just shook his head and got his wooden ticket box from a crate at our feet. He handed me tickets with various numbers on them totaling the 34 quarts I had picked. I hugged him, which I rarely did, and ran up to the house to show Mom-mom.

"Look Mom-mom," I spread my blue tickets with Pop-pop's name on them out on the table.

She nodded in approval and when questioned about the bee, she nonchalantly said, "It's only a small welt."

We had leftover lunch for supper. When we were nearly finished, Bruce asked Pop-pop when he was going to the auction block with the berries. The reply was, "Tomorrow morning, before light, them strawberries cain't wait till Monday."

"I want to go!" I pleaded and waited. *Please, please, please,* I begged silently, *the only place I've been for weeks is school.* I was ready to go somewhere, anywhere, but I got no answer, which to me was yes! "Yay!" I said, and settled in a rocker on the front porch to make plans.

Pop-pop and Bruce went outside to bring the crates of strawberries up from the field. Once they were finished, those strawberries sat in the shade of the maples to cool until sundown. Just at dusk, Pop-pop backed the car he had borrowed, a 1949 Ford, near the large maple in front of the well. The back seat of that car had been taken out and that is where they stacked crates, from floor to roof. They packed the trunk of the car with crates as well, and tied the handle of the trunk's lid to the bumper. Suddenly, Bruce yelled out and searched his arm. He had been stung. Pop-pop promptly spit tobacco in his hand and plopped it on Bruce's sting. "Yuck," I said out loud, and thought, *talk about adding insult to injury.*

I yelled to Mom-mom in the kitchen. She came out onto the porch asking Bruce if he needed 'baking-sodie', but he said the tobacco was already taking the pain away. I continued to sit in her porch rocker and plan tomorrow's trip.

Mom-mom always packs a bagged lunch for each person going to the auction, so I decided to ask her for a ham sandwich, not spam from a can or canned corn beef.

She had gone to fill the hanging feeders in the long chicken house, the chickens that would be sold at market. I pitied those cooped up chickens. They never got to run around the yard and to have baby chicks, but Mom-mom had said that people in the big cities needed to eat chicken too, and rounding up 5,000 chickens running around loose wouldn't work out very well. That vision came to mind and I realized she was right for another reason, *There would be too much chicken poop to sidestep.*

Back to envisioning tomorrow, I made promises to myself. *The ride is always fun, but I'll wear pants so I won't get the skin of my leg pinched by the crack in the seat of that old car. I'll try and be quiet so maybe Pop-pop will let me go next time too, and I won't ask for too much candy from the store when we get there.*

Mom-mom's bedroom with the wide featherbed was downstairs across the hall from the living room. Beside the bed was a walnut washstand with pitcher and bowl; sometimes her Bible was on that stand. Where the Bible lay depended on which room she had been in while reading, but she never left it in the kitchen. Sometimes she put water in the bowl for washing her hands and face in the morning, but mostly, she used the washroom, like now, to wash and change into her nightgown. I sat upright in the feather bed waiting for her. I watched as glowing golden reflections from the lamp she was carrying moved like ghosts through the hallway and into the bedroom. Dark shadows wavered and shrank into the corners of the bedroom as she entered. The flame made her small frame appear as a monster on the wall and ceiling behind her. She put the lamp on the washstand and cupped her hand above the chimney, then blew it out. The smell of the oil wafted through the room.

I began to talk immediately. "Bruce and I nearly upended the basket bench today," I confessed.

"That bench for makin' split oak baskets is made from a white oak log. More like that bench would'a upended you."

"That would have hurt!"

She simply said, "Uh huh, Now, turn your back to mine."

Whenever I stayed, we slept that way, back-to-back. But I wasn't done talking, "May I have some ham in my biscuit?"

"No corned beef or sausage?"

"No."

"Yes, but come daylight, you'd best be inside that car when it pulls out or your Pop-pop'll leave you here."

"I'll be there, I can promise you that."

And I was. Crawling up into the car, I sat squarely in the middle of the seat clutching my lunch bag before the car was ever started. Pop-pop took his time traveling the back roads to Princess Anne, where strawberries were auctioned. He and Bruce cranked the windows down and turned the latch, opening the small window vents. With a nice breeze swirling through the car, the scent of strawberries and pine trees filled the air. *I couldn't be happier,* I thought, *except later today when I hand Pop-pop my tickets to get paid.*

A bonnet made by Eva Pusey and baskets filled with strawberries inside a carrier similar to the ones used.

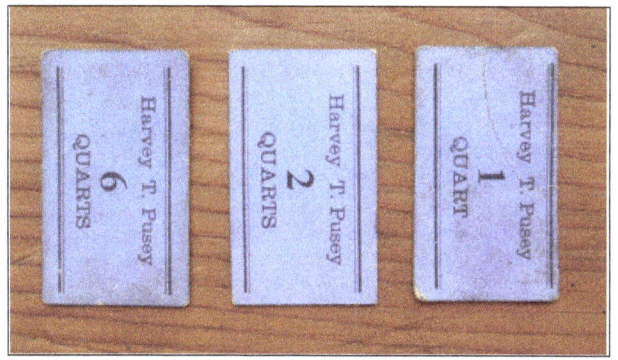

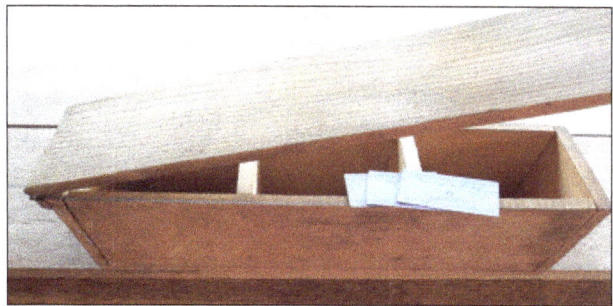

Harvey Pusey's strawberry tickets and a ticket box. His ticket box had been painted green.

Never mind the egg sucking dog, snakes will rob eggs from a nest as shown above. This black snake, just having swallowed an egg that can be seen just behind its head, made no movement while I leaned over to take its picture.

A familiar foggy morning scene in past years at farms on the Eastern Shore of Maryland, especially on Sundays when they might have company stop in for a visit.

A lilac bush with a mockingbird's nest in its branches. Lilacs wafted through the yard sending a strong and sweet, recognizable scent.

Hoeing

Strawberry picking gradually ended as there were fewer and fewer strawberry blossoms. The amount of berries dwindled down to grazing the field for a bowlful for the table. Later we found only the occasional stray strawberry, but they were all gone by the end of June when hoeing the truck-crops had already begun. Hoeing was a chore that no one liked, except maybe Pop-pop who loved the out-of-doors, but more than that, he felt it was his duty to be outside working, accomplishing something. To Bruce and me, shelling corn was about the only chore that never got old.

The corn-sheller groaned and squeaked as Bruce cranked the long handle operating the wheel, grinding corn off the cob. He shoved husked corn from last fall into the top of the sheller. The shelled corn spit into the bucket, and how hard it hit depended on how fast Bruce turned the wheel. The cob came out perfectly clean. Even though I liked to call the chickens to come for what I considered their breakfast, some were already there. Others heard the corn hit the bucket and came running, even flying directly to the sheller. I decided that the birds already waiting must have an internal clock that adjusted each day according to the sunrise. The ornery roosters did, crowing just before dawn with a call nearly as shrill as Mom-mom's, but not quite. One hen always seemed to come closer than the rest. I stood perfectly still and reached down to pet her. She allowed a couple strokes before moving away.

Dad had dropped us off just before dawn and headed back home. He had some cultivating to do today and Pop-pop needed our help, so we volunteered. Mom-mom had her own internal clock just like the chickens. She did not use an alarm clock to get up, but was up by dawn. This morning had been no exception. She was in the kitchen cooking when we arrived. The salt and peppered eggs with yolks that were a deep sunset hue had been cooked in grease leftover from fried bacon. Both tasted like heaven.

We all had enjoyed the breakfast, even Pop-pop seemed to linger at the table, but he finally scraped his chair backward and said, "That's enough lollygaggin' this mornin', time to get hoein' and turnin' them vines." His statement had not been directed at us. We helped with chores anyway, partly for money, partly because there was nothing else to do, and because Dad liked for us to help. There was also a tinge of guilt if we didn't. No demands were made by Pop-pop or Mom-mom, just strong suggestions for our safety, such as wearing the bonnets, hats, and shoes; staying clear of the pigpen and the bee hives; and looking out for wild dogs. One order we never challenged was to not stand or sit on the boards at the top of the well. There was room enough to sit a good sized bucket on that wood under the pump. The thought of plunging several feet below ground into water was enough for me; I was never tempted to even lean on the wood.

"Did you see my hen come up to me this morning?" I asked Bruce as we chopped around cucumber plants, the sun now high in the sky.

"Yeah."

"I didn't really try to make her a pet, she just started coming up to me."

"Uh. Huh."

"Why do you think she did that?"

"Don't know."

"The guineas though, they don't seem to warm up to us. The way they move in a huddle they'd all come close or none would. Even the one that watches from the shed roof doesn't come."

"I guess that's true."

Changing the subject, I said, "Lyn wanted to come this morning, but Mom said she's too little to be out in the field."

"She's just six. You've only been working in the fields a couple years now."

"I can't hardly remember what I was doing when I was six."

"You were talking all the time, just like you are now."

I ignored his jab, but after hoeing a little further down the row, I asked, "Where is Pop-pop? He said he was going to hoe."

"He's hoeing the squash in the garden. He'll be here soon."

"Well, I'm tired of hoeing," I complained.

"We're both tired," Bruce agreed.

"I don't want to do it anymore."

"You don't have too, you know."

"I know, but I can't jump rope and play hopscotch all summer."

Bruce stood on one side of a row of cucumbers and I on the other. We were turning young cucumber vines that had grown out between rows. By picking the vines up and pulling them in line or by gently moving them inward with the hoe, we placed those creeping lengths into long straight lines. We hoed out the cucumber plants that were less than four or five feet apart, as well as weeds dotted here and there in the rows and furrows. Looking back, we could easily see how far we had come, having worked about a quarter of the small field into neatly formed rows. The prickly cucumber vines had irritated my hands and this was only the beginning, they would need turned at least one more time before the cucumbers were big enough to pick.

Not able to think of anything else to say, I just kept on hoeing until my hands began to burn. "I want some gloves," I said, "just look at my hands."

"Have you ever seen anyone, even Pop-Pop or Mom-Mom use gloves?" Bruce questioned, stopping to lean on his hoe.

"No."

"Well then, stop fussing."

"I know they make um."

"Of course gloves are made, we just don't have any. Think how many they'd have to buy if all the family members who worked their fields wanted gloves. Mom-mom just wears them when making wreaths."

"I'm getting blisters, see," I held out my hands to him.

Bruce leaned across the row and rubbed his fingers across my palms, "They're just red, besides, nobody ever died of blisters. Remember that time down at Public Landing when my shoulders got all blistered. That was bad, but I healed and I'm still here."

"Yeah, but you were sick to your stomach."

"There are different kind of blisters, ones from the sun and ones from a hoe handle. The only ones you might get today are from the hoe handle."

"What's the difference?"

"You won't get the bad kind from the sun cause you're all covered up with a hat and white shirt, which by the way, looks suspiciously like mine."

"It is. I couldn't find my long sleeve blouse and you and Dad were waiting in the car."

"How about asking next time?"

"I'd of had to go downstairs and outside to the car and then back and upstairs, put it on, and come down the stairs and outside to the car. That don't make no sense when you were going to say yes anyway," I replied.

"Doesn't make any sense," Bruce corrected.

"At least we agree on something."

"Oh, for Pete's sake, will you stop? Look, if you want to take a break, wade in the ditch here beside us or go on over by the woods and sit, otherwise hush."

"Will you turn both sides so when I come back, I'm up even? Don't like hoeing when I'm too far away from anybody."

Bruce just nodded and pointed toward the woods, "Remember, we dug a hole over there at the edge of the field by the tallest pine; that is where we put the jar of water so it would keep cool. Get a drink and when you feel like it, bring the jar to me."

The water was still cold and tasted sweet. I sipped and watched Bruce. He hoed both sides of the cucumber row for a few minutes and then paused, looking across the farm at the various crops. The watermelon and cantaloupe vines would need turned into rows before another month was gone. The tomato plants across the road stood strong and erect, yet still small. With weed season coming on, those rows would need hoed or cultivated until the plants were thick enough to stop weeds. *When hoeing is finished, the long neat rows of loupes, melons, cucumbers, and tomatoes will show just what a truck-crop farm should look like*, I thought.

Now would be a good time to take the water to Bruce, but the sun across the field had turned into waves and I wanted to lay down on the cool ground, yet I didn't want to fall asleep. I took another sip of water and settled it in the dirt again. Kicking my sneakers off, I dug my toes into the cool sand shaded by the pine. After pulling my knees up to my chest and wrapping my arms around my legs, I settled. The sounds of summer were like a lullaby. They soothed my swimming head. There was the constant whoosh of wind through the pine needles and maple leaves. Birds called and toads croaked along with the small rodents rustling ground leaves in the forest. I rested my forehead on my knees and nearly fell asleep, when all of a sudden those sounds stopped.

Raising my head, I scanned the field and found nothing in particular. Bruce was still as a statue leaning on his hoe beside the ditch where banks of grasses waved in the wind. Through waves of heat several yards away, I saw one dog and then another come out from the woods and into the field. Both looked thin and unkempt, even scraggly, far worse than Fred when he had appeared. A deep fear crept over me like ants crawling over my skin. I did not move except my eyes in Bruce's direction. He had seen them. Ever so slightly, with one hand he made a motion to stay still, which was no problem; I may well have appeared a growth, one of the forest's fixed forms in the shadow of that old pine. Even the forest creatures had the good sense to cease all sounds so as not give away their position. We watched the two dogs move straight across in front of us and head for the ditch in search of water. Then another appeared from the woods and followed the first two, and then another. After getting their fill and coming up from the shallow ditch, they looked mucky and drenched. They lifted their noses into the wind with faces turned away from us. The wind was in our favor. If we had the senses of the dogs, we could have caught their scent. Moving north, they slunk along the bank, trotting away from us.

Time passed and we did not move a muscle and did not utter a word until they had been in the far woods for several minutes. Finally, Bruce came over to the pine, but before he could speak we heard the steady clomping of feet, a sound we knew well. Pop-Pop stopped beside us with hoe in hand, and saw Bruce with both our hoes, and me sitting with a ghostly expression. Bruce explained and Pop-pop promptly produced a pistol from his pocket and said, "Don't you young'uns head for the field without me no more. Let's git up to the house." I nodded, grabbed the water jar and handed it to Bruce. Then I took Pop-pop's outstretched hand to help me up, an unusual offering. He seemed worried.

When we reached the house, Pop-pop retrieved his shotgun and explained to Mom-mom that he was going after wild dogs. He handed her the pistol and turned to me, "You look peaked; go lay down. And, don't even look at them pigs, they's growed some, but that sow can still get riled." I couldn't answer him, it seemed the sight of wild dogs had forced me to lose my voice. Leaving the hoes leaning against the porch, they headed for the north side of the field and walked along the ditch. They were not going to hoe crops. They had gone hunting.

Even young pigs, one of the cutest baby animals on the farm, failed to peak my attention. I was shaken by the mangy dogs and besides that, had to admit that I wasn't feeling too perky. Mom-mom and I went into the house. She walked back to her bedroom with the pistol and came out wearing a different apron, one with deep pockets. I could only guess, but it looked to me as if that pistol was weighing down one pocket.

Looking down, I caught sight of my dust covered feet on the cool kitchen linoleum. I had walked from the field to the house in bare feet, shoes forgotten, left under that tall pine. The washing-machine on the porch was in full thrashing mode and seemed dizzying and loud.

Mom-Mom glanced at my face. I didn't bother to say anything. She grasped my flushed cheeks in one hand and felt my forehead with the other. Then she ordered me to sit and put a glass of lemonade in front of me. She had been eyeing me a lot lately. "You got a bit'a fever. Has your woman's time come yet?"

"My what?"

"Next birthday you'll be twelve."

"Don't get a fever with that."

"Some do. First time especially."

"Don't want to talk about it."

"You will when your time comes. I'm going to git you somethin' for that queasy stomach; you got one ain't you? I can tell." she said.

"What are you getting?" I asked, worried. Usually, if she thought I had an upset stomach, she would get the blackberry juice, but I feared something foul tasting.

"Blackberry juice," she said, "it'll settle you."

"Thank goodness."

She watched while I drank the half cup she had offered. It was straight squeezed blackberry juice. Nothing added, and it tasted really good.

Finally satisfied, she went onto the porch to feed clothes through the wringer.

I poked my head into the washroom and looked at my face in the time-stained mirror. *Just a little red, maybe it's nothing*, I hoped, and went to help her with the clothes.

As she fed each piece of laundry through the rollers, I caught them on the back side of the washer. Each piece could just as well have fallen into the basket on the floor she had placed perfectly to catch them. I saw how flat each piece became after it rolled from the wringer. *Pants and shirts alike look flat as a pancake,* I thought. When we were finished she picked the clothes-basket up and pulled the small basket of clothespins off a nail and headed outside with me on her heels.

"You stay inside. Set at that kitchen window and if you see somethin', you can give me a yell," she said.

I nodded. Finally managing to talk, I asked if Pop-pop had gone to kill the dogs, knowing full well he had.

"He's got to. He worries about you grand-young'uns all up and down the road."

"He doesn't say anything."

"That's not his way. See, them dogs is starvin' animals, poor things, and we cain't be lookin' over our shoulder all the time wonderin' if they might go after us. Some of um turned bad because of people treatin' um bad and they is starved."

Mom-mom moved on out to the clothesline, lowered the pole, and hung her clothespin basket on the line. She began to hang shirts one after the other, then pants, and then her dresses by the hem. She constantly glanced around. Fred had joined her and I was sure we would be alerted by him if anything came near the yard, just like Plato did at home. Both dogs were good guards, protectors of family. Mom-mom moved on down the line hanging clothes, a chore for her that never ended week in and week out, just like toting wood for her Home Comfort, feeding the housed chickens, and fixing three meals a day.

At the window, a slight breeze blew through the screen. She had raised the window far enough for a short screen to fit the hole. Both ends of the screen pushed open to widen so that it could fit any window. I watched intently through the wire mesh. Fred appeared to be comfortable with his surroundings and was sniffing his way around the smokehouse. He looked up once in a while, sniffed the air and then nosed his way around again not seeming to be alarmed.

I called to Mom-mom, "May I come out now?"

She said. "Just for a couple minutes."

I followed Fred in his circles around the smokehouse and spied a flower, a most beautiful flower that sat upon the top of a long stem. "What's that?" I asked Mom-mom.

"What's what?"

"Those purple flowers there with a funny shape. Looks like they've been crowned."

"Maypop. Your Pop-pop's mother keeped them in her garden."

"How about that clump with purple flowers along the stem over there with leaves that look like skinny greens?"

"Don't tell me you don't know chicory when you see it?"

"I forget year to year."

"The roots'a them is good for you, got medicine. Truth be told, they's lots of plants that folks think of as weeds that has got medicine. My Aunts knowed their medicines!"

"Don't need none of um," I spouted. My experience with her medicines was that they seemed to work most of the time, but to my mind, *The bitter taste would gag a goat, and a goat will eat just about anything including the seat out of a car if the door was left open.*

Suddenly, the shotgun sounded twice, and then twice again. I looked at Mom-mom. She stood still as if counting, but said nothing. One more shot sounded. When the blasts stopped, she calmly walked toward the porch with her empty clothesbasket and pins. Fred picked up his ears and poked his head around the house in the direction of the shots, but then followed us to the porch steps.

Back in the kitchen, she wet a cloth and handed it to me, "Wipe your feet and go stretch yourself out on my bed, at least for a few minutes." There was no use in arguing and once I laid down, sleep came fast.

I awoke alone in the house. My shoes were beside the washstand and Fred lay on the floor beside the bed. Fred was not allowed in the house, but probably, Mom-Mom had done that so I wouldn't wake up alone. *Better take no chances,* I thought, and jumped out of bed, ignored the shoes, and took Fred outside. "No need to get fussed at if you can help it," I said to him, "That's a good one to learn, Fred."

From the looks of the table, lunch had passed. There sat a half-eaten platter of scrapple, a couple links of sausage, and dirty dishes were in the sink. Bruce and Pop-Pop had come to the house, eaten lunch, and gone back out again, Mom-Mom with them. She had left my lunch on the stove, a plate with a large helping of greens, two biscuits, a sausage link, and pears. *Pop-Pop worries! My foot! If so, he's not the only one*, I thought, but I didn't feel like eating.

The next day, when it came time to hoe, the fact that I had slept all afternoon the day before was proof enough for Mom-mom that I was not fit to go in the field. "Well, I'll bring you extra water mid-morning. I can do that," I argued.

Pop-Pop said, "Ring the yard bell if need be," and turning to Fred he said, "Stay Dog," and then they were gone.

Why won't he call him, Fred? I wondered. *A dog needs a name and Fred is a solid name! Strong*! "Fred," I exclaimed emphatically. Fred wagged his tail. Looking at him, I knew that he could have been one of those wild dogs if we had not taken him in and fed him. I wondered if they had killed all of the dogs they had hunted yesterday. If they got all four of them, one dog had to be shot twice, unless there were five. No one had said.

I patted his shaggy head and looked at the yard-bell remembering stories of how important those bells had been out in the country before telephones had been installed. Pop-Pop had an Aunt, Aunt India, who had lived about a mile down the road. She got sick and weak, sometimes she would fall. So, her husband, Uncle Will would ring his yard bell for Pop-Pop to go help put her back in bed. No telephones had been installed down many local roads during the 50s, a fact that crossed my mind every time something urgent happened now. *But*, I thought, *telephones don't reach out into the field anyhow. How can they?* My imagination could not come up with solving that problem. "No telephones out there, Fred," I said, as I pumped water into his pail. He lapped thirstily for a couple minutes and then knocked it over. Tired, I settled under the largest maple and promised him I'd fill it again later.

He settled beside me as I started making roads in and out of the roots with a small metal truck and building bridges with small twigs while brushing away the ants crossing my roads. A doodlebug hill caught my attention and so I clapped my hands just above the hole, but none came out. Finally bored, I watched the work going on out in the field.

Everyone moved steadily down the rows tucking the vines into straight lines. The field began to look neat and orderly. The breeze blew Mom-Mom's dress as she walked along. No skin could be seen. Her dress was nearly to her ankles, and she had a thin long-sleeve shirt over her arms, and a bonnet that nearly covered the side of her face. Her eyeglasses held the rim of the bonnet outward. Occasionally, Pop-Pop took his straw hat off, wiped his forehead with his shirtsleeve, and capped the hat back on his head. His suspenders made his pants jerk slightly with each chop of the hoe. Bruce didn't take his hat off and moved ahead, on up the rows. Their movements began to seem dizzying until the realization hit me just like before—*I don't feel well.*

My eyes watered and felt sunburnt. *Better get some water*, I decided and moved from the maple tree to the well. Priming the pump, I splashed water over my face which felt strange, tingling. I went inside and looked in the washroom mirror again. *Yesterday my face was just red. Today it is speckled.*

No one had ever rung that yard-bell so loud. I just kept ringing and ringing. They hurried from the field looking around for the problem, but when Mom-Mom glanced at me, she simply said, "She's got the measles," and then ordered, "You put a lightweight nightgown on and git into my bed." I didn't argue. All my energy was gone. She added, "Should'a had them shoes on; you'd wish you had one of these days if you step on one of them big red ants." But her chiding was half-hearted. She did what she does best, take care of things as they happen, and so she took charge of me.

She had Bruce pump some water and fill the washbowl by the bed, and then asked him, "You've had the measles?" Bruce nodded. "Well, it's likely you won't catch um from her then," she added, and continued to move around doing things I couldn't see, but I heard the shades being drawn, liquid shake in a bottle, and then she wet a cloth and laid it on my hot forehead. "Now, you're not to set foot outta this bed."

All I could think about was castor oil and niter, "No castor oil or niter!" I managed to say.

"No," she affirmed.

"Or chicory!"

"You've not lost that sense'a humor'a your'n, I can see that."

But, I wasn't joking.

"This is cherry tastin'," she said shoving a spoon in my mouth before I could protest, "It'll help you sleep." She leaned down and smiled; then she patted the cloth on my forehead. Her comforting gestures were given in so many ways that I did not doubt her love, even when she sternly cautioned against this or that.

Bruce stayed when she went out. The medicine was sweet, but I frowned at her leaving. "She'll be back," he offered, "She probably went to get a chicken from the yard to make you some chicken broth. You know how she is about her broth."

"Not the one that lets me pet her. Not that one."

"She knows. She won't."

"She's mostly white so I named her, Snowball," I whispered to Bruce. "But don't tell."

"Better keep that to yourself then," he said with no irritation in his voice, just caution.

"You remember when we walked past our house and on down to Fleming's Mill Pond the other day when we were fishing for catfish?"

"Yeah."

"Well, we could have come across those dogs then."

"I thought about that too," he agreed.

"I've decided that I don't want to catch catfish anymore, anyway."

"Why?"

"That spike on their back; it almost poked me good. I gotta wait till they're still and grab them quick, getting a finger on each side of that spike. Makes me nervous."

"Just takes practice." Bruce said.

Gazing at the wall, I focused on the framed picture of an old woman, so old that a saying I'd heard many times came to mind. 'Old as Methuselah.' The picture had been hanging in the living room, but now hung over the old pump organ at the foot of the bed. I wondered why the woman had been moved and wondered who she was, a great-grandmother? Turning to Bruce I asked, but he didn't know.

Getting sleepy, I asked, "How come you don't get sick with different things like I do?"

"I've already had most of this kind of stuff. I'm nearly four years older and besides, I'm far more superior in ways to avoid such things," he said with a grin, but I was too tired to take the bait.

Yet rousing for a moment, I questioned him about the dogs, "We heard shots yesterday. Did Pop-pop get them all?"

"Yes, all," he said.

"That's good, I guess." Then, thinking of Fred, "Fred's pail is beside the well. Will, you pump him some water. He spilled it," but I didn't hear an answer. The medication knocked me out.

Not wanting to hoe cucumbers and watermelons had become a reality. Two weeks of bed, burning eyes, headache, and chicken broth had been endured before I began to return to my usual chatty self. The first round of hoeing cucumber and watermelon plants had passed and Pop-Pop had already cultivated between the rows. After that, rain had come just at the right time. There was another stint of turning vines a couple weeks later, but even then I was not allowed since Mom-Mom announced that I was still 'weak-eyed.'

I had created my own superstition—the fact that I had complained had caused me to become sick. I made a solemn vow to be more careful about shirking chores from now on. Afraid of how sick I might become if I complained about hoeing or other chores, I quickly defended going in the field, "Baloney, I'm fit as a fiddle."

"Broth from the feisty rooster done you good. Lord knows, you got back the gumption to speak your mind." Then she grinned, "Let's hope you don't start to crow."

Passion Flower, also commonly known as Maypop.

A variety of chickens always ran Eva Pusey's yard. Some were chicks from the chicken house such as the Rock chicks and others were bought, such as Banties and Reds.

"The Guinea Watcher" - nothing escapes his all-seeing eyes.

Guineas, sentinels flowing like silver across the landscape. Their white heads with black dots for eyes can be seen jerking back and forth as they move. They will also send up a screeching signal should anything unusual enter their range area. They are watchdogs on the farm and unlike chickens, they form pairs.

Harvesting

"Sure is hot. The sun is just barely above the tree tops," I fussed snatching the bonnet off my head. Mom-Mom had insisted that I wear one today, saying that the sun would bake my head if I didn't. "Keeps you from gettin' giddy-headed," she'd added, saying the same thing from strawberry through tomato picking. At least in the spring during strawberry time, the mornings were cooler and the baskets were so small that a child could carry it with little effort, but the 5/8's basket of tomatoes got heavier every day and my 89 pounds staggered while dragging it down my row. Bruce was right. I should have appreciated the strawberry picking season. And after the bout with measles, I had sworn not to complain about chores. But tomato picking would tempt the angels from heaven—I was sure of it.

Arching my back while wiping sweat from around my hairline, I fussed, "Giddy-headed my foot, I'll pass clean out if I don't get some air to my face." I began to fan my head with the bonnet. My cotton knee pants were soaked through to my skin from the morning's dew, dew that was slow to leave the thick tomato vines. Breakfast seemed long past and although I knew it was nowhere near noon, my back ached already. I looked across the rows seeing Aunts and Uncles, Cousins, Bruce, Mom-Mom and Pop-Pop, all up and down the field, bending and stooping while filling their baskets. A couple of my Uncles had just entered the field, starting new rows next to a few neighbors who lived a few miles away and had just arrived as well. The neighbors were ribbing each other about something and laughter rang out across the field. With every newcomer, Fred had roused from his sanctuary under the largest maple, but had settled quickly.

A slight breeze stirred loose dirt from the sandy road forming a dust devil that whirled around me, filling my eyes with fine grit. "Must be past 90 degrees already," I sighed while tucking the bonnet brim inside the waist of my pants. *Let that thing flop on my backside instead of covering my face*, I thought, and turned to see Pop-Pop eyeing me. Guess I couldn't get away with going barefoot just now. That brought on a bigger fuss than not wearing the bonnet.

Sometimes we kids took our shoes off and tied the strings around the top edge of the basket. They would hang down so nobody could see them above the plants as we moved the basket down our row. We had boldly said to one another that our fear of snakes was not enough to keep us from wanting to feel the cool moist dirt between our toes; however, when either one of us was sighted by a grown-up, that feigned courage endured a scolding. I reasoned that we had to contend with spiders and green horned worms on the tomato plants while we are picking and we didn't wear gloves. *So snakes are the only real problem and Bruce said they would move out of our way. I doubt if snakes bite feet anyhow, more like ankles and legs.*

Since I had recently learned to wink with either eye, I used that communication at every opportunity, picking which eye to leave open and which to close. So I winked at Pop-Pop using a closed right eye, the most recent learned, and saw him try to keep from grinning as I skipped back down my row for an empty basket. Thankfully, my baskets were not new, but not too old, so I was less likely to get splinters in my hands. They were worn enough to bend, but not break.

However, that appreciation didn't last long. When turning to wink, I skipped into the baskets, sending me sprawling and driving splinters from one broken basket into the back of my hand. The wound stung like the dickens. I quickly looked around to see if anyone was watching, but everyone was busy, even Pop-Pop had turned back to work. Gingerly working one fingernail under and another over the biggest splinter, I pulled out a strip of wood that felt inches long. I left the small ones in the wound. *Doggone it*, I thought. *Before the small pieces of wood can be wiggled out, it will fester and need pinched out along with the pus that will form.* Embarrassment would not allow me to get Mom-Mom out of the field to pick at my clumsiness with a needle. Pulling the unbroken half-bushel baskets away from the broken one, I went back to work, although not quite as peppy as before.

Earlier in the morning, Pop-pop had backed his truck up to the barn. A couple helpers, who had arrived early, lent a hand pulling half-bushel baskets out of storage and pitching them onto the flatbed. As Pop-pop drove along the road beside the tomato field, they rolled baskets off the truck and onto the ground up and down the entire length of the field. As the helpers began to pick, Pop-pop separated the baskets into piles and since the rows were so long, he placed several baskets at both ends of each row for all the pickers. Once in a while, if time allowed, he would place baskets in the middle of every-other row. That way we pickers did not have to waste time retrieving baskets piled at the end of each row or the side of the field. We got paid by each basket picked, not by an hourly wage. He got paid at the canning factory for the amount picked, so everyone benefited by not having to waste time walking too far for baskets.

Two rows were picked at a time. The grown-ups stooped while picking, moving predictably down the middle of their rows, swaying over one row and then twisting and swaying over the other row reaching the far sides of each one. This morning I crawled along on my hands and knees while lifting and parting the vines in order to find the recently ripened tomatoes. Those vines were higher than my waist. This seemed easier to most of the children who did not have the height to sway over and see the far side of each plant. I jumped up once in a while to drag my basket with me.

When I reached the end of my row and looked back, the rows seemed a mile long. We all knew that tomatoes were heavy on the vine in August and must be picked or they would rot. *Even though there are less acres planted than last year or the year before, it's still going to take a lot of people to pick even this many rows*, I thought. But help came not only from family and our neighbors, but from other families in the area as well.

There was a loud backfire and we all looked up at two cars and a pick-up that had parked along the edge of the road. One of our neighbors raised his hand to his eyes to gain a clearer view. "Here come some colored folks to help us pick. Not as many today as yesterde'," he voiced so Pop-Pop could hear. Then to anyone listening he said, "I expect they's fewer pickers cause vines is heavy all over the county just now and Old Man Townsend's tomatoes, cucumbers, and watermelons is needin' picked all at onced, too, them cantaloupe fields over on Court House Hill Road is bigger this year so I expect Roger's done good gettin' this many." But, he had simply stated the obvious. Everyone already knew that tomatoes ripened at the same time across the county and even across many states. I marveled that he had said all that without taking a second breath.

Roger's group laughed and carried on so that I was curious about the merriment. He got out of the old Ford pickup and went over to Pop-Pop. Their conversation was lost on me, but I suspected he was telling Pop-Pop that he had done the best he could finding help for today. Pop-Pop nodded to him and bent back over his basket. Fred had stood and growled, watched everyone take their places in the field, and then laid back down. So everyone found rows not yet started and began to pick in rows next to each other.

Some folks who had not come this year as Roger had, were Slim and Rose. They were from Florida, and in years past they had lived just through the woods near where Roger lived. Each year, they had stayed from early summer until the first weeks of December. I had been told that during some of the war years between '41-'45, they had stayed year-round. They had become as regular as clockwork arriving on a certain day in the late spring and leaving on December 10th, perhaps leaving to pick oranges in their home state of Florida. Slim and Rose were tall and slender. She came to the fields each morning very neatly dressed in perfectly clean shirt and jeans. While they had helped pick many crops on the farm, their favorite had been string-beans when Pop-pop had planted a few acres for sale. Yet, they were masters at husking corn.

They had been middle-aged during those war years and became very closely attached to Mom-mom and Pop-pop. Rose would come inside the house with Mom-mom for a while, but Slim did not go inside. He would sit outside on the porch steps or maybe find a chore to do while Rose and Mom-mom visited.

After all their years helping to pick crops on the farms that Pop-pop and Mom-mom owned, I wondered why Slim and Rose had not come the past couple or so years. Perhaps they were now too old to travel all the way from Florida. Or maybe they just became too tired to travel and work on the various farms along whatever route they had taken northward from Florida to here. I wasn't sure if I really even remembered what they looked like, or if I was recalling descriptions of them told to me. Suddenly, I realized I had been staring in Roger's direction as if Slim and Rose were going to magically appear.

As far as I was concerned, lunch break arrived just in the nick of time. Although it was plenty hot by noon, the hottest part of the day was yet to come. "This August heat is what strokes is made of," I heard Mom-mom say. She'd said the same thing about January's freezing weather when she carried wood to the house for her cook stove.

When the house was too stifling, our family ate outside. When it was cooler inside meals were spent with cousins as we wolfed down sandwiches in the kitchen, then chased each other in and out of the house. Mom-Mom could be heard yelling, "Stay in or out and quit bangin' that screen door; it'll fall off'a the hinges." Eating inside meant an extra treat, maybe leftover dumplings or jelly biscuits. Everyone other than family brought their own lunch, usually in a small brown paper bag and nearly the same things, a sandwich of bologna, spam, or smoked ham and an apple or pear. All were permitted a tomato from the field. Since August was so hot everyone ate outside most of the time and there was no lemonade, which was one of Pop-pop's favorites, we just drank cold water from the well.

A young girl, who was about my age, came with Roger today as in previous days. Although I was a distance away, I could have sworn I heard someone called her Marge. Catching glances, we were shy, curious about one another. When going back into the field, we were a short distance from each other while walking out the lane. Face to face, the shyness came again when I said, "Hi."

She said, "Hi."

I remembered how I had found a worm in my half eaten tomato making me want to heave. I was sure she had experienced that same trauma and I wanted to ask her, but I didn't. I wanted to ask her what grade she would be in and when her school started. I was curious to know what her school was like. Surely everyone played hop-scotch, and jumped rope, and girls had to wear dresses and could not wear pants. Very unfair, having to wear dresses, and I wanted to talk about that and about how many baskets she had picked so far today. But, I didn't. Neither of us said anything except, 'Hi,' and then we walked the short way to the field in silence. After crossing the road, we quietly moved away from one another going back to our individual rows.

There were other places where that same separation came to mind, the movies for one. My Aunts and Uncles promised some of us children a movie on Saturday nights after picking tomatoes all week. Many times, we went to the drive-in theatre and promptly fell asleep in the back seat of the car. Also, on rare occasions, after Pop-pop had taken a load of tomatoes to the cannery on a Saturday, he took us to the horseraces in late afternoon. We got all dressed up and at the racetrack we watched the long white Cadillac fold its gates while pulling away from the horses as the race began. But, in order to see special movies, we went to the movie theater in town. "Please take us to the Marva," we begged often. Our mind centered on the popcorn machine and being able to sit by ourselves, away from the grownups!

The lines were long one Saturday night that summer. There was a line for black people and one for white people. Marge and I stood in those separate lines and stared at each other. We had picked tomatoes in the same field and eaten lunch in the same yard, but when the weekend came we went in separate doors at the movies. We sat in separate rooms; she in the balcony and I downstairs. That separation seemed absolute by some invisible line that I could not see, in the fields, at the movies, in school, and even places to eat. All those places crossed my mind as Marge and I continued to work in the same tomato field together and sit with our own families under separate trees. *Separate lives doing similar things*, I concluded.

Each afternoon seemed to get hotter than the last. One afternoon while bending over my basket to pick it up and move it, a hard knot of a tomato hit my butt and hit it hard. I spun around to see who the culprit might be, as if I didn't know. Bruce was grinning like a Cheshire cat. I shook my fist at him, threatening him with bodily harm. He was not phased. Rubbing my butt, I vowed to get him back. *The fact that I had picked green tomatoes to finish out his basket before he got back in the field couldn't have had anything to do with it. Could it? That's okay*, I thought while rubbing my welt, *He'll get his.*

Reaching the end of my row, I picked some blackberries in the corner of the field. The juice was hot, but tasted so good. The vines were prickly, but I was careful and stood in the shade for quite some time before sitting, sweat still beading on my forehead. A toad hopped at edge of the woods where the rise dropped off to the water. I was too tired to even catch and play with him. No one chastised me for taking such a break and would not have, even had I quit and gone up to the house. Looking up, Pop-Pop saw me, but said nothing. He sure kept an eye on everything. While I looked out over the long, narrow field, sudden laughter would ring out from various sections and echo in the woods, bringing a sense of well-being, comfort in knowing that all was well with the grownups.

After a few minutes, Pop-pop called for a break to anyone who wanted watermelon. He sent Bruce and Roger over to the four acre watermelon field to bring back what they could carry. He then produced his pocket knife and wiped the blade with his handkerchief. So under the shade of a cypress tree next to Burk's Mill Branch, our family and neighbors had slices of watermelon as did Roger and his friends under a large oak protruding from the woods. The random biting fly found its mark and the occasional slapping of a hand on an arm or leg could be heard. Those flies seemed to hover around the woods daring anyone to come near. The mosquitoes didn't seem so bad this year and that was another relief. Someone mentioned snapping turtles coming up from the branch behind us, mainly to razz the younger ones, me included. That teasing made me realize that I had not looked before settling myself. We all knew that a bite from a snapper could be serious and the conversation grew to the yarn about someone's toe being bitten off. We were young when we had been taught the difference between box turtles and snapping turtles.

As I ate, I glanced around for movement in the grasses. *Holding the slices by the rind seems like we are more civilized than bursting a melon open in the field and scooping out chunks with our unwashed hands*, I thought, remembering last year. Juice still ran down my arms, but the fruit was as refreshing as a swim in the creek might have been, that is, if we were allowed, which we weren't. We were told that the murky, cypress-stained water of Dividing Creek contained dangers. The limbs and leaves that had fallen for many years into the water around the banks had created the illusion of solid ground. Swamps and bogs surrounded Dividing Creek and in many spots, a person would have to know where to step in order not to become mired in the muck.

"Them watermelons is gonna need picked sometime next week, cucumbers too. That little patch'a cantaloupes might not turn out to be much, but we'll break with these here tomatoes to git that done," Pop-Pop was thinking out loud. There was no need for an answer from anyone. He was the first to reenter the field. One-by-one we all straggled back to our individual rows and began picking once again. Bruce and I started new rows near the woods. I didn't mention my sore butt, but had plans to surprise him when he least expected it.

I had eaten so much watermelon it was sloshing around in my belly. Feeling sluggish, it seemed the afternoon wore on too slowly. Bruce moved ahead of me, working faster than I could. Gauging my timing, I chucked a couple of rotten tomatoes his way. He dodged well. When Pop-Pop was at the opposite end of the field, Roger chased me with one of those fat green worms with horns. I screamed and ran even though I knew he wouldn't put it on me. He knew that I knew, he wouldn't. It was all a game.

Today had been filled with events that had helped break the monotony of picking. Breaks such as lunch, watermelon in the shade, and playing around, whether tormenting each other with tomatoes or worms, helped us all to make it through the day. Suddenly another event jerked us all upright looking in several directions at once. A shotgun blast resounded through the woods.

My eyes finally settled on Pop-Pop. He was facing the woods still aiming his gun. *Where had the gun come from that quickly?* I couldn't figure and shaded my eyes, wondering what that thing was now laying at the edge of the field? It looked the size of a dog. "Bruce," I yelled. "What is that?"

"Looks like an otter," he shouted.

I was confused. *Why in the world would anyone shoot an otter?* I looked at Bruce. He shrugged his shoulders.

Pop-Pop walked over to the animal making sure it was dead. "Git me a shovel from the truck," he bellowed across the field to Roger. A couple more men walked with Roger over to the edge of the woods. Roger started to pick up the otter with the shovel, but Pop-Pop took it from him and said, "I done it. I'll take care of it." Pop-pop scooped the animal with the shovel and disappeared into the woods with his heavy load. It was several minutes before he returned. Nothing more was said.

That afternoon, I paid more attention to my surroundings and knew that the feeling of unknown dangers would stay with me. The event made me feel as if there were other threats besides wild dogs in the woods, dogs like Fred, that had been dropped off in the country one by one, left to starve and roam in packs. But I had never thought of otter as being dangerous. I was sure that the otter had been killed for a very good reason and wanted to know what it was, but that would have to wait, at least until evening.

Just before we all quit for the day, I picked some green tomatoes for Mom-Mom and carried them in my bonnet. Some were for frying and some were used for removing vine stains from our hands. The smell of tomato vine on me was strong. I hoped she didn't insist that a bleach bath was necessary tonight. We never really seemed to get rid of that vine smell on our bodies until the season was spent.

Pop-Pop counted the baskets in everyone's row and gave each of us numbered tickets equaling the amount of baskets picked, just like in strawberry time. Then the men carried the baskets over to the edge of the field by the road, placing them in one long line. There had been a particularly large number of baskets filled. Everyone was tired. Without talking, family members and other pickers slowly walked to their vehicles and headed home. It was nearly sundown, late for a day's picking, and that made for a late supper like during planting time. *All this work will make for a good night's sleep. I'm exhausted.*

Even Pop-Pop seemed to be shuffling his feet on the way to the house. After lunch, I had taken my navy oxfords off and tied them together by the shoe strings. Having grabbed one shoe, the other trailed behind me bouncing on the ground. He was too tired to notice and I was too tired to put them on.

When we reached the well, we hand-pumped water for one another, splashing our faces and arms. But that wasn't good enough to remove the tomato stains. I opened the porch door and put the bonnet of tomatoes inside the porch. "Here are the green ones," I called to Mom-mom, "I guess I ate too much watermelon; my belly is still full, feels sloshy." That was a mistake. Before I knew what happened, I had a teaspoon of sugar doctored with niter shoved in my mouth.

I got my toothbrush from the sink and took it out to the pump, brushing and rinsing the taste of niter out of my mouth. Pumping more water, I splashed my arms again and moved into the backyard. Walnuts had begun to fall to the ground. Bruce picked up a few walnuts and threw them into the corn-sheller. Hearing the grinding sound, a few chickens came to us and I got to pet Snowball, the friendly hen again. But, they quickly moved away, realizing there was no corn.

"That won't work," I said to Bruce as he ground away, "the walnuts are going to grind to pieces."

"No. Just watch."

Sure enough, that sheller hulled those nuts, spitting the hulls in one direction and nuts out on the ground. I gathered more nuts and dumped them in the top of the sheller and he turned the wheel until Mom-mom called us to supper.

Her normally shrill call sounded muted, tired. She had filled basins with water and sliced a green tomato in half and handed it back to me. "Go scrub your hands and feet and then rinse with water," she said and added, "Had them shoes off quite a spell today, huh?" But I didn't answer. She already knew by the looks of my heavily stained feet. I hurried outside to scrub the juice onto stained skin before she could mention bleach.

There was no sparring between Bruce and me at supper. A quiet tiredness engulfed the kitchen. Pop-Pop made one comment, "That otter come up from the crick into a field in the midst'a people in broad daylight. Had to be somethin' or t'other wrong with it. I only seen such a thing once before. Otter can drown you in the crick tryin' to play, but water's their natural place. The field ain't."

So that was why; safe rather than sorry. I was glad to have that question answered at least, but my interest in everything else seemed to fade as my head began to nod at the table. Watching me, Mom-mom said, "Had that bonnet off too! You know, sweatin' under a bonnet cools your head and gives you shade besides." I had to admit that she was probably right. I felt as if the work and the sun had drained every last ounce of energy I had. She sent me to bed, that is, after retrieving my dirty clothes and wetting a cloth to scrub my neck herself. I hadn't even tasted the green tomatoes she had fried so perfectly. But shortly after going to bed that niter began to work. And as Pop-pop had said many times, "Niter makes your waterworks run smooth."

The sound of helpers arriving to load baskets had already roused me from sleep when Mom-mom came in to wake me the next morning. She said nothing. It was still dark so she lit the coal-oil lamp and stood waiting for me to get dressed and then walked behind me out to the table, an unusual occurrence. We children could always tell when something was wrong, the grown-ups became silent and grim. Their actions changed, sometimes beyond description. My own silent alarm went off. She pointed to a chair for me to sit and said, "Don't ask no questions and stay put." I was sure she was going to explain, but she began to busy herself with breakfast.

Every sound on the farm seemed to have ceased. *Has everyone left?* Mom-mom moved around the kitchen, even placing her pans quietly on the stove as if someone were sleeping in the next room. Finally I couldn't stand the silence any longer. "The men have come to load that old Dodge Truck of Pop-Pop's this morning; I heard um before light," I said, swatting at a fly that had landed on my nose. "But they are awful quiet now," I added, figuring I hadn't said anything that required an answer. I should have looked out the front bedroom window at the road, but it was probably too dark to see anything. Silence drew in like a dreaded plague. "Might be they had some drink last night and are a bit out of sorts," I reasoned my own explanation.

That simply drew a look of disapproval from her. I had been told before that what the men did or didn't do when they were together, did not involve me — it was none of my business. My imagination took a turn. *Has somebody died,* I wondered, *or become sick? Maybe the truck won't start. Then they can't take the tomatoes to the canary and the sun beating down on those baskets of tomatoes all day might ruin yesterday's picking.*

The Home Comfort was hot which added to the heat of the early morning. She had taken a ham from the smokehouse and boiled it to remove heavy salt. It sat steaming in a pan while she chose a knife to use for slicing. The sun was coming up and there was quiet except for her movements, removing the top of a lard tin to spoon some lard into two spiders, then cutting ham slices, and finally placing them in the sizzling fat to fry. The kitchen took on new sounds. Taking down another spider, she dipped more lard in that pan for frying eggs. She got a dipper of water from the reservoir on the stove, and poured it into the sizzling ham. Steam flew to the ceiling as the pan crackled and spit. Then removing the ham, she placed each slice in an aluminum cake pan. Then lightly dusting flour over the ham juice left in the spiders, she stirred and stirred making a thin gravy they called red-eye gravy, which was no longer red, and she poured it over the ham. She got a bowl of eggs that sat on the back shelf of the stove, and cracked one at a time on the edge of the last spider and dropped each one in the hot lard.

Whenever Mom-mom put a pan of ham on the table with the juice in the bottom like she had just done, Pop-pop would break open a biscuit and place the soft centers face down in the pan until they had become soaked with that gravy, and then fish them out and eat. Usually, I might have taken a morsel of something while waiting for everyone, but today was different. I felt glued to my chair without knowing why.

Her well-worn tin of flour caught my attention; it had a brightly colored chicken painted on it and I wondered how long she had had the tin. Her lard tin was plain and had been filled from the big pots of lard stored in the sewing room. That lard came from the rendering of hogs during the cold winter. I had rarely seen anything new in the house, except maybe a screen for a window. The screen in the window behind me may as well not have even been there; the heat was building in the kitchen.

"You want to git the flyswatter and kill some of these flies. They is terrible this year. Don't swat none on the table."

"Sure," I said, grateful for something to do. I took the swatter off a nail hammered in the back door jamb and began waving the flies away from the table so they would land somewhere else. They seemed to land mostly in the sunshine on the floor and the side of the electric stove. After squishing them, I brushed them off each surface and onto the floor. All would be swept up later after the men came in and left again, leaving sand from their shoes. There was sand in the yard all the way up to the porch steps and Mom-mom never seemed to get rid of it in the kitchen, especially in the summer when people tracked in and out all day long, day in and day out. A dirty floor could not be helped and the best she could do was to sweep every evening.

When I was done, I went back to contemplating the painted chicken when the screen door closed quietly. I jumped. Pop-Pop and Bruce came in and sat down at the table without washing their hands. My eyes darted from face to face, but their expressions told me nothing and no one looked at anyone. Pop-pop took off his hat and dashed it to the floor. While he waited, Mom-Mom hurried, scooping the eggs onto our plates with the spatula and sat down. One after the other, we each reached for a slice of ham, and Pop-pop broke open two biscuits placing them face down in the gravy. Mom-mom stuck a large spoon in the jar of syrupy brown pears and then stuck a fork in one of her eggs. The yolk ran, surrounding her ham.

Many times, we had seen Pop-Pop crack the top of an eggshell and eat the egg raw. He loved eggs, morning, noon, or night; he would eat them anytime, occasionally grunting approval. But for all the pains Mom-mom had taken for this meal, there were no hints of approval. We ate in silence. With breakfast nearly finished, the pickers from the previous day arrived. Pop-Pop grabbed his hat from the floor and was up out of the chair at the first sound of a motor, leaving unfinished ham on his plate. Quietly, Bruce followed him outside. The silence had been painful. I turned and looked at Mom-mom still sitting at the table.

That was when she explained to me what had happened. During the night someone, probably teenage boys from town, had ridden out into the country and down our road lookin' for mischief. "This road is mostly traveled by our family what lives here, so it was outsiders that come," she said. "They upended nearly all them tomato baskets as a lark. None'a us heard nothin'. Your Pop-Pop raised up early thinkin' about our biggest pickin' so far, needin' to be loaded and taken into town. That's when he seen what they'd done."

When she finished speaking, she arose and began cleaning off the table. Since the flies were so bad, she covered the lazy-susan and stepped onto the porch. Whistling for Fred, she pitched the scraps onto the ground. Fred gratefully ate the small scraps, but looked guilty as he snatched Pop-pop's left over ham and ran around the side of the house, out of sight. Looking through the porch screens, Mom-Mom and I turned our gaze from Fred to the road and tomato field. Half empty baskets lay every which-way. Tomatoes were scattered up and down the road.

Neighbors, as well as the men who had come to load, were standing in the road, no laughing, no joshing each other about this or that. And Roger's group, a little smaller today, were still standing beside their vehicles, no merriment not a single conversation could be heard except for Pop-Pop selecting men to clean up the mess. Once the group of men began righting the baskets, everyone else went out to pick, dragging their own baskets into the field.

When it was still dark this morning, Pop-pop had loaded baskets from the barn for today's picking. He was going to place them in the field at the ends of the rows as usual and then load the tomatoes, but upon passing in front of the house toward the road, he had seen the damage. Now, Mom-mom and I gazed at the mess and then at empty baskets he had left on the truck. I was shocked at the destruction. Feeling the pain of sweaty work for better than 30 people, now ruined, I said, "Damn," instantly realizing I wasn't just thinking, I'd said it out loud. I fully expected a reprimand from Mom-mom for cursing.

"You young'uns worked as hard as everybody else. You've earned the right to speak you mind," she said emphatically as if the scene were too much for her too, "but," she added, "cursing mightn't be the best way to express it."

That was the moment when I realized that we grandchildren working the farm was not child's play. We were a part, a link in keeping the family farm going, enduring. And in that moment of recognition, I understood that everyone had felt the seriousness and pain of the situation down to the core, even we kids.

"That was hard work yesterday. It was so hot, I sweated in places

I didn't even know I had," I offered in a lighter tone.

Such a statement would usually force a grin to light her face, but I was not joking. I was serious. I had sweat terribly, pulled muscles in places I shouldn't have, and driven splinters into my hand—which suddenly came to mind. Too tired last night to have Mom-mom dig them out, the splinters had been ignored this morning as well. Glancing at my hand, I saw that they were festering. I picked at my pus-filled sores and squeezed them. The small splinters popped out. Looking back at her, I noticed her expression had not changed. Suddenly, she returned to the kitchen, grabbed a big butcher knife, and headed into the dining room through to the sewing room where the balance of last winter's hams had been taken out of the smokehouse, wrapped, and stored.

"What are you doing?" I asked unsteadily.

"Them people should be fed somethin' better than the bologna sandwiches they brought. That one I cooked this mornin' and another ought to be enough."

"What should I do?"

"They's plenty'a older ones to make out what tomatoes is still good and what's not. You stay with me. Rest yourself."

So, through until lunchtime, she made two large oblong pans of biscuits and placed them in the open window to gather natural yeast from the outside. Next, she boiled some salt out of the ham and then fried it all. When the biscuits had finally been baked and cooled a bit, she started to slice them and stuck an overhanging piece of ham inside. She had me get out the wax paper and cut squares big enough for two biscuits on each and lay them out flat on the table. "Go see if you can count how many men is cleaning up the mess, and then count the pickers too." She asked.

I went through the dining room and living room to the hallway and opened the screen door to the front porch. Looking across the road at everyone, I said, "Looks like eleven grown men including family. Then there's Pop-pop, Bruce, and two boys. The women and kids are picking, maybe seven of them." I yelled, noting that Marge was not here today.

"Well they's no need to tell them about it," she fussed.

"Sorry," I was embarrassed.

"Will you start slicin' them biscuits while I stuff um?"

"Sure," I said, and she handed me a knife.

I was confused. Today all the workers would get treated to lunch. It had seemed as if hired help was just that, hired help, but when it turned into some of them lending a hand when they didn't have too, that was different—hard times called for different actions. This reminded me of the story Dad told me about when so many people were hungry in the 30's and walked up and down the roads asking for a sandwich. He said, Mom-mom had fed several of those people, and one day an older black couple came. She brought them in the house, sat them down at the table, and fed them. I was still figuring out the rules of grown-ups, interaction between black and white, and the rules for children. I guess if children acted grown-up they got treated that way and if seriously hard times knocked on your door, white or black, black or white, you answered, but that area was still gray to me.

The day waned into afternoon before the men finished. I gave up trying to count the baskets of saved tomatoes, but from the way they were lined on the road, it was less than half. *How can she and Pop-pop accept this loss?* I wondered, *and how did he manage not to cuss, not to throw a fit, or react to show his feelings? He had been so tired last night, his age showed in the bend of his body. But today, there is no reaction from him that I can see.*

Everyone who had filled baskets found a tree and ate the biscuits stuffed with ham offered to them by Mom-mom. Some of the pickers politely declined the ham sandwiches and some didn't. The quiet was unnatural with so many people and no words spoken. I knew how hot it had been in the field and all the work that had gone into that harvest yesterday.

The broken baskets and smashed tomatoes had not been just a prank, but the destruction of a full day's work by many people and part of a crop that could not be recovered. Pop-pop still paid everyone for their baskets picked the day before, the same amount per basket. He took cash from his pocket for those who had repacked baskets. The damage was a big loss, but it was clear from the gloomy mood of the pickers throughout the day that everyone felt the same despair.

As soon as the truck was loaded with the repacked baskets and the baskets the pickers had finished, Pop-pop went to the cannery in Pocomoke, but I did not ask to go. I just couldn't stand to ride during what was bound to be a somber trip. I hadn't helped with the clean-up or picked today, neither had Mom-mom. *What was she thinking as she spent the day catching up on laundry and cleaning?* When evening came, she didn't talk then either. From the expression on their faces, you could not tell whether things were getting better or not. *Have they ever weighed the whys and the wherefores of the good times as opposed to the bad?* The only indication that I could see when something was wrong, would be a slammed door, or a pitched hat, but that was rare.

As intolerable as the day had been, that was not the end. The destruction was attempted again a few days later. That second time, boys from town were caught in the act. Pop-Pop had a man waiting, sitting in the field all night where he couldn't be seen—waiting every night. In the late hours of the third night, they tried the same destruction again and were dealt with right there on the farm. The law was not called. We never had that problem again. We grandchildren were only told that the perpetrators had been well-dressed boys from town. We were not told how some things were handled and that was one, but that had not kept us from wondering.

While back in the field a couple days later, a neighbor was passing me two rows over. I questioned her, not about the tomato event, but about Marge. "We're living in the 60's now. How come that girl who came with Roger, I think her name is Marge, and I shouldn't talk together and can't sit together here or in the movies? Who decides that?"

"Well," she said, "They's sweets, drinks, and bathrooms upstairs just like they is downstairs, and the seats is all the same. They's lots'a theatres like that."

But she had not answered my question so I repeated, "Why the separation?"

She thought for a moment before trying again, "See, for a while now, I don't think nobody has said nothin' about where colored or white folks has to sit. It's just that old ways is hard to break I s'pect. No one, not white, not black, is comfortable with gettin' started on them changes. But them changes is comin'; you can count on that!"

I didn't ask again. *Old ways! How old?* I wondered. Neither did I ask about church. I saw no separate door, no separate line there on Sunday morning. Thing was, I saw no black people there at all; their church was across town from the Presbyterian. I decided that getting an answer from grownups as to why black and white people stayed separate was about like the time I'd asked how babies were made. I was told how things are, not how they got that way. School didn't teach us answers to those questions and the older ones, whether family or neighbor, weren't about to do it either.

When the day came for picking and loading those Charleston Gray watermelons, all I could do was sit and watch as the men loaded those melons on the bed of the old Dodge. Men were lined up in the field, tossing melons forward into the next pair of waiting hands, until the melons reached the men on the ground at the back of the truck. Each melon seemed to float from one man to another, to the next, and so on, then skyward, up into the waiting hands in the truck's bed as it idled down the rows. Rails had been placed on both sides of the truck. Broken bales of straw lay on one side in the back of the bed. The men were stuffing straw between the rails and melons and between each melon. Depending on the yield, watermelons might be picked only once, sometimes twice. It seemed that this was a onetime picking. When it looked as if the rails might break, the men began to pile the next layer of melons inside of the outer row on the previous layer, and then each layer continued to be stepped further toward the middle as well. When loading was finished, they put the tailgate in place. It was late afternoon.

I asked if I could go with them to the auction block in Salisbury, and added, "I'll be up in plenty of time, I like that little store with all kinds of candy."

Mom-mom pleaded my case, saying, "Might be the last time she has a chance this summer."

In answer, Pop-pop shrugged his shoulders and that was that; I could go.

I had gone to Salisbury's auction block last year. I pictured the little store where I'd get an Orange Nehi, some squirrel nuts, orange jelly slices, maybe some root-beer barrels. I also remembered playing with other kids until Pop-pop pulled his truck forward for his watermelons to be auctioned.

Still fully dark the next morning, we piled out of the house together with lunch bags in hand. I was perched between Pop-pop and Bruce as we lightly bounced across the dirt road on our way to the auction. I remained quiet, but wished for a radio. The old dashboard didn't even seem to have a place for one. Listening to new songs, was now a favorite pastime of mine. With nothing to amuse, the trip to Salisbury seemed long since Pop-pop drove so slowly. But when we arrived, we weren't too far back in the line of trucks.

Once inside the little store, I went straight for the candy bins and one after the other searched for the Squirrel Nuts and jellies. I found only the orange jellies, root beer barrels, peanut butter logs, and one empty bin. I settled back in the truck with the barrels, jellies, and Orange Nehi. Chewing and chewing the jellies and then sucking away on the barrels, I fell asleep with the side of my cheek bulging—not even knowing what was in my lunch bag. The auctioneer was steadily chattering away, bidding off Pop-pop's melons when I awoke. Bruce was standing beside the truck, watching with Pop-pop. I could see from the expression on Pop-pop's face that he was pleased.

So he pulled his truck around and waited in line once more. This time the tractor trailer from the city had three farm trucks in line in front of Pop-pop's. We had to wait until those trucks were unloaded into the tractor trailer, before ours could be unloaded.

Since I had slept through my chances of finding playmates, I figured maybe Pop-pop, Bruce, and I could have a conversation on the way home, but I was wrong. I was simply told not to ask such silly questions, "What color were squirrels when they were born?" and "Who made up the rule that girls had to wear dresses or skirts to school?" *Those are pretty important questions*, I thought, *but clearly not to men.*

Pop-pop and Bruce had the windows rolled down with their elbows stuck out. They began to talk about a whining sound in the motor of the old Oliver tractor, so I turned around backwards with knees on the seat while grasping the high back of the seat with my fingers. I stuck my face against the back window of the truck watching dust from the road swirl and blow in thick clouds behind us and up on the flatbed. Pop-pop traveled much faster going home, so fast it seemed as if a tire might pop when we hit an especially deep hole in the road and every once in a while, a bump would send my head near the ceiling which added to my entertainment. That is when Pop-pop would say, "If I gotta slam them brakes, you is gonna bust the back of your head on that dashboard." But, it was half-hearted disapproval, and so, we continued home that way, me looking where we had been and they watching where we were going.

The harvest season finished quietly as the same routine had played itself out. Before dawn, Mom-mom began by lighting the coal-oil lamps, stoking the woodstove, and cooking breakfast. After Pop-pop arose, he went outside to load stacked tomato baskets from the barn onto the flatbed and dump them into the field. Usually, men had arrived to help with the placement of those empty baskets in the field and, if there was a harvest from the previous day, they would help load the truck as dawn was breaking. Pop-pop would wolf down some breakfast before leaving for the Pocomoke cannery. After he came back, Mom-mom was already in the field with all the workers who had arrived. He would begin to pick as well.

Just before lunchtime, Mom-mom left the field to fix a meal for the family that usually included the morning's leftover biscuits stuffed with sliced ham or pork, sometimes just bologna. Our family lunch was similar to what all the other workers had brought to eat. Everyone came out of the field to rest and eat lunch in the shade of the maples in the front yard. Brown paper bags could be heard rustling and the pump handle could be heard squeaking up and down. Once lunch was over, a steady stream of people could be seen leaving the yard for the rows each of them had left. Work in the afternoon wore on much the same as the morning, only hotter. Occasionally someone rested in the shade.

If the day had been spent in the watermelon field, only men would load the truck. Mom-mom did not enter the watermelon field except to thump a melon for ripeness and check stems in an attempt to find a good one for after supper. She rarely helped with the loading of the melons, or the loading of cantaloupes which had produced just as Pop-pop had expected—not much. Some had rotted on the low ground near the end of some rows.

Toward the end of tomato picking, I sat on the front porch and watched the men form a line in the field and swing baskets from one to another until reaching the last men near the road who placed each basket in a long line at the edge of the field. No factory assembly line worked any smoother. Similar to the loading of watermelons and cucumber baskets, the loading of tomato baskets seemed streamlined as straw-hatted heads bobbled in turn from receiving the weight. Even the occasional wiping of foreheads and the handkerchiefs being stuffed in the back pocket of overalls and suspendered pants was blended with the smooth action of loading.

Each day, the Pocomoke cannery had a set price for tomatoes. At the Salisbury Auction Block the cucumbers were bid on by the basket, cantaloupes by the pair, and watermelons by a single melon. Pop-Pop was usually among the first in line at the cannery so he could get back to the farm. He tried to arrive early at the auction block too and hoped for the best price as his crops went up for bid.

After Mom-mom left the field at dinnertime, she rarely plucked, cleaned, and fried a chicken when she had picked tomatoes all day. But one late summer day, an old rooster wound up in the stew pot for chasing more than one grandchild around the yard. She had simply said, that a rooster's spurs could leave 'pretty nasty scars on a young'un.' It was clear to those watching, that she had had enough of that rooster's actions. With more than her share of work to accomplish before winter set in, chasing a cocky rooster every time he tried to spur a grandchild was one less thing she would have to do.

A couple times we had come out of the field a little early. So while she was fixing dinner, Pop-pop had treated all the young family pickers to a trip into town. Hickman's Market was located near the Pocomoke River, just before crossing the bridge into town. Mr. Hickman's market had fresh fruit from Florida during the winter. But in the summer, we children were looking for Nehi sodas and candy. Since soda bottles were reused, we took bottles from our previous visit back to the store and got credit for each one. Searching the candy bins, I always wanted the squirrel nuts first. Small ice-cream cups with little wooden spoons were a real bonus. Of course, we would be full of candy when dinner was ready.

After dinner was over, Mom-mom might pick greens, sweetcorn, beans, or any vegetable that had ripened in the garden and needed to be canned. She even made a few trips out into the field to find the exact size cucumbers for making pickles. In order to get out of picking cucumbers, I would offer to do nearly anything, pick greens or pole beans from the garden, anything to keep the small fibers on the cucumbers from pricking my fingers, but she did not seem to mind. She helped workers pick and pack the larger ones in bushel baskets. Her fingernails had split from too much farm work, but that did not seem to bother her even when she pulled the wire bales on each side of those wooden baskets up over the ears of the lid. Her hands were calloused and cracked too, but I never heard her complain, only rub her salve over one hand and then the other.

Pop-pop was the last one in the field at night giving out tickets to the pickers and packing up tools used during the day. The Dodge truck had broken only one axle during August, and thankfully that mishap had happened on the farm where it was promptly fixed. One day when Pop-pop was taking the Dodge flatbed to park it beside the barn for the evening, I struggled to pull myself up on the back just as he started the motor. I rode that flatbed all the way from the field and across the road while standing with my arms outstretched to catch the wind. As soon as he parked in front of the barn, I swung down and casually walked away and he went on to do his last chores of the day. He fed the hogs and pumped water into the cypress log. The kick-start pump in the chicken house could be heard after that. Either he or Mom-Mom had fed those chickens before the sun went down.

With the last tomato picking, as with the last picking of cucumbers, pickers left the baskets right where they had finished them. The men did not have to carry them over to the road this time. With rails removed, that Dodge idled slowly down the rows while men on the ground swung baskets up to men on the bed of the truck. Plants were being smashed by tires as the truck continued on its slow roll, hardly stopping while turning up and down the rows. The first round of loading filled the bed with cucumber baskets. The second layer was stepped just inside of the outside row of the bottom layer. The stacking continued that way, and looking at the back of the truck, the baskets began to form a pyramid. Three rows high was usually the maximum Pop-pop would ever stack baskets. Neither the rails nor tailgate were used. He drove the truck very slowly to the auction block in Salisbury, just as slowly as he had done taking tomatoes to Pocomoke. The truck-crop season had finally come to an end.

Some plants remained unharmed by the truck wheels, so folks would glean the fields for their own consumption over the next few days. The left over crops would also become food for the hogs. Now that the shoats were full blown hogs they could eat nearly anything. Adding to his warnings about hogs, Pop-pop had said, "Too, that breedin' boar can turn meaner than that sow with babies." He didn't need to say anything about the boar, it was a threatening looking animal just standing still. I wasn't about to go anywhere near his pen.

Marge and I did not have the chance to speak again during those last days of August, and I continued to wonder about things we had not been able to mention. I had wanted to talk about a movie coming to the Marva in September. I didn't though. Best not, I thought. Once we caught ourselves staring at each other and looked away suddenly. Something had changed. Although we were shy and had only said, 'Hi' to one another, there was a bigger distance that I couldn't fully grasp, but one thing was clear: as children, we had not chosen that distance! I had heard talk that in a year from now, some black children might be bussed to the white high school where I would be starting seventh grade. Then black and white could go to school together. I would have to wait and see.

After that final day of picking tomatoes, I sat on the porch steps while Mom-mom fixed supper. Trucks and cars went in separate directions as usual. The scene was bittersweet. Even though we were glad to be done with the truck-crops, the end of the season meant that school was about to start. Not knowing if I would see Marge again, I watched her disappear in a cloud of dust while sitting in the back of a pickup truck bouncing over the potholes in the road. After the truck turned the corner by Miss Stella's house, the dust cloud settled within the trees of Burk's Mill Branch.

I stared at the clouded trees for a moment and then turned my gaze back to the farm. I saw the spent crops in the fields, and the apple trees with fruit yet to ripen, the beloved pear tree, the persimmon trees against the woods that would bear ripe fruit in late September, and the mountain laurel past its bloom. Next year came to mind. I would only be twelve: becoming a teenager seemed far away. I had been waiting for 1964 like it was a magic year, and I still had over a year to wait. I felt older, having worked with the harvest this summer and thought that years should be added to my life, not months, but Mom-Mom said to me, "You'll sprout up quick enough; they's no need to rush it along. 'Sides you'll change then. These times'a small worries'll be gone and you'll miss um."

Bet me, I thought.

After pumping water and drinking from the spout. I plopped back on the porch steps and rubbed Fred's head, frustration taking hold. I shifted my gaze from the fields to the moon that had risen without the benefit of the sun going down. I considered what I had been told about how everyone's life changes from year to year, yet as we get older, we see life more clearly. *I want some of those changes*, I decided. *There are many things I want to see clearer. Surely, Marge and girls our age everywhere feel the same impatience with all of this waiting. In the meantime, we will have to be content with feeling awkward and barely noticeable, a lot like that pale new-moon.*

Mountain laurel found in the Pocomoke Forest.

Vintage postcard of Pocomoke tomato canning (circa 1930-1945)
Image within the public domain

Harvey Pusey's Dodge truck used for hauling baskets of tomatoes was abandoned on this Fleming Mill Road Farm where he lived.

Split Oak Basket of tomatoes.

Cucumbers in a decorated handle, buttocks basket made by author from an oak on her grandparents' farm.

Snapping turtle from a Pocomoke Forest Pond.

Box turtle from the Pocomoke Forest woodlands.

Corn Husking and Pear Tree Climbing

Corn husking time had arrived but Slim and Rose still had not come. Once again, I wondered why they had not shown up this year and if they had called anyone lately. So without the couple, Pop-pop and Bruce had gone out beyond the barn to begin the corn harvest. They were armed with hand huskers that looked like can-openers. Pop-pop showed Bruce how to hold his gizmo and they began. Leaning up against the largest maple, I was curious as to how they were going to husk that field of corn. I had not paid much attention in previous years, except when the husking was complete and corn had been piled in the barn for the pigs and chickens. But to me, that corn was also there for me to climb up to my favorite perch and view the world.

Pop-pop had already borrowed a conveyor elevator. But first, he had hooked his trusty Oliver tractor to his wagon. Manual labor was all they needed to finish the job. Grasping an ear of corn still on the stalk with his right hand, Pop-pop raked the corn husker that he held in his left hand across where the corn connected to the stalk and husk. Some of the husk was left on the stalk and some on the ear of corn. Then he grabbed that ear of corn, pulling backward in one swift move, then twisted. He tossed the husk on the ground in one spot and the corn in another. That ear of corn had come out clean with most of the husk still on the stalk. Bruce followed by doing the same, but came away with most of the husk on the corn. He kept trying.

On and on they worked until the corn pile was too far away to toss the ears, so Pop-pop started a new pile by tossing corn ahead and they worked their way up to that pile and on past it tossing backwards, and then started another pile ahead of them once again. In years past, there had not only been Slim and Rose but neighborhood men to come and help. When my Father and Uncles were younger, they were in the field shucking corn. They made several piles as they moved up and down the field, a field much larger than Pop-pop had planted this year. *What a great family photograph that would have been*, I thought.

I turned to look as a rumbling from the road caught my attention. A pickup truck with a few men I did not know had pulled into the field. They got out of the truck and after a conversation with Pop-pop I could not hear, they started shucking corn in rows not yet begun. With the little I knew about shucking corn, I could tell that they had shucked corn many times. Within only a few minutes, the men had moved well into the field.

Searching for Mom-mom, I found her in the sewing room rummaging through a small old trunk and started to say something when the phone rang. It was such an unusual sound in their house since the phone rarely rang. "I'll get it," I said, and ran for the phone. It sat on a small two door stand that matched the dining room set. The phone was an older desk model and the handle was heavy, just as heavy as the telephone receiver in the drugstore phone-booth. Looking at Mom-mom's receiver reminded me of the telephone booths on the corner of the street and in the drugstore in Pocomoke, but each phone call had to be paid for in a booth; change was dropped in the money slots. "Hello," I said, delighted to get to answer. "Some man wants to talk to you, Mom-mom," I yelled.

She raised her eyebrows at my blatant statement. "Hey-O," she said and after listening, she simply said, "Thank you," and went into the kitchen where she had a calendar hung on the wall by a nail left of the kitchen-porch door. A pencil hung from a string around the nail and it would not make a mark on the calendar, so she got a paring knife from the drawer and began to whittle it to a point. Satisfied, she licked the lead and began to write. She always licked the lead of a pencil before she started to write as if the pencil would not write unless it was wet.

Poking my nose up to the calendar, I asked, "Who is that doctor appointment for?" Neither of them went to the doctor unless something was seriously wrong and it seemed Pop-pop had to be forced, which nobody forced him to do anything anyhow.

"Mind your own business," she said. "Tell you what, go see if I got any eggs in them nests in the shed and in the coop. That coop door stays open unless I pen um at night, they just might lay an egg or two inside." She handed me her handmade split oak basket.

Once outside, I went from one place to the next. Nearly everywhere I went, there were spider webs and morning glory climbing wherever it could attach onto something. I went from one place to the other and found thirteen eggs. I'd never found so many eggs before. Pleased with myself, I ran inside to show her the eggs and tell her that morning glory was blooming.

"A baker's dozen," she said.

"Look at that really big one!"

"Most likely a double yolk! That means a young hen is startin' to lay."

"Will you save it for me?"

"Yes, I'll try to."

"The morning glory is climbing inside your shed. It is so beautiful; the blue is bluer than a bluebird's eggs."

"That stuff takes over this time of year, climbs them corn stalks and all. I expect Harvey will be battlin' them vines gettin' out that corn today."

"Do they have medicine in them?"

"Not that I'm gonna use. Some old widow woman used the seeds for somethin', but don't go tastin' no plant. They's some that can kill you. Workin' with herbs and wild plants is for grownups who know what they is doin'."

"Went through a spider web big as I am," I said wiping my face over and over, feeling as if it was still there. "How does a spider spin a web from the smokehouse to the walnut tree anyhow? Seems like they would have to fly."

"Don't know. Now, go play or push that mower under the clothesline. Grass has got thick there. I got to git myself cleaning out that old trunk."

I wandered into the backyard and swirled myself around the

clothesline post, sneakers in at the bottom of the post and my body leaning out, round and round I went until I was dizzy. Wrestling the push mower out of the shed, it seemed quite a chore to get it through the grass, but after I got it going, steady back-and-forth pushing kept it moving. A constant clicking sound sounded out into the yard. Finally finished with the small patch of grass that she seemed bothered by, I was hot and sweaty and kicked my sneakers off.

The watermelon field caught my attention. *Maybe there is still a watermelon or two that has not been smashed*, I thought and walked the edge while looking out into the field for at least one melon that had survived. I ran out to a busted melon thinking it was whole. It was just the top half laying in the sun. Reaching the edge of the cucumber field, I saw a worn-out bushel basket that had been left behind after the bushel baskets of cucumbers had been loaded and taken to market. The ears of the lid stuck through the bale wires on the side. The morning sun glinted off the top. The basket sat in the tall grass between the nearly spent lavender-blue chicory, and the rarely seen white chicory.

I kept wandering until suddenly realizing how far I had gone. My bare feet were stepping on pears. Unconcerned by my disturbing them, the large hornets moved out of my way and seemed to pose no danger. Looking straight up, I saw just how tall the pear tree was, a monstrosity that still bore fruit every year and was impressive even in the winter, standing like a monument in a barren field. While quenching my thirst on the fattest and least rotten pear, I convinced myself to climb, reasoning that it is probably not too much taller than the thin pine trees in our yard at home. *Maybe Bruce was right. Maybe we can see the creek or even a tall building in town from up there.* I decided to give it a go.

"What on earth is you doin' runnin' all over creation and scarin' the daylights out of your grandmother? You was missin' from the yard and you got her wringin' her hands. What possessed you to git all the way up near the top anyways?" Pop-pop said, looking at me squatted on a branch at the top of the main trunk of the pear tree.

"Bruce said this tree is so tall that the creek could probably be seen from here, maybe town. After each higher branch I could see more and more."

"You cain't see the crick for the tall pines and cypress trees, no how."

"I know that now."

"Sent Bruce lookin' for you. When he come back to the house, I could hardly believe what he said—that you was all the way up top and wouldn't come down." Then eyeing the first branch which was better than six feet off the ground he asked, "How'd you git started?"

"I got a foothold in that big knothole under that first limb, it was a cinch from there. I told Bruce last week that I wanted to climb it and he said, 'Bet you can't.' Guess I showed him," I said proudly. "Climbed it just like the trees at home, but I hadn't planned on doing it today. It just happened." A tremor of fear crept through my bold statement. Those three pine trees in the front yard at home were short and stubby and I had not realized how tall this pear tree was until I got to the top. I had climbed steadily not looking down. When I finally glanced down, I realized it was a fearful drop if I was to fall. "Got up here so fast, makes my belly do a flip-flop to look down," I added.

"Nothing wrong with lookin' down if you got the stomach for it. That's where you started from ain't it?" He pulled at his chin while talking. "You already stepped on every one'a them branches on your way up. Do the same thing on your way down."

The order to climb down made me shaky and anxiety took over. I suddenly remembered falling out of one of the pine trees at home. I had fallen flat on my back, knocking the wind right out of me. "No!" I said and gripped the main trunk tighter. I looked out at the other branches that were smaller, but that only made me feel dizzy since they seemed to move with the breeze.

He continued to stare at me while pulling at his white stubbled chin as if in thought and then started to walk around the tree still stroking his week-old whiskers and eyeing the pears on the ground. Finally he said, "Evie's already put up the best'a these pears. These ones on the ground is mostly rotten now and they's jugger hornets a plenty. You is lucky their nest is not near this tree. They'd have lit you up."

"They aren't as pretty as bumble bees or the little honey bees are they?" I said trying to make conversation to ease the tension, but the anxiety was mine.

He looked up scanning the tree, and ignored my question which hadn't really required an answer. We both knew one bee from another and this was not the time to discuss the various bees. "They's a nice ripe pear about three branches down from you; git that one for me and toss it here. I been huskin' corn and you cut short my break for lunch, corned beef and cabbage. It was salty as all get out, so I got a powerful thirst. Don't look all the way down, just at that next branch, and then the next." Then he coughed, as if his throat had gone dry.

I hesitated. I knew how thirsty someone could get out in the field, and a salty meal besides, well that was bad. Anyone could nearly feel like choking from a dry throat after that. I began to feel guilty as I sat there, perched on the branch with my toes curled tightly and sitting on my haunches like a chicken, my arms around the tree. I looked down at the next branch. It was thicker than the one I was on. Still holding the trunk I stepped down, and the next branch looked even thicker, and finally I reached the third without looking at the ground. Sure enough, he had eyed a nice fat pear from all the way down there. Reaching out with fingertips, I retrieved the pear and then looked down. "Here," I said and dropped it.

He caught the pear perfectly and immediately bit into it as if it had reached him just in time. My stomach seemed to have dropped with the pear and after staring at Pop-pop for a second, I looked up again. Suddenly a crow perched just above me and Pop-pop had not missed its arrival. "You best git down here before that crow pecks you on the head. Come on down like you just done, lookin' at one branch at a time—further down you go the bigger they git."

Regaining my nerve, I glanced down again and watched him wipe juice out of his whiskers with his sleeve, and walk away from the tree talking over his shoulder, "Besides it's gonna git dark in a few hours and I wouldn't give a wooden nickel for you lastin' the night up there."

Now that made a lot of sense. Cautiously, I picked my way down the tree, only looking at each limb in turn and not the ground. It was a slow process as I gained and lost my nerve to continue several times. When reaching the lowest limb, he was halfway to the house and I called to him. "Help me down from this last branch. It's too high off the ground."

He didn't miss a step as he headed for the house, "You managed to git yourself up; you can git yourself down."

"I found the knot hole going up, but I can't see it going down." I was getting mad.

Pop-pop turned and looked squarely at me, "Swing down."

When my feet hit the ground they stung like the dickens all the way to my knees, but I refused to make a sound. Recovering, I worked my way around the small volunteer pear trees and weeds and ran toward the house ahead of him, but he called to me. So, I waited. I didn't look at him. I looked at the ground.

"Evie had a distant relative broke a leg fallin' from a tree at The Old Home Place, could'a broke his neck, gimpy from then on, and now, she's in the kitchen wringin' her hands, frettin' about you breakin' your'un—so git up to the house and show her you is alright."

I bolted for the house, paying no attention to where I was stepping, but well aware that he having to come after me meant that I had messed up this time for sure. Since neither Grandparent ever punished the grandchildren, my anxiety wasn't that I would be made to do anything or something might be taken from me, but they had a way of just throwing a meaningful glance my way, especially Pop-pop. When he sent me that look, my behavior changed quickly. The glance told me, 'straighten up or else' but there was never any 'or else' that happened, perhaps because the hard drilling look just worked on me. I didn't want to test 'the stare.'

Fred met me at the corner of the house, wagging his tail, and followed me to the porch where Bruce sat on the steps. "I'm in big trouble," I whispered to Fred, then I stuck my tongue out at Bruce, and ran into the house. Sure enough there was Mom-mom, standing by the kitchen table, curling one hand over the other.

"Your feet is bloody and your hands look tore," she said evenly, trying not to show emotion in her voice.

I looked down at my feet in surprise, and saw the bloody tracks I had left on the linoleum. "The field briars, I guess," I replied.

"Too, the spikes on them pear tree branches is bad."

"Tree's old. I stepped between, at least I think I did."

"Them big hornets can git you good if they've a mind to; you is lucky. Set down and eat your lunch. I'll git the salve. School is gonna start next week and you with cut feet. How in the world is you gonna wear shoes?"

"I'll just put them on and go, I guess."

"Mm, mm," she mumbled.

I realized they had eaten the noontime meal without me or Bruce. They had sent Bruce to find me and Bruce had gone back to report that I was stuck up the pear tree. He had eaten his lunch while Pop-pop had gone to get me. That was not good. I sat, obedient to her command. There sat Pop-pop's unfinished plate. She handed me a plate loaded with corned beef and cabbage; it was still warm. She must have kept my food atop the stove. It was salty, like Pop-pop had said, but tasted really good. I felt ashamed that he had to cut his lunch short because of me. There were too many things that had happened, things that had forced him to leave food on his plate.

The dryness had not left my mouth, so I drank a whole glass of water. I felt hot through and through and the salty meal had not helped. Suddenly, the vision of homemade ice-cream we had fixed at home came to mind. Mother had set everything up. Bruce and I traded turns cranking the handle on the ice-cream maker. We added ice between the wooden bucket and metal container that held cream, sugar, eggs, and peaches. We had cranked the handle until it got too hard for me to turn. *I can taste it now.*

Mom-mom came into the kitchen, bringing me back to the present. She carried a wet rag, basin, and salve. After my feet were washed, she applied that thick gooey salve and ordered me to stay put until supper. With legs not propped this time, but dangling, I sat at the kitchen window looking out at the buildings while she got busy in the sewing room, bringing canning jars out into the kitchen.

The clop-clop of Pop-pop's boots had come to a stop in front of the porch before I realized that I had heard him coming. I looked out the kitchen door and through the porch screen to see him stop in front of Bruce. With no real tone in his voice, he said, "Quit putting ideas in that child's head. Lord knows she can think'a enough on her own," he paused, "Come to mind though, first cool day what keeps them bees away, we'll gather up baskets'a them rotten pears and feed um to the hogs."

Finished with what he had to say, he pumped a jar of water, downed it, and plodded away toward the corn field. Bruce turned to see me watching through the front kitchen door, so he crossed his eyes and then stuck out his tongue returning the favor, and then followed Pop-pop back out into the cornfield. I had to sit the rest of the afternoon with salve on my feet. The only things to do for entertainment were swing my legs and watch Mom-mom walk back and forth, hauling wood to a corner of the porch, and carry more loads into the kitchen to fill her wood-box.

She was getting ready for another round of canning. I turned to look out the back kitchen door and saw the pear tree standing stately in the field seeming to reach the sky. I went weak in the knees and turned once again to watch Mom-mom. In between her trips, I turned to the window to watch and looked beyond the clothesline to the cornfield. The men had left for today, so Bruce and Pop-pop were left alone to get the piles of corn into the barn. They threw one pile of corn after the other into the wagon until it was full. Pop-pop placed the wagon next to the elevator that was overhanging the high hole in the barn. He unhitched the tractor from that wagon and hooked it to the elevator. They threw corn onto the rotating conveyor that dumped the bright golden ears inside the high window. Although I couldn't see the high hole from where I was sitting, I could visualize the barn filling up with corn.

In the next few days, Pop-pop will finish husking the corn and Mom-mom will finish her canning. That corn will pile up inside the barn under that window and slope toward the door, I thought, as I began to make plans for making a climb once again. *After all, that pile of corn is much safer than that pear tree from where I have just become a seasoned climber.*

A hornet's (Jugger Hornet) nest taken out of a building. This shows the smooth front-side and the backside where it was attached to wood. Approximately three feet tall and appearing as condominiums.

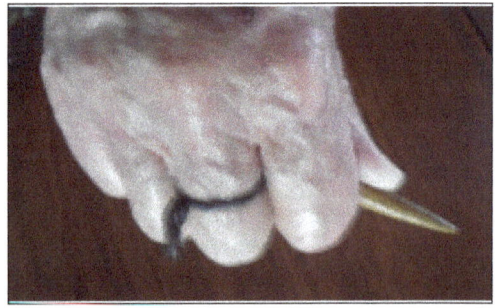

Wooden corn husker-shucker from the early 1900s that belonged to Harvey Pusey's father, Emory Asbury Pusey.

A bushel basket with lid sitting in the middle of lavender-blue chicory and the rarely seen white chicory.

Wild morning glory making itself at home in a shed.

The magnificent pear tree in springtime that stood in the field north of Harvey and Eva's house.

The porch off the kitchen and dining room that held chopped wood, the washing machine, and rockers and where tubs were hung on the wall.

A telephone like the one used by Eva Pusey. The runner was stitched by Dorothy Gibbons Pusey.

A telephone that was used in telephone booths on street corners and in drug stores with slots for quarters, nickels, and dimes. (Flea Market 13 Antiques & Used Furniture, Pocomoke, MD)

Canning

The first couple weeks of school had been so warm that classroom windows and doors had been opened so air could circulate, but then chilly weather came. Our classroom windows and door were then closed and the heat turned on, but it had not worked. We girls buttoned our sweaters and the boys zipped their jackets as we all began to think about winter coats. So, since the heating system in the middle school had needed some unexpected repairs, classes had been canceled for today while those repairs were made. I considered a day off from school a gift and planned to take advantage of the break by getting outside before another round of cold weather forced me back inside.

The dress I had planned to wear to school had been flung across the end of the bed; now I could wear pants. I pulled my clothes from the chest-of-drawers and went in the hallway to dress as quietly as possible because Lyn was still sleeping in the double bed we shared. Lickety-split, I pulled on jeans, socks and oxfords, blouse, and a thin car-coat. Outside, Dad and Bruce were working on Dad's John Deere tractor and the repairs did not appear to be going well. Tools and parts of the tractor were spread out along a bench in Dad's double bay shed. They hardly noticed as I teased Bruce about being a grease monkey or when I told them where I was going.

I pedaled slowly down the road toward my grandparents' farm and shivered in the thin coat. *No need to hurry though,* I decided. *The day is too perfect to rush.* Fall flowers lined the road along the edge of the woods. The geese flew overhead in great flocks searching for cornfields near a pond or the creek. Their wings whistled a tune, the sound becoming clearer the closer they came. Once overhead, black and white feathered bodies easily contrasted the blue sky as they winged through the green of the pines, the red, gold, and yellow of maples and oaks. Their honking hailed the beginning of fall's cooler weather.

When reaching the open fields, the wasting tomatoes filled my senses. The trucks had rolled over the vines after last picking and splotches of red dotted several acres of ground. The watermelon field was similar, although not as brightly colored. I could see a variety of insects in the morning sun hovering over the ground and busily consuming leftover juices, even though that melon field had been disked. With the heat and the smell of tomato vine still fresh on my mind, I felt little sentiment about harvest's passing. Pop-pop had finished the corn harvest quickly and Mom-mom was still canning.

When I arrived, the sight was one of a busy farm kitchen. Steam was clouding out of the kitchen door, filtering through the porch screens, and disappearing into the two brilliant maples. With autumn's arrival came the chore of preserving the food that was left in the gardens and fields. I bounded up the porch steps waving my arms in circles trying to disperse the clouds of vapor. Mom-mom was a silhouette appearing and disappearing through the vapors as she stood in in front of the woodstove stirring two huge pots of tomatoes. She had gleaned the field of the last good tomatoes. As soon as I called my hello, she asked me to heist the window cattycornered to the porch kitchen door. When it was raised the steam-filled kitchen cleared.

"There you are! I can see you now!" I said.

"This is the last'a the tomatoes and I'm tryin' to git um boiled down so's I can git um canned today. What takes you home on a school day?" She asked, while wiping the steam from her eyeglasses.

"Something about the heat at the middle school and today is Friday, that means I've got three days off," I explained. Then, standing on my toes, I peered into the pots, "You've been at it a while cause its getting thick. Looks like stewed tomatoes to me." Sweat beaded my forehead. "It's a cool fall day outside, but it's hot in here," I said, removing my coat and chucking it on a kitchen chair.

"Indeed it is," she added, "Best put that school coat in the dinin' room where nothing'll get on it."

"Guess I shouldn't have worn it, but I was in a hurry." I said in defense. "Where's Pop-pop?"

"Helpin' Filip round his cows up. They got out again."

"Oh." I said, knowing Mr. Facejew's cows just seemed to walk their way out of his fence whenever they wanted. Looking at her pots on the stove, I stated the obvious. "Well, it looks like its canning time, but soon it'll be wreaths, and then after Christmas, hog rendering."

"Makes me weary just thinkin' on it."

"Yeah! But after that comes quilting time during the freeeeeezing cold," I said, drawing out my e's for emphasis. "You said you'd show me the feed bag material this year and some of your finished quilts. I'm in sixth grade now and next year I will be in high school, seventh. I will have Home Economics and I'll start to sew."

"That's good," she said.

"Well, this January, you can teach me how to use your treadle sewing machine. I hope we get a deep snow; that would be fun. We would be all snowed in and could really get to sewing."

"Snow causes problems."

"Pretty though."

She changed the subject, "Glad I got them batches of pears and peaches done. These two pots is the second batch'a tomatoes," and she beat the long handled wooden spoon on the side of one pot, then laid it on a saucer.

The kitchen table was half full of glass canning jars which included some of the pale, turquoise, Mason jars—even an Atlas. Canning lids were in a pile, some were zinc having white milk glass inside with a pile of rubber rings along-side. Other jars were newer, clear glass with rubber ringed metal tops that sucked in when in the canning bath. Noticing some pint jars with the quarts, I asked Mom-mom what was going in them.

"Apples," she replied.

"Apple butter?"

"Yes."

"Yay! Where are the apples?"

"Back'a the stove."

Looking in the narrow place between the big pots, I could see a smaller one.

"Want to hand me the tin'a molasses? It's inside the corner cupboard in the little washroom." She grabbed a tea-towel and pushed one pot of tomatoes aside and pulled the simmering apples to the front. Taking the can of King Molasses from me, she pried the lid off with a butter knife and poured the entire quart tin into what looked like three gallons of apples. Reaching for her spice shelf, she got out the cinnamon and cloves. She only added one clove but three tablespoons of cinnamon. "Now," she said, "it's gotta be stirred until it gets real thick and poured quick into them jars that I boiled in water this mornin'. S'pect I'll melt paraffin to seal them."

Moving around the kitchen, she went from one task to the next, stoking the stove, stirring, and adding ingredients to the pots. She raised and lowered the window opposite the stove, raising one to let steam out, but when cooler air crept into the kitchen, she closed it. Bobby pins were still in her hair from the night before, so she brushed stay strands away from her face. She even managed to fix us a quick lunch in between her tasks; all the while, her soiled apron fluttered back and forth with her movements.

On the table, she placed fried bacon and biscuits left over from breakfast. She sliced the biscuits in half, then sliced a tomato, and said, "Fix yourself a sandwich." Changing her mind she decided to fry us some eggs. "I found one of the biggest eggs yesterde' I ever seen. I'll fix you that one, bound to be a double yolk. We ate that double one you found a few weeks back." She placed a frying pan on the woodstove, grabbed her lard tin and tablespooned some of that hog grease into the pan. But when she broke the egg open, she exclaimed, "Come here child and look at this!"

I leaned over the pan. A triple yolk covered nearly one-third of her large pan with each yolk as big as the ones in a regular egg. "I've never seen one!" I shouted.

"Been quite some time since I've seen one myself," she said. We stared at it!

"See, like I told you, a young hen will lay very small eggs and then extra-large un's until she gits herself used to layin'." She explained, "The difference in the color of some yolks comes from the foods they eat. My yard hens eat bugs, and grasses, and seeds that's nearly 'bout everywhere they walk, fresh not packaged. The hens that lay in layer chicken houses only git bagged dry feed, not fresh like grass when it goes to seed, or seed from the tomatoes in the field, or crickets and grasshoppers, you see?"

"Yes," I said, and I did see. Even though she didn't raise the layer hens in her chicken house, I saw other differences between her housed broiler chickens and the wandering chickens, not only in what they ate, but their actions toward people. I loved eggs and so I savored this one with its three yolks. Even newly picked vegetables tasted better than her canned vegetables.

Mom-mom did not linger long at the table. She ate quickly and grabbed her pan, wiping it out with a cloth from the nail. She did not wash her frying pans. They were just wiped out for the next use. If something had stuck to one while cooking, she would simply scrape it off with the spatula, and then wipe the pan. If a pan got too crusty, like a big iron one, she would open the woodstove grates, two side by side and then take out the middle section. She would then settle the frying pan down in hot coals. After a time, the crusted food around the sides, practically hard as that iron, would flake off. She said that once a pan was seasoned, soap shouldn't touch it.

Putting the pan away, she asked me to get her more jars from the pantry closet under the stairs and explained, "Most of the canning jars is in the sewing room, but I got a few in the pantry closet. On your way to the pantry, look inside that pot beside the dining room stove. It's full of persimmons."

Oh, the dreaded persimmon, I puckered my lips at the thought. The art of catching a persimmon exactly ripe had escaped me. I considered any unripe fruit that could injure a person just by the screwed up face it forced upon them, was not worth the trouble. The memory of eating that unripe assailant was not one that is easily forgotten, but with Mom-mom's guidance, maybe I'll try just one since the fruity flavor of a perfectly ripe persimmon is one to savor. I gingerly took the lid off the pot of persimmons. It appeared as if she had picked the fully ripe, deep orange and squishy ones, but I decided I wasn't going to take any chances. I slammed the lid back on the pot.

The hinges made a grinding sound as I opened the pantry door. I pulled the chain on an overhead light that had been mounted on the bottom of a stair tread. The electric wire had been stapled in place and ran along the stair tread and down the wall. The closet was long and narrow. The ceiling slanted downward toward the back until it reached the floor. The underneath of each stair step could be seen. Both sides of the closet were lined with shelves, each one longer as they neared the floor. Every shelf was lined with white shelf paper boasting a flowered print. Atop that paper stood her canned goods and canning items. Beautiful colors came not only from the shelf paper, but from her canned fruits and vegetables.

Quarts of red tomatoes ran the length of the two top shelves. On lower shelves were her brown syrupy pears, green peas, black-eyed peas, a milky-green citrine jam, and on the other side, were two rows of peaches and peach preserves, jellies, more pears, apples which were so brown they were nearly indistinguishable from the pears. Another shelf held greens, lima beans, pickles, something so dark brown I couldn't see what was in the jar, and blackberry juice which was only used as medicine.

The blackberries became ripe only a few at a time, so she had been constantly picking the ripe ones for juice. Her squeezing blackberry juice through cheesecloth was a sight to behold. First she mashed the blackberries with her potato masher, and then placed the pulp in cheesecloth and squeezed the juice through the cloth, the juice running through her fingers. She then put the pulp in a pan, added a little water, heated that mixture, and then squeezed more juice. The canning process I did not see, but I suspected that a fermenting process took place with some of that juice.

I guessed that some of the dark brown jars were persimmons,

some of which had been placed on the floor in the back of the closet along with empty jars and lids. Three gallons of honey sat on the floor and I recalled the hot mixture with honey she had fixed for my bouts of sore throat. There was more to that concoction than I knew since a woozy feeling quickly followed. I guessed that Pop-pop had robbed the bees, but he always left enough for them to winter over.

In boxes under the bottom shelves there were dried peas and beans, probably for planting next year if they could not be ordered. She always prepared for hard times. A jar of pickled pig's feet left from last January was pushed back on one of the bottom shelves as if the contrast with the mouthwatering fruits was too much.

Staring at the jar of feet, I questioned, *Why do they call them pickled pig's feet instead of pickled hog's feet, since once pigs are grown they are called hogs?* The pink and white pig's feet in a jar didn't startle me. I realized that I had watched them boil on the stove until done, just as I watched a chicken boil to make chicken and dumplings. I couldn't even remember the first time I had seen hog rendering, work that took several days to complete. I had watched the different stages of that rendering one year to the next. To my mind, the killing of hogs was done in order to have meat through the winter and lard for cooking, a necessity that must be accepted, and a taken-for-granted survival, just like fruits and vegetables, and quilting too.

Long ago I had concluded that we would freeze to death if there weren't a pile of quilts on our beds in winter. That survival seemed to include keeping enough food stored a year ahead. I guessed that ritual was done in case of disasters like poor crop production due to no rain or bad storm, or sickness among the hogs, or even an epidemic among the people, or in case of an economic depression when money dries up. I'd heard them say, 'It's better to be safe than sorry.'

My eyes were drawn back to the peaches again. *Since we haven't had any desert after our lunch, maybe we can have some peaches. Even though she has just canned them within the last month, there aren't any fresh ones left on the trees.* So I grasped a box of the empty quart jars, laid a jar of peaches on top, and kicked the closet door shut.

When I set that jar on the table, Mom-mom didn't hesitate in saying, "Yes, indeedy". She simply picked up a folded tea towel and reached for the pan of apples and pushed them to the back of the stove where the fire was not so hot. I pulled out two chairs, one on each side of the table and then sat on the one by the window. Afternoon sunshine had flooded the table catching the peaches just right. At that moment, there wasn't a thing I could remember that was prettier than those golden peaches in that glass jar lit by the sun. "They's pretty in those new clear glass Mason's I just got," she said proudly.

Mom-mom placed two bowls on the table, unscrewed the top ring and pried the sealed lid up with her paring knife. She poured the fruit equally in each bowl. We sat at a sunlit table eating those peaches like two starved beggars, even drinking the juice from the bowl, and gracefully settling the bowls back on the table grinning at one another. We had been satisfied with the bacon and tomato sandwiches, that is, until the peaches. The sweetness of the fruit or perhaps the rare moment when our eyes smiled together, gave me a great feeling of contentment until the guineas made a ruckus.

"Why don't the guineas come up to get corn with the chickens," I said.

"They wander around the yard and fields; they's more like geese than chickens."

"I know, they're like a herd of geese."

"You mean, flock, a gaggle of geese in the field."

"Yeah, where one goes, they all go. They herd up together."

"Guineas is good at eatin' bugs on the farm. They keeped the bugs outta my garden this summer—I'm partial to guineas; always was," she said, as she got up to stir the tomatoes. The comfortable silence took over once again. I thought about her statement, how much she liked her guineas, but there was so much more she cared about.

She works hard to see that food is grown and canned, starting in the planting season through to canning season. During the winter she prepares meals from her hard work. She is determined to cure whatever illness she sees right down to the slightest snick-up. She likes to see the beds covered with quilts. She cares about the animals, even Fred. She makes sure that the best food she has goes on the table at Christmas. She makes sure the people around her are not hungry, even strangers during the Great Depression. She earns money from Christmas wreaths, even enough to buy some farm equipment and a car years ago. She works steadily at her daily chores. She has a good heart and, at times, a temper, which I think is a good thing, 'You gotta find the gumption to stick up for yourself,' she's said in many different ways, and she follows her own advice. Thinking about all she had accomplished gave me an unshakeable respect for her.

I was drawn out of my thoughts by a noise and turned my stare from her at the stove to the chickens outside. They had started such an uproar that we both glanced through the window to see what was happening. Two roosters were flying at one another bumping chests. Another rooster joined the show. Then the hens began to titter. "One or t'other of them roosters needs to go in the stewpot," she said mildly, and added, "Forgot where I laid my hook."

Once the fight had concluded, the winner strutted confidently around the hens. I was content to just sit and watch Mom-mom, but I began to yawn. She told me to put my head down on the table if I wanted and turned to stir the tomatoes again. I fell fast asleep. Resting my head on folded arms, I did not hear her wash and boil jars, fill them with tomatoes and apple butter, wipe the glass rim, tighten lids in place for the tomatoes, or melt wax to seal the butter. All the methodical movements of canning had gone on around me and I had not awakened.

Having seen my bicycle, Pop-pop came inside and asked, "Where's that young'un'?" I raised my head above the neatly finished, now red and brown quart jars. "What's the matter with you napping middle'a the afternoon? Have you took sick?"

"No!" I blurted defensively. With the sweet taste of the peaches still in my mouth, I sure didn't want it replaced by some dreadful cure-all.

Turning to Mom-mom, he said, "Put a patch job on Filip's rail fence and helped him run his cows back in. He's got quite a bit of mendin' to do," and then he downed a dipper of warm water from the reservoir. Mom-mom just nodded and continued to wash the last huge pot. With water running from his chin, Pop-pop headed for the living room, "Gonna set a spell," he said, and added, "Them walnuts in the path to the house is bound to throw a body down."

"From spring peas through turnips in early winter, it seems like cannin' don't never want to end," she said as if exhaustion had overtaken her. She did not comment on the walnuts.

"Didn't see any turnips on the shelves," I said.

"Don't do up too many. Ones planted in the fall gets picked with dirt left on the roots and put in a cold shed or left in the ground 'til a hard freeze comes to stay. Seeds can be planted in the spring too, but those, we just eat um as they git ready. Turnips don't like warm weather."

"I know what!" I piped up, my mind switching to Pop-pop's griping, "I'll pick up walnuts while you sit and watch. It's still warm enough for being outside."

"Sunning for a few minutes won't hurt none," she agreed, and picked up a glass from the sink and a sweater from her rocker. She headed outside, dropping the last clean pot in the porch. Pumping a glass of water, she pulled her sweater on, and settled herself on a wooden stump facing the sun. The edges of her stained apron touched the ground in front of her and the pins in her hair were askew which added to her look of fatigue and I saw it again, the weariness of age on her face. Her glasses had slipped down her nose. Fred walked up to her and sniffed her clothes to see if there was anything he could retrieve, but he soon gave up and laid down beside her.

Not going near the pigpen at the back of the barn, I opened the big cypress door on the storage side. After wrestling a bushel basket from the others and plopping it near the clothesline, I began to toss walnuts into it as if I were playing basketball, but that became old quickly, so I scooped with my hands putting several in at a time. I kept up a fast pace until I had all the nuts under the clothesline cleaned up and then started on clearing the path to the double bay shed. It was a good half-hour before I had a bushel of nuts.

Mom-mom sat quietly while I made lots of clatter by chucking nuts in the basket and rambling on about school and how I wished I could stay here with her instead. While I darted around the yard, she just sat and listened, occasionally glancing one way and then the next until the sun sank low, casting tree shadows across the field, followed by a sudden chill.

With the sun nearly set, she got up, dashed the last of her water on the ground. "You grab the handle on one side and I'll get t'other. We'll fill some holes in the driveway."

We carried the basket to the lane and dumped walnuts into two holes. They had done the same thing last year and I had forgotten that sure-fired way to hull nuts. Once cars and trucks have driven over the filled holes, those nuts will be hulled, then retrieved later and stored in a basket on the porch. It took a hammer to crack the hard shell of those bittersweet black walnuts, a chore I never volunteered to do.

As we walked toward the porch Mom-mom said, "You best git into the washroom and scrub that walnut stain off'a your hands. I got a remedy for that." I groaned, but followed as expected. Fred fell in step beside me, nuzzling my hand, hinting for dinner.

Canned jar of peaches with zinc lid.

Eva Pusey's canning jars.

Persimmon tree mid-summer. They will not ripen until early fall.

In late September, the persimmons are ripening. The darkest ones are ready to eat.

On left, a ripe orange persimmon. On right, shown is the inside fruit of a very ripe persimmon.

The darkest blackberries are ready for picking.

Black walnut tree at Milburn's Landing State Park along the Pocomoke River in September.

Black walnut tree in summer.

A common sight on the Eastern Shore of Maryland—Canadian Geese flying through the pines.

A triple yolk egg from a Red Ranger hen.

Grandfather's Gift

Pop-Pop was what folks called complicated, ornery, and quietly stubborn to a fault. Gradually, I had begun to relate him to the vision of others, but I saw that there was much more to his puzzling nature than that. He seldom talked and rarely changed his mind about anything. I could see his orneriness due to the warm slimy tobacco being propelled directly onto my toes. Sometimes we grandchildren had miss-stepped into chicken poop, but the slimy tobacco had no less effect upon us. We could expect either of those 'yucky' events during the summer as we played under the great maples just outside the screened porch. But, I allayed most of his traits to a long life on the farm, work that demanded a continual hard-fought survival that deserved respect, thus bringing me close to forgiving him his mischievous hurling of tobacco and unresponsive temperament.

Some days during the crop seasons, I could be found jumping from one of his footprints to the next while following him when he checked on the tomato or watermelon plants or whatever crop needed attention. Whenever I saw him take off for a field or the woods, I would stop playing and trot after him. Few or no words were spoken; that seemed to be an unwritten law.

Since neither he nor Mom-mom talked very much, many evenings we had gone through entire meals, clean-up, and had sat in front of the woodstove with hardly a word spoken—not that I didn't try. I usually thought of some last minute thing to say before going to bed or talked nonstop in the mornings. With wet flour pasted up to my elbows while helping Mom-mom make biscuits this morning, I had pulled at the thick dough on my fingers and talked about how that reminded me of making mud pies after a rain. I was proud as a post when those slightly irregular biscuits were promptly eaten. This morning, we had lathered them with strawberry jam.

Recently, I had given up playing with dolls and wore dresses less often. Forced to wear dresses during school was enough. I held onto my calico blouses with peter-pan collars and short puffy sleeves. The knee pants or the longer corded pants were favorites too. But today, I wore a pair of bib-overalls that I had begged for out of the catalog. Quite sensible to me since those overalls offered more freedom, especially when crawling in and out of the corn crib and searching the scattered chicken nests for eggs.

After breakfast Mom-mom had busied herself cleaning in the sewing room, while I rocked on the porch mulling over the stack of corn rising to a high seat overlooking the farm. So when lunchtime came she simply opened a can of corned beef for sandwiches and went back to cleaning out the sewing room, sweeping the floor, and rearranging stored items. I suspected she had the making of Christmas wreaths on her mind and was cleaning out one end of that room for storing those wreaths. Pop-pop had gone outside and I waited a few minutes before gingerly creeping toward the barn, looking around for him. He was nowhere in sight. I jumped up on the stump, then on tip-toes, I turned the knob, opened the door, and scrambled inside pulling the door shut behind me.

Peering into the right side, I saw his horse and mule collars, harnesses hung on the far wall, and above them was a huge opening that had once been used for the conveyor to dump potatoes into that side of the barn. Left over half-bushel baskets were neatly stacked, as well as larger bushel baskets, burlap bags, broken iron, and leather straps from some bygone era. Turning to my mission I looked to my left at the mountain of gold.

The corn had been stacked all the way up to the open hole with the ears sloping down to the floor toward the door. I began to climb, sliding backwards at times when the corn gave way. Finally making it to the top, I sat at the window with knees resting on the corn and elbows propped on the sill. That way, I could lean my head out the window with no chance of falling and little chance of being seen. I could see just a glimmer of the water that ran under the road near the Facejew's house, and some brilliant colors of fall shone in the trees, but most leaves lay on the ground. Some corn stalks still stood with husks attached and waved this way and that as they rustled in the breeze. Some husks blew across the field catching on a stalk or briar here and there. The bright gold ears of corn that had been missed had fallen to the ground and were easy to see from way up here, but Bruce and Pop-pop hadn't missed many. Stalks had been cut and stacked in the far end of the field. The sound of the wind in the husks was musical. There had been little rain and the field did not smell of mold, but held a fresh clean corn-scent. I inhaled deeply.

Perhaps it was the height of the window and looking at the farm from a different angle, but I suddenly felt as if anything were possible. Glancing over to the right I saw the towering cypress that had been there forever and had not been cut when the cypress trees had been logged better than a half century earlier. Then looking down, I saw the big fat healthy hogs, but not as big as the sow with them, or the boar well secluded in his own sturdy pen. I threw a few ears of corn into the large pigpen and then pitched a couple more ears to the boar. Cob and all disappeared quickly. Glancing beyond the pens, I saw movement in the field. It was Pop-pop! He was walking toward the creek and was nearly halfway to the woods!

I didn't bother to climb down from my perch, but slid down the corn, first wedging then snatching my underwear and jumped out the barn door. I lit out after him, giving the pigpen a wide birth. Upon catching up to him, I breathlessly reprimanded him for leaving without me. There was no response from him. I hadn't expected one.

The cut corn stalks protruded from the ground in neat rows. We walked between two rows in single file, passing one shock and then another. So Pop-pop led the way and I trailed behind trying to take strides as long as his, but failed. His overalls smelled faintly of woodsmoke and I got a whiff of a new chaw of Beech-nut. His rubber boots made thudding sounds as they pounded the ground. I would have known him by sound and smell, even if I couldn't see him.

Bored with trailing behind, I looked back toward the house for Fred, but no Fred. I skipped over some rows and circled Pop-pop as we went, and even though I wore shoes, I carefully picked where I stepped. He said nothing. It would seem that I could have been the wind whirling around him, a natural event that he seemed to accept. I wasn't sure. His stride remained even; he chewed steadily on his wad and his eyes were fixed on the woods ahead.

Perhaps he didn't know I was there at all, but I deducted that he had ears and could hear, so I broke an unwritten rule. I began to sing, making up the words about our dog as I went along, "There was a dog and his name was Fred and he had just three short legs to walk on." I peeked sideways at Pop-pop as I passed in front of him. Nothing.

"So we fashioned him a hick-ree leg and strapped it to his back one Sunday noon." This time his face held the expression of holding back a grin.

"Come Tuesday Fred walked with a slight limp, but come Friday that stump was toothpick size."

"Git som'mers now," burst from him, and he guffawed loudly, "Haw, Haw, Haw!"

I was satisfied and more pleased with myself than ever. I fell back into line, single file and began to look around. We had reached the woods. Pop-Pop paused, for far too long to my mind. I shifted from one foot to the other. He looked to his left, deep into the woods where Burk's Mill Branch met Dividing Creek. Then he looked up. I wished I knew what he was thinking while looking at that old Virgin Cypress that I had seen from my corn perch. We couldn't help but see it, even up at the house; it towered above the other trees. 'Older than the hills,' people had said whenever the tree was mentioned. 'Someday that one will fall,' they'd said, but it hadn't yet.

I waited, contemplating the wonder of cypress. It varied greatly in height and width producing short knees that stuck up out of the swamp, from tiny nubs to nearly five feet in height that produced no needles. The trees themselves varied in size as well, but grew needles that I considered hair. In a swampy area near Dividing Creek, I had seen one so large that a few people could stand inside the hollowed out trunk, but I had been told not to tell where it is because townspeople would come out to gawk at it and nobody wanted people traipsing through their fields. The trunks of the large trees seemed to have huge hands with fingers that went in all directions. Those trunks could clearly be seen, especially when the tide lowered in Dividing Creek. I peered into the woods seeing cypress hair from a long branch trailing in the moving water. I looked up at Pop-pop and waited.

Finally, he turned and walked into the woods, straight to a high bank above the creek where he stopped and said, "Let's set here by the crick." He sat on an oak log felled for firewood. I scooped some leaves into a pile and plopped down.

Immediately my eyes found a tree that had been bent over many years ago and had grown its own personality. "Look," I said, "there is an animal with an eye, a snout, and a big horn growing out of its head."

Pop-pop turned halfway around recognizing a tree he had seen many times and said, "That snout is pointing out a direction, I expect."

"Well, which way is it pointing?"

"You tell me."

"That's north, I think."

"Yeah, that's north."

Only a few leaves remained on the trees. The real color was now on the ground, with the exception of red berries left on some vines by the bank. Those bright berries stood out, pulling my eyes to them just as the holly trees did with their shiny, deep-green leaves and red berries. After studying my surroundings, I began to twiddle and then thought of Fred and how strange it was that he had not followed us.

The sudden noise of blackbirds filled the air and looking through the trees, I could see them coming, rising over the chicken house and settling in the cornfield. Some had red and yellow under their wings and when flying past appeared mostly as red streaks.

"Look!" I said, "Look at the blackbirds. Some have red under their wings! They are going to eat what corn you left in the field. Do mice eat corn? I guess what crops you leave in the field, the animals clean it up."

Suddenly, Pop-Pop said, "With your eyes closed, tell me what you hear."

Surprised, I did as ordered, "Well, I hear an airplane and the sun has been out a while because my back is right warm."

There was no reaction from him for what seemed a long time. I was confused at the strange turn our walk had taken. Finally he said, "Listen out yonder, past the plane."

The plane? Droning from the plane's engine had long since gone. Had he even been conscious of the dying sound? Had it reminded him of war? In World War II his son Orville had been stationed in the Pacific. When Pop-pop and his other sons were working in the field, planting and harvesting crops needed for the war effort, they would stop and watch as the planes flew over, even watching until the planes had disappeared from sight. *Had he wondered if the planes were ours or if the enemy was attacking the east coast? After seventeen years was that droning sound of war still stuck in his mind?* I mused questions that I didn't dare ask.

"Well, I hear a Caw! Caw!" I ventured tentatively after a bit. "What is it?"

"It's a crow I think, can't see it."

"We'll wait."

Wait for what, I thought. *I know I am right, so why doesn't he say so?*

The sun began to sink behind the trees and gradually the warmth was fading. The blackbirds took off suddenly, filling the sky, flying back across the farm.

The sounds of early evening began to resound through the woods. One particular bird deep in the woods began to tweet in a fast, high pitched murmuring and I told him. Then I asked, "What kind is it?"

"You tell me," he replied.

"I don't know," I answered and thought—*or I wouldn't have asked.* Far away I heard another plane, but didn't mention that.

He was silent.

There was something he wanted from me, something I couldn't figure, so I sat motionless trying to tune out the plane. Then something began to move in the grass. A scratching sound down under the leaves and twigs, maybe a mouse or a ground squirrel. The difference between wind in the grass and the animal was slight, but even with my eyes shut, I knew with certainty that this sound was animal. I almost shouted while explaining how I had figured the difference between wind and animal sound. Still no reply.

I blurted suddenly, "Well, I'll tell you one thing right now, those cypress trees are a confounded puzzle the way they grow, but I love them just the same," and took a peek at him and saw a twinkle at the corner of his eyes.

Minutes went by and then he spoke so softly I wasn't sure whether I had really heard or just imagined his words, "Put all them sounds together."

My confusion grew with what I saw as unusual behavior, especially for him, but newly found instinct told me not to answer right away and allow his words to sink in. *What is he looking for? Perhaps it is the feel of wind brushing skin with the dampness seeping into my overalls from the leaves.* Then I heard the water in the creek moving; not rippling or gurgling, but simply movement of the water like a soft murmur that was very soothing. "I feel that water moving." With that spoken I snuck a peek at him.

But he raised a few fingers as if to say, wait. I shut my eyes again.

I had been expecting a flock of geese to fly over, headed for the Pocomoke River nearby, or maybe some ducks, squawking, being spooked by the otter along the bank of the creek, complaining to the world—as they often did—that they had been disturbed. Or some of those strange sounds from across the creek that left even the most knowledgeable perplexed. I tried to pick up on a strange sound, one that could pass for a bobcat or a wolf. Some folks think there are such animals still living here today that were known to have lived on the Eastern Shore better than a century ago. My mind began to wonder and wander and everything became mixed, one with the other. Quite some time passed before I spoke again for I didn't hear anything new, but the air got chillier. Night was close. I eased my eyes open watching shadows form, longer and longer. The faraway droning was gone. Suddenly, I saw an Eagle wing through the woods, and snatch a mouse from the opposite bank which in turn, that mouse dropped something that it was eating, maybe a cricket.

Pop-pop's view between nature and man snapped to mind. He had mentioned his admiration for nature beginning with seeds. The corn seed knew its job, to produce corn on the cob supported by a stalk. Same for the tomato seed, it grew into a vine that produced flowers that, fed by the vine, turned into tomatoes. Same for the watermelon seed, and so on. Too, he said that the male and female bluebird build their nest together. She lays the eggs and sits on them while he guards and they both feed the fledglings. They do that year after year not varying their actions. He had said that each animal followed a certain course that helped the next one survive, and so on, from the otter in the creek, to the birds in the trees.

We knew our chickens were going to scratch the ground, nest, and lay eggs. We knew the hogs would snort, wallow in mud, and grow fat from farm feed. We knew that the sow would become overprotective and the boar temperamental. We could predict the geese flying in great flocks toward the creek and ponds in the fall. In his own traditional language, Pop-Pop had said that man is the only creature who varies in his actions, goes off and does something contrary to his nature, disrupting the course of all other creatures and even himself.

Recalling his conviction about nature, I began to think about it all as a single flowing stream. The movement of the creek water continued to soothe and I could hear it move, on and on. Then the murmuring water began to blend with sounds from the birds and the wind in the trees, even becoming one with the rustling grass. Something happened. A peace settled over me—contentment so strong that all worries and problems had been replaced. All the natures of the Forest became a single harmony and I was a part of it.

I marveled at feeling perfect and utter peace in such a simple way and thought—*If I dare speak it, the peace might disappear.* Tentatively, quietly, I breathed, "I'm a part of everything that is living and moving and breathing, right here, right now—same as the ground squirrel, same as the cypress tree." Then I sighed and opened my eyes.

He knew. He had been a part of it, the same as I. Gazing steadily into his pale blue eyes, I saw that his face held none of the foreboding and sadness I had seen many times before, the reasons of which I never knew. But, I now understood how he found peace. He nodded his approval and said, "By the by, my cane is made of hickory and it don't wear down."

He was paying attention, I thought with great satisfaction—*though it will not do for me to say so.* With that said, he got up and headed slowly for the house. I followed, comfortably producing my own leisurely gait.

Looking toward the farm he said, "Somebody left the barn door ajar," with a glint of teasing in his voice. I realized that he had known I was up in the window before he ever started for the creek. *Where he gets himself off to sometimes, especially when I am really searching and can't find him, is a mystery,* I mused. Now, he just kept walking the long way down Dividing Creek, then down Burk's Mill Branch, and on around the bend, out to the road, and on up toward the house. The smell of burning wood and bacon drifted over us in greeting. The smells let us know that we were having breakfast for supper. Mom-mom must have opened the doors to relieve herself from a hot kitchen and I would make my amends with her for not saying where I had gone. Fred suddenly spied us and bounded in our direction. Even though Pop-pop moved in an easy gait, his long legs covered vast ground and never faltered, even when Fred met us. So, I started to move in a kind of a skip walk, which fit my mood. I had learned how to be quiet and listen, but even better — *I fit. I belong to something that no words conjured by man can describe.*

The foreground behind the barn was the cornfield and not in view on the far left was the chicken house. The two bay shed can be seen on the left, cypress barn and attached sloped shed, smokehouse, walnut tree, and home with two maples in front of the side porch, larger maple to the right. Crabapple trees are in the middle background. The small opening on the right side of the barn was the hole where the elevator dropped the corn and children viewed the farm. Beyond the house, across the road was the tomato field.

Blackbirds and Baltimore Orioles have gleaned crops from the fields and are rising above a chicken house.

A massive cypress with lily pads along the bank of the Pocomoke River.

A view of that huge cypress tree from across the river.

From some of the old stories heard in the Pocomoke Forest—this cypress tree shows that it really is possible for some of our ancestors to have hidden inside a cypress for safety. The inside is rotting out, but the tree is still alive. Perhaps this tree is several cypress trees that have grown together over the last century or so. And perhaps it is only one of many sanctuaries throughout the Pocomoke River and its creeks. This shows the massive cypress tree in comparison to the cypress trees around it and how thick cypress knees can grow in the swamp.

An Eastern Shore Native American (First Nations Peoples) mortar among cypress knees.

Cypress tree growing on the edge of the Pocomoke River.

Cypress tree and knees showing their trunks at low tide.

A fox den in the Pocomoke Forest.

Although a person might be able to crawl into this opening, smaller cave dwellings in tree trunks are used by animals and can be found throughout the Pocomoke Forest.

Often the lower trunk of an older cypress might look like these two, appearing to have many legs.

Bald Eagles in the Pocomoke Forest, photo taken through a telescope with a Nikon camera.

Cooper's Hawk.

Red-Tailed Hawks in the Pocomoke Forest, side and front images taken through a telescope.

Huge tree with branches that had been bent over many years ago.

It is not hard to understand why children who love nature can find entertainment in the simplest of sights. Intriguing wonders can be seen within the Pocomoke River tributaries and forests.

Basket Making

Mom-mom trudged along the creek looking for the perfect white oak tree as I strolled along behind with my newfound vision of peace through the harmony of fauna and florae. My canvas shoes were wet, but not nearly as soaked as the hem of her long dress which had caught on a briar, then broken loose and caught again, and again. She moved through grasses and weeds with a low slung pouch of tools hung over one shoulder. Finally finding what looked like an acceptable tree, she raised her hands and touched middle fingers to thumbs around the bark, her measurement for the perfect sixteen inch circumference. She then moved her hands up and down the tree feeling the feathery soft bark. Passing all tests and growing on the edge of the creek in a soft mossy bank, here stood the perfect basket tree—straight with very few knots. Having found the exact wood she needed so early in her search, she appeared elated. I was disappointed, hoping that we would make it back to our ancestor's old abandoned farm. Suddenly, a sound of disappointment in the form of a grown escaped her lips. A huge rotten spot had been found. We moved on.

Water rose and lowered in Dividing Creek with the tide from the Pocomoke River and today it was low, showing the occasional slippery slope of otter slides along the bank. The ferns were still plenty green, but the red and blue berried bushes along the creek had lost most of their leaves. The north sides of many trees were covered with moss. Even a few rotten trees that had fallen had a soft moss covering. "Look at this," I exclaimed to Mom-mom. A clump of white that looked like hair, hung from a fallen tree.

"That's a mushroom," she said.

"I've never seen anything like that before!"

"It's a pretty fungus, but some is not so pretty so don't never touch or try to eat any mushrooms you might come across in these woods! Some of them can kill you or make you wish you was dead!"

She didn't need to tell me that twice. I got the point. It was the same point she had made about berries in the forest. So we continued to move on along the old woods road that most people wouldn't see as a trail, but one we knew. It was a road from the past that was taking us into the past. I knew we were getting close to the brambled farm, since the land began to rise and we had passed the two old boat landings. As we rounded one more bend, there it was; the woods had opened into farmland containing a treeless mass of briars and grapevine, wandering creepers and climbers of all kinds.

"Ticks are probably still out," I said, thinking about pulling a tick out of my skin.

"Well, they is not much of a problem, but if the deer population grows like it's been doin', we'll not be able to walk in the woods in the summer or early fall no more."

The thought of not walking in the woods when the trees were leafed and the flowers in bloom, a time when the woods was most beautiful, seemed an impossibility to me. Once we finally reached my destination, I begged to look around the old homestead.

"Not without me," she said. "They's a deep well hereabouts that's never been filled in." She pointed to the old house with its roof peak barely seen, laying on the ground, covered with vines, and said that the well was at the right corner where the kitchen had been. "I remember seein' it years ago," she said wistfully.

"Finally, I know where it is," I said more to myself, but she heard me.

She glanced at me, realizing that I had been here by myself. But she said nothing. Both she and Pop-pop had a way of not mentioning deeds of the past or talking about what anyone had done. I guessed they figured that what was done, was done and there was nothing that could be changed now.

"Where was the root-cellar?"

"Under the kitchen, back corner there; it was very shallow." She said while pointing.

"Who lived here besides John and Mary?" I asked partly to change the subject and because I had often wondered.

"They was my and your own ancestors. They was good people!" she said defensively.

"They were native people from this land, weren't they? What really happened to him?

But I didn't get an answer to either question and had not really expected one. I had asked before.

"Look! There is the old cow tree sticking up above the other trees! Boy, it's a big one!"

"That it is," she said, "People needed meat to survive and when he slaughtered a cow, he hung it from that old hickory tree to be rendered."

Since she had offered that much information, I told her about going up to Holland's Church Cemetery to see John Frank's grave, pointing northward as I talked, as if she didn't know where it was. She knew though. His wife Mary had attended that now abandoned church in the 1880's.

I said, "Their gravestones are worn now, but I wrote down everything that his stone said and it was nice." Mom-mom didn't comment so I continued, "His family thought a lot of him. They said they wanted him to sleep peaceful and they were sorrowful he was gone. And what a joy it will be to meet him in heaven and that they miss him being home in his place. They said he had sunshine in his face, and how well he took care of them, and he was kind, and everywhere they look—they miss him." I paused for only a moment, "So this was a happy place and I like it here."

She did not move or change expression.

"You know," I said, "Holland's Church looks like it's about to fall in. It needs a roof. And, that old place where Shockley's store stood down by Whitesburg Bridge, the buildings have vines growing all over them. Pop-pop said that had been a big store with stuff stored upstairs too."

But I could see, she had said all she had to say, so I turned away looking across the ruins and spied a grapevine hanging from a massive oak tree. I pleaded, "May I swing that grapevine? It's not near the well."

"Yes, go ahead."

I pulled the end up from the ground and tried winding that end upward in order to make a loop to sit inside, round and round I wound and pulled the end back through my wound vine. Satisfied, but still holding onto both tightly I began to swing. Looking around, she found a low limb that protruded straight out from a large oak. Half leaning and half sitting, she rested. I swung and swung.

"Not too high," she said half-heartedly for she was content, just as I was.

I called her attention to a few cardinals that had settled along a bare spot of ground. How beautiful their red looked against such a baron looking place. After a few minutes, I noticed something I hadn't seen before, a single fence post with rails that seemed to disappear into the ground. Grapevines trailed down from a high limb of an old cypress and wrapped and curled around that post and its trailing rails. That vine seemed to insist that the last of that old fence not be lost to time. I pointed out the vine's self-appointed duty to the fence. Mom-mom said that baskets were made from grapevine too.

"How so?" I questioned.

"Easier than Oak, that's for sure. "The ribs is wound down across the bottom, up the sides, and then form an arch at the rim. Then that same vine is wound down across the bottom and up the sides to the rim again, forming another arch and so on around the basket. The same size grapevine is woven in and out of the bottom and standing ribs leaving the half circles at the top for the rim. Most times, the handle is vines woven together or vines twisted like a rope. I got an old one in the sewing room."

"Really?" I said, looking up at the vine holding me, I considered just how strong a grapevine basket might be if it was made right.

"Baskets is made from grasses too."

"Must take a lot of grass."

"Not so much as you'd think," she replied, but neither of us pursued the conversation. I feared that something else might escape my notice that I might want to mention. Discussion could be had later, if Mom-mom was willing.

A pair of ducks flew low over the old home and settled in the grasses on the other side of the creek. I listened to the sound trying to commit it to memory so that I would know it when I heard it again. The peacefulness of the sound was sweet. Pop-pop's lesson had not been lost on me.

Hardly noticing, the vine had begun to cinch around me like a hangman's noose and cooler air had forced me to pull my sweater closer over my chest. Mom-mom noticed. "They's a chill now so we best find that tree," she said, sounding almost as wistful as I felt at leaving the comfort of the old farm that wasn't there.

We moved on up the road further. I jumped when we flushed ducks from the grasses on our side of the creek, then reached out to touch some of the fernlike leaves of a cypress. Some of those feathery cypress branches hung so low over the creek that I thought, *What fun it would be to swing on them and let go, crashing into the murky waters.* But I was not brave enough for that. The fact that an otter might want to play with me in the water was enough to make me shudder, plus the fact that I didn't know how to swim anyhow. I was twiddling with the ball-like cones when I heard Mom-mom call for me to keep up.

Just a few feet further she found her oak, clean of knots, feathery soft, straight, although a bit smaller around. Slipping the small crosscut saw from the low-slung pouch on her shoulder, she surmised the best five-foot stretch and began to cut around the trunk to fell the tree. In just seconds, new basket material lay before her. After inspecting that section, she realized the tree would provide enough strips for better than two large baskets, providing the peeling went well. She huffed breath on her cold hands. A whippoorwill sounded, sending music ringing through the woods. Then a dove called, sounding more like an owl and that is when Mom-mom said, "We best git to the house."

As was usual in mid-fall, the warm weather had abruptly changed to a cold wind and the clouds threatened rain. She drug her treasure up onto the old overgrown forest road, a road that in years previous to 1900, ran along the creek for miles. She then hoisted it up on her left shoulder and maneuvered as best she could along the road toward the field at the back of the house. Trudging straight from the woods into her backyard, she rolled the log off her shoulder onto the ground. That was the end of the day for us. We were hungry and tired.

Pop-pop was sitting in the kitchen and simply raised his eyebrows at us, but said nothing. "We were busy basket searching," I offered and those were the only words spoken. Mom-mom fixed a quick dinner and by the time we were done the sun was going down. It didn't take me many minutes to get ready. I jumped in the bed, landing hard to see if I could bounce on the featherbed like on my mattress at home. I sunk with a thud and promptly decided I wouldn't try that again.

The next morning Mom-mom was up and dressed, breakfast over, and out at her treasured length of oak when I, sleepy-eyed, walked into the kitchen and glanced out the window. I tapped on a pane. She looked up and smiled and then continued to arrange her tools necessary for carving the wood into sections. I stretched, loaded a biscuit with jam, and walked outside to stand beside her while she organized her tools. Yawning, I said, "I know what the wedges and maul are for from watching Pop-pop chop firewood, but what do you do with the rest?"

"They's for whittlin' the wood. When I get to that part, I'll give you a call." She pulled a Barlow pocketknife from her apron pocket, "And this does lots'a things, used mostly to separate the wood at the air-holes so as I can peel the splits."

I eyed the old grayed, white oak bench and seat, with a wrapped around clamp that was bolted through the bench. She called that her basket bench, but some people called it a shaving bench since the draw knife shaved off the bark and the heart. No one could walk into the backyard and not wonder about such a contraption. As if reading my mind, she said, "The men cut down that old white oak and made that for me. Still solid after all these years." She paused, "You best go git a bite to eat and git a glass of milk out of the icebox. Put a jacket on 'cause it's chilly this mornin', and best comb that hair too."

In answer, I yawned again, and went back to my seat by the window. Heck with the hair, I filled another biscuit with the sweetest peach jam anyone ever made, and poured some applesauce into my plate. After slicing a biscuit in half, I poured King Syrup on it, then cut a slice of ham into two pieces and placed them on top. What a sloppy mess, but I dove in using my fingers. Pop-pop came inside to get a cloth to wrap around his neck. I marveled at him sweating as chilly as it was outside and guessed he must had been doing something strenuous. Looking at me with hair in my face and syrup to my elbows, he grinned, grunted in greeting, and headed back outside.

While I ate I watched Mom-mom begin to split the wood. With oak log placed on the ground and using a maul, she tapped one wedge into an end near the edge to begin a split in the log. Once the wedge had a solid grip she then hit the wedge with the maul until a large split began down the side of the log. She placed the other wedge in the crack and hit it with the maul, took the first wedge out and put it on the other side of the second wedge and continued likewise down the length of the oak. The two wedges moved down the log, one after the other, until the oak length was cut in half showing two full lengths of the tree with heart exposed—a darker wood. She then took each of those halves, and using the wedges once more, she placed them in the middle of the heart of each half and placing wedge after wedge, split those two halves in half. Four long lengths lay on the ground, triangle shaped.

Putting one strip on her basket bench with the bark side down, she clamped it, swinging the clamp closed with her foot, and taking her froe and hammer, she began to hammer, pull, and wrench the handle of the froe sideways to break the heart away from that quarter piece of tree. She only stopped to move the length further away from the clamp in order to hammer and wench, removing the heart. With most of the heart out, she now had a slightly bowed, but straight length of wood and used the drawknife to finish taking out the heart, then flipped the clean side down and bark up, and clamped. Taking the drawknife again, she began to pull the bark off the remaining wood, clamping and unclamping, sliding the strip and drawing the bark off. With that done she came in the house and sat down, "I'm tuckered out," she said, "and what in the world happened to you?"

"I fixed my own breakfast," I answered proudly, "and it was good! Don't worry I'm going to wash up," and with that I went outside and pumped water over my arms. Fred found me and tried to lick me clean.

"Got syrup in your hair," she called from the kitchen.

"I know."

"All that syrup is gonna draw ants around that well," she yelled again.

"Don't worry," I hollered back, "I'll pump enough water to wash it away."

She knew and I knew that I'd be creating a mud-hole around the well, but she said nothing about that.

After she had downed a glass of water, she went back outside and began to hammer the butcher knife in the end of one long length. By the time I had finished washing, and running Pop-pop's brush through my hair, she had cut that one of the quarter pieces into four long lengths. She continued that way with three of the four quarters, saving the fourth for hoops that would become the rim and handle; some of the ribs could be made from that piece as well. Basket making was hard work and not one that could be done in a day or two.

Bored with the whole process, I played within the roots of maple, drawing pictures in the sand. Suddenly, I heard her yell, "Git back here with that!" Fred had taken off with one of her lengths and was playing keep away with it. "Who taught him to fetch twigs anyways?"

I didn't answer that, but I got in the chase. Fred thought it was a game, "I'll get it," I promised while chasing him around the smokehouse and toward the house. I got close enough to grab his tail, he yelped and dropped the oak. The chase was over. I handed the wood to Mom-mom as if nothing had happened.

Pop-pop had passed by watching the mayhem with an amused look on his face, until he had gone into the washroom and used his brush. He bellowed, "What in tarnation is syrup doing in my brush?" That left me wondering once again, *What does he use that brush for?*

The next day, Mom-mom began to peal a few of the lengths to be used as splits for weaving. With each length she placed the Barlow knife directly on the airholes at one end, tapped the knife with a short stout piece of wood, and began to peal strips one at a time along each line of airholes. She had told me many times that air holes tell the years of a tree and the thickness of a split told how little or how much rain had fallen that particular year. Some of the twelve lengths may not be fit to peal for one reason or another, perhaps too many little knots in one spot, so they might be cut in shorter lengths for ribs.

The one quarter of the tree she had left whole, she cut lengthwise into two long halves and not into fourths. Part of one half was peeled into wide pieces to make the hoops or mainframe of the basket. One as a handle and bottom, which was held vertically, and around that another hoop was placed horizontally for the rim. Each side was woven at the connecting X on the sides which made a sturdier mainframe. Then, with one of the twelve lengths she made ribs, carving and shaping them round with her Barlow knife. The length of the ribs varied with longer ones around the middle and got shorter as they reached the top near the rim and bottom. She had fit just one side of the basket with ribs, and asked, "Is it lunchtime yet?"

"Can't be," I said, "I just finished breakfast."

"You got up late again this mornin' and dawdled around the kitchen, eatin' all the syrup again, I expect."

"There's a plenty left."

"A plenty on your face."

I grinned sheepishly realizing I had forgotten to wipe my mouth, but I had not created the mess from the previous morning.

"Can you go git me some kindlin' for my cook-stove? Them corn cobs under the sheller will work just fine. Get me 'bout a dozen. I'm gonna fix some lunch. I'm hungry as that dog, but he'll wait 'til we eat. You make sure that animal don't take off with nothin' again." She added, "When you come back inside, look at the old apple basket hanging on a nail in the porch. I repaired it with some'a my new splits. I done that this mornin'."

While they ate, I looked at that apple basket. Probably sturdy enough to carry me, I thought, and sure enough there were her new golden brown splits clearly defined against the faded blue and gray-brown wood. But Fred caught my attention, so I ran outside again and kept on running with Fred chasing from behind. We ran out in the field as far as I dared without fear of a scolding. We rounded the garden of greens and crossed the road into the wasted tomato field. I walked along the edge of the woods by the Burk's Mill Branch and could hear the water running. The woods that was so lusciously green in the summer had lost some of its luster, but was still shadowy and welcoming—I stepped inside. A sea of cypress knees stuck up out of the muck. I went as close as I dared while eyeing a big cypress and decided that climbing it was out of the question.

Suddenly, I heard growls and barking coming from the woods further up the branch. Fred's head went down and he growled low in his throat like I'd never heard him do before. It had only been a few months ago, in the spring, when the last wild dogs had been a problem. We knew all the dogs owned by our family and neighbors. No one had more than two dogs.

I grabbed Fred by the hair on his back and forced him to run with me out of the woods, across the field and to the house. I shoved him up the porch steps and slammed the screen door hooking it and flew into the kitchen while yelling about wild dogs across the road.

Mom-mom glanced at Pop-pop. He got up from his chair, scraping it backwards and disappeared into the living room and up the stairs. He came back through the kitchen with a pistol in his belt and carrying a shotgun. One pocket of his pants bulged with shells. On the porch, with double barrels aimed toward the screens, he shoved two shells in place and snapped the barrel too. He nearly went through the screen door trying to push it open, not knowing it was hooked. I shrunk, but my kneejerk reaction brought no comment from him, he just unhooked the door and clomped down the steps.

Across the road he went. Neither of them had said a word. Mom-mom continued to eat. I didn't know what to do, so I just stood frozen holding onto Fred's hair. He whined. I waited. Finally, she got up and put her plate on the floor, a small piece of ham and half biscuit left in syrup. I released his hair. He must wonder what he had done that was so good, getting to eat in the house, I thought, but I still didn't move.

She said, "With two episodes' a wild dogs now, I reckon you can understand why we like you to stick so close to the house."

"Well, we went in the woods yesterday, all the way back to John Frank's farm. If there's a pack, we both would have been in trouble," I said with my voice trembling, "Should've taken Fred."

"I had the pistol in my pocket and I'm a right fair shot. Gun scares um, see, and yes, I expect Fred would've tried to protect us, but even I never dreamed that another pack would form this soon."

"Oh." I paused, "Well, how about me riding my bicycle that mile from my house to here?"

"Most times we know when them packs is wandering. Somebody hears um and sends word. But here on this farm near the branch and the crick, don't know as a pack of dogs would swim the branch, and they's nobody between us and that branch to hear um. Stella's on the other side. Too, soon as you leave your house, they's one Uncle across the way, and then two more Uncles in view'a here. And, you've got enough sense to stop at one if you hear anything."

"Oh."

She looked at me and started to say more, but instead took the lid off the stove reservoir and dipped the corner of her apron in the water, turned to me, and wiped dried syrup from my mouth. We heard both barrels of the shotgun go off and then the pistol retort time after time. I grabbed her around the waist, hugging. She put her arm around me, hugging me back.

"He's gotta kill them dogs before they hurt somebody. We been through this before."

"They were named by some people before they dumped them!"

"Most likely."

"They are just all the Freds that have gone wild from hunger."

"I know, but they is too dangerous now."

"People from town oughtn't to drop them!"

"But, they do, honey, they do anyways."

I dried my eyes with the back of my hand. Crying was not something I did easily. It made me feel weak, like I couldn't handle whatever was happening, but the reality of the situation had become clear. Looking at me, Fred had cleaned his plate and jerked his head with ears alert at the sounds of the shots. He licked my hand. Mom-mom turned back to the stove, stoking embers that didn't need stoked.

"Gotta git back to my basket," she said easily. "You come with me. We'll be close to the porch and we got Fred. But, most likely, everything is taken care of."

She had me sit back on the chopping block again and hand wood to her while she whittled some ribs. Still nervous, I made Fred lay beside me. With handle and bottom made by one circle of wood and another piece around the center which formed the rim, she put a couple carved ribs in place and whittled one at a time to fit. It was a long process. While she worked Pop-pop returned from across the road with shotgun draped over his arm and entered the house. She gave no indication that she had seen him. When he came out of the house toward the backyard, she began going into detail about her work. She talked about how the shortest ribs went on both sides of the bottom and then both sides of the rim. As they went out toward the middle, they got longer.

Her splits lay in a tub of water. She began to weave the wet splits in and out of the ribs near the X where handle and rim met. In and out, pushing each in place, weaving and pushing. "When each split dries, it shrinks, so that if you was to weave one wet split after the other they'd be spaces and gaps. Each one is near dry by the time I've done weavin' it, but not quite. To push it in place, I use this screwdriver, and weave the next one when the last one is dried."

She made sure that she held my attention until late afternoon, but she had not finished the basket when suppertime had come. I could see that so far the weaving was tight and consistent, and she had purposely left little room for me to ask Pop-pop questions as he came and went finishing his chores for the day.

After supper she got a small tub from the porch and pumped water into it and put a rock in the bottom of the basket settling it to the rim. She cleaned up her tools and arranged all her pieces of wood in order. When lifting her basket out of the water, it leaked like a sieve out of the section she had finished, even after she had done the finest carving, weaving, and tightening she could manage— it still leaked. She had felt that this was her year for the long sought after water-carrying-basket. She explained that she had only seen one basket that ever held water and scolded herself for not having paid more attention to the detail in the weaving and the width of strips and ribs.

"They must'a cut notches in them ribs for the splits to fit tight; first the outside of the rib then the inside and so on. May be that's it." Her voice revealed her disappointment. "I know what they done! They made it with all splits, not ribs like the old one I got, only they made it real snug. That must be it. I could'a sworn it was ribs."

"Well," I said, "I think it's a grand basket. Look how beautiful it is turning out. And, it came from the bank of the creek near the old family farm that isn't there anymore."

She relaxed and smiled, "I got me enough material to make another basket, and indeed, it come from the bank'a that crick and the ancestor's farm. I guess it don't git no better than that." Climbing the steps to the porch, she patted Fred on the head, which I'd never seen her do before, and breathed a contented sigh.

Ann Bloom and oak basket bench made by husband, Robert. She made the baskets from a small white oak from Harvey and Eva Pusey's property. Tools used were a butcher knife and Barlow knife stuck in the top of the clamp, drawknife hanging on the side of the clamp, froe in grass beside baskets, wedges and maul beside length of oak on the ground. Note, half an oak length is clamped and ready for the bark to be stripped by the drawknife.

The top half of the vertical circle will be the handle, bottom half will be the bottom of the basket. The rim is the horizontal circle. The ribs are placed in a circular pattern from the rim to the bottom on both sides. Shown are parts of an old basket, a two-hoop frame, and a few ribs.

An old apple basket with side handles, bottom rewoven by the author.

Pears picked from Harvey and Eva's pear tree in a grapevine basket.

Grapevine basket with crabapples that were picked in mid-1980s from Harvey and Eva's trees beside their house.

Close-ups of various basket weavings and designs. The use of oak split by hand rather than machine can be seen in the rough lines in the various rims, handles, ribs, and weaves, as well as the inside and outside bottoms of these baskets (carved swing handle basket and feather basket with lid). All of the following baskets were made by the author.

On left: swing handle basket with kicked-in bottom that was begun over an old shoe last stand. On right: outside of that bottom.

On left: the bottom of the Feather Basket. On right: the top of the lid that pulls up and down the handle. That feather basket could store down from geese or ducks.

Long, carved handle, loosely woven, farm basket used for gathering asparagus.

Large field basket.

Two-handled, lightly woven, sewing basket.

Examples of a smaller berry basket with some weaving stained by strawberries.

A pair of matching half-baskets that fit against the wall, one boasting guinea feathers. Baskets made by the author by carving matching handles, rims, and various lengths of ribs a pair at a time.

Ground mushroom in a Pocomoke pine forest.

Fungus growing on the side of a pine tree in the Pocomoke Forest.

Mushrooms growing on the sides of trees in the Pocomoke Forest.

A mushroom that children called Stacked Pancakes.

A mushroom called Lion's Mane.

Berry bushes along the banks of the Pocomoke River.

A Winterberry on the bank of the Pocomoke River.

Believed to be Partridge Berry or Squaw Vine, found in Pocomoke Forest.

Moss growing on a fallen, dead tree near Dividing Creek in the Pocomoke Forest.

Raccoon Hunting

My curiosity had a hold on me all night. Men had come around midnight, unlatched the pens on the back of their pickup, and let the hounds out to go raccoon hunting. Pop-Pop had latched Fred in the chicken coop while he and Bruce had been waiting for the men. Over the years, many wild tales about raccoon hunting had been told and retold, mostly in the evenings down at one of the country stores, so I could hardly sleep waiting to get firsthand details from Bruce. At intervals of waking during the night, I listened for sounds of them coming home from the hunt. Finally, I heard the whoops and whistles for the hounds to return to the pens and I listened as the sound of the pickup motor faded away—followed by Fred's whimper when Pop-Pop let him loose. Pop-pop and Bruce finally lumbered upstairs to go to bed. Only then did I fall sound asleep.

Waking with a start, I dressed hurriedly while shivering uncontrollably, sincerely believing that the temperature had dropped to zero during the night. Just a few weeks ago I had been running all over the farm in short sleeves and knee pants. This cold seemed a drastic change to me. Running into the kitchen and hunkering over the Home-Comfort, I leaned as close as possible to the only heat in the house. Mom-mom grinned at me. "It ain't that cold. You is gonna get fire-burnt pretty quick this winter," she said and then went out to her wringer washer on the porch. She had already started washing clothes.

Still shivering I followed her out onto the porch, "Are they up yet?" I asked.

"Child, you tossed and turned all night—kept me awake," she said, while wiping her hands on her apron before handling the clothes.

"Couldn't help it. But, have they got up yet?"

"No and they is upstairs in bed. Don't you go botherin' um just now. They'll get up when they is good and ready!"

"Rats!" I said, knowing I would have to wait.

"Girls don't go coon huntin', you know," she stated consolingly, while feeding each piece of clothes through the wooden rollers at the top of the washing machine.

"It's not fair!"

"May be, but its men's doin's and no woman belongs in the mix." She said and continued with her chore by shaking out each piece of clothing and dropping them into a wicker basket.

"Where's the raccoons?" I asked looking out the porch door for the animals that would be latched inside bushel baskets.

"They ain't none."

"None?"

"None! And most times that ain't what it's all about anyhow. And, don't go pesterin' your brother too much and your Pop-Pop not at all. You'll catch 'what for' if you do. Now," she continued, "git me the sausage outta the icebox." With that said, Mom-mom moved into the kitchen, slipped a pan of her biscuits into the oven, took down two spiders, and began cooking breakfast. She cut one long sausage link in four inch lengths and then sliced each one down the middle of the casing and flattened them out in the pan. They sizzled as they hit. Glancing at an empty wood-box beside the stove, she added, "Honey, git me an armload of wood for this stove." an endearment that passed for please and rarely for sympathy.

Slumping my shoulders, I did as she asked and snatched a jacket off a nail in the porch not knowing whose it was, pulled it over my sweater with my arms fully engulfed in sleeves, and passing the thrashing washing-machine, went out to the woodpile. It really wasn't that cold outside for the end of November. A stray cat scurried under the smokehouse with Fred on its heels. "Fred, why can't you leave that cat alone?" I admonished him knowing it was futile and bent over at the waist peeking under the smokehouse. The cat hissed. Not today, I decided. But instead of gathering wood, I absentmindedly sat on a stump that was yet to be reduced to chunks.

Raccoon hunting stories had drifted down through the years as the men loved telling stories on each other. Arguments ensued as to the truth about what the other fella was telling and some of those half-truths and creative tales were told with great humor at home as well as the store. The men recounting the yarns at home were unaware of children listening intently and we had learned far more than Mom-mom thought any of us knew.

The little bits of information I had been able to gather were few and constantly contradicted by new stories, but those tidbits ran through my mind as the hard and fast process of the event. *Naturally, hunting raccoons has to be done at night since that is when the masked bandits are on the move. So, the men bring their trained coonhounds, a mule, shotgun or .22 rifle, burlap bag, coal-oil lantern, food, and booze, some of which is homemade. Then, a fire is built in a choice spot in a clearing in the woods so the men can keep warm. The hounds roam free running through the woods, howling when they have a raccoon on the run, or have one treed, but the mule is a puzzle to me. If the hounds are chasing a raccoon, the mule has to keep up. Surely when they get the dead raccoon in the burlap bag, it is time to come home.*

The outrageous possibilities as to whether there was such a thing as a coon-mule varied—The mule followed the hounds throughout the hunt, treed raccoon or not; The mule took off running by itself when hearing the sounds of the hounds once a raccoon had been treed; The mule could sniff out a raccoon on its own and didn't need the hounds; The mule had been given a bottle of beer and stumbled where it wanted to go; There is no such thing as a mule that will run through the woods at night for any reason—but most of these seemed impossible since I thought, *No such mule exists.* My reasoning was that the mule was simply led by the rider toward the sounds of the hounds once a raccoon had been treed. Because if there was such a thing as a coon-mule, then that mule would take off across the pasture after any stray raccoon in sight, morning, noon, or night and I'd never heard of any such thing happening.

It was easy to picture the men sitting around a campfire in a clearing in the woods. And probably there was some whiskey drunk, perhaps none at all, but one thing was for sure—there were lots of stories told. There were fearful hunts, such as men coming back with faces cut to pieces, looking as if the masked bandit had clawed them bloody. If a mule with a man on its back had run a beeline into the swamp toward the barking hounds, it seemed that mule and man would be slapped senseless by branches and briars. I imagined a pitch black night and the man running blind to the unseen danger of a thick wall of tall briars.

One story, sworn to be the truth, was about a man who was convinced that his hounds were lost in the woods. Cold sober, he left the other men sitting around the campfire to search for his prized coonhounds on a moonless night. The further he got from camp, the less light he had. He stumbled into huge briar patch. Complete darkness closed in. He had mashed the briars by laying down in order to move forward and continued that process, all the while calling out to the men and hounds. Once the men heard the lost man calling, they scattered in all directions. Just one man carried the lantern. He was the only one with light enough to see. The lost man, confused with voices coming from all sides, didn't know which direction to take and floundered around in a circle mashing down a huge patch of briars. Finally, the men came together by following the sounds of the barking coonhounds, hounds standing at the edge of a wall of briars where their owner could be heard calling for help.

What a spectacle the procession must have made as they all came back. One man in the lead and holding the lantern was followed by the man who had been lost and appeared to be cut to pieces with clothes shredded. All the other men followed with faces and hands scratched, clothes torn and muddy from the rescue, carrying no raccoons, and their hounds yipping at their heels with the mule they had left at camp bounding behind the hounds. They had not put out their campfire, and luckily it had not caused a woods-fire before it went out. The men on that excursion had not talked much about the hunt for the lost man, but the scratched faces told it all. Neighbors had needled the truth out of one of the men. The story had survived and several new yarns had been added.

I giggled with the memory of those scowling faces and zipped lips, but now, I was waiting to hear a firsthand account about a brand new hunt from Bruce. Fred pushed at my leg wanting a pat on the head, so I absentmindedly patted him. Then smells from the kitchen drifted outside snapping me out of daydreaming and reminding me of my errand. I quickly gathered an armful of wood and entered the kitchen whereupon Mom-mom asked, "Fire's low! What happened to you? You've had enough time to chase a bandit'a your own." I slung the coat down on the rocker in the porch and hardly heard what she said since Pop-Pop and Bruce were at the table. Neither looked the worse for wear. I knew neither one drank whiskey, but no scratched faces! I was disappointed.

We ate quietly. I knew better than to start asking questions, so I would wait until Bruce and I were alone, but Bruce began. "You're just dying to know what happened last night so I'm going to tell you—nothin'!"

"What do you mean, nothing happened or you're not going to tell me nothin'?"

"Right." Bruce said.

"Pop-Pop, he's teasing me." I said accusingly.

"Well, leave him be," Pop-Pop answered and took one last swipe with his biscuit at the runny egg on his plate, strode onto the porch for his hat and coat and promptly fussed, "Somebody's chucked my coat on the rocker and not back on the nail," and then he banged the screen door on his way out.

"He started it. I never said nothing." I called after him, not bothering to address the coat.

Bruce wiggled his ears at me. He had a knack for doing that without any assistance from his hands—both ears wiggled.

"Mom-Mom did you see that?"

"See what?" She asked, gathering the plates and dropping them in a basin of cold water.

Bruce got up from the table, patted me on the head and headed outside, but I would not be put off and stuffed a crumbling biscuit into my sweater pocket and chased after him.

"Come on Bruce, tell me!"

"Curiosity killed the cat, you know."

"Hang the cat, I want to know what happened. Did you even see a raccoon? I heard the hounds. Couldn't help but hear them a ways off. Must have been a chasing something."

Mom-Mom, wearing a scarf and heavy sweater, passed hurriedly by us with basket on her hip, headed for the clothesline and looked at both of us with no coats, "You young'uns will catch your death."

We paid no attention as I trotted behind Bruce out to the barn. He climbed the corn up to the hole and began to toss corn to the hogs. Turning to watch me climb through the barn doorway, he said, "Maybe next time, probably in January, we will come back all bloody and then you can tell us what happened," and he turned back to his chore.

I stood in the doorway with my hands on my hips, staring at him, and waiting.

Finally he turned to me and said, "Really! Nothing happened! We built a fire and sat around telling stories. The men from the other side of the creek were entertainment enough. The hounds chased shadows or something and I fell asleep and woke up as they were packing up to come home. That's all!" He paused, "Now, why don't you make yourself useful and go help Mom-Mom hang clothes on the line before I feed you to the hogs."

"Jeez-whiz, you don't have to get huffy," I said and jumped down to the ground, yanked the biscuit out of my pocket, took a bite, and tossed the rest to the nearest hog, careful not to get anywhere close to the pen. "That raccoon hunting is just playtime for men is all," I yelled backwards at him, "and it doesn't come close to accounting for a season of work, because it ain't."

Mom-mom had hung her basket of clothespins on the line and scooted it along ahead of each piece of clothes she had jabbed in place. She had lowered the pole attached to the line in order to reach the line to hang her clothes. As usual, each pair of pants was hung separately and the shirts were pinned next to each-other as were dresses and underwear. I began to hand her each piece of clothes. We worked silently, moving down the line until nearly reaching the end. With basket empty, she walked to the middle of the line, gave the pole a shove skyward and the clothes began to flap in a breeze that had kicked up. Mom-mom looked up as clouds moved over the sun. She said simply, "Rain'll make um softer and the wind'll iron um out," and then she grabbed her basket, tossed the clothespin bag inside, and walked toward the porch. I knew the clothes would stay on the line in rain or shine until dry, whether today or tomorrow.

Fred was barking at something under the house and would not stop even when I called to him. "Must be something or other under the house, "Mom-mom said. Trailing behind her, I was considering what to grab to get Fred's attention, when I heard the sounds of faint mews, baby kittens under the house. Mom-mom heard them at the same time and groaned, "Git a bowl'a milk out of the icebox and slip it under the porch for the mother."

"Oh boy, that cat has had baby kittens!" I said excitedly and got the milk, pushing the bowl under the porch as far as possible without getting scratched by the Momma cat. I ordered Fred to come and we ran out to Pop-Pop in the chicken house where he had started the Maytag motor and was checking the barrels for leaks as water ran to troughs on both sides of the house.

"We got baby kittens under the porch!" I announced proudly.

"Git me the tow sack," he teased.

"When they grow they can catch mice!" I offered knowing that some people did drown kittens and puppies they couldn't feed.

"They'll all be around my feet while I'm tryin' to git into the house! They's gotta be moved."

"But it's warm under the kitchen where the woodstove sits and winter is coming on. Only thing is Fred."

"When Fred gets his eyes near scratched out, he'll leave um alone. They's plenty of farms with cats and dogs runnin' around together. Now, when them cats is weaned, you best find homes for a couple of um 'cause that is the only way for um all to make it. And, don't name um cause all of um ain't gonna last."

"No worry there; can't even get close to the Mama to see what name she deserves."

Running back to the house, I was on a new mission—homes for the kittens in just a few weeks. I could give them away as Christmas presents. Sitting down at the kitchen table, I got pencil and paper, and headlined the paper: Christmas Homes for Kittens. But, try as I might, there was not a single person I knew who would want one. Most of the surrounding farms already had more cats than they wanted.

Mom-Mom leaned over my paper and then patted me on the head, "Been talkin' to your grandfather ain't you? Well, don't worry about it, these things got their own way'a working out."

"That's what I'm afraid of," I replied. *Well*, I thought, *I can probably have one to take home, but that's about it.* Lifting the grate on the woodstove, I threw the paper in the flames and sat down at the table again. The warm fire and lack of sleep took over. I fell fast asleep until Bruce came in, plucked me on top of my head with a knuckle, and dangled a little calico kitten by the nape of the neck in front of me.

"Why are you carrying it like that?" I fussed, wiping my sleepy eyes.

"That's the way the mother cat carries her kitten."

"Looks like you're choking it."

"You said hang the at-cay!"

"It's a wonder that mother cat didn't slice you to ribbons and stop that Pig Latin!"

"You have to know how to do these ings-tay."

"Let me hold it."

"You won't give it back to her. We've been through this before, just wanted you to see it."

"Ive-it-gay." I said rounding the table.

"Watch out for that coal-oil lamp on the Hoosier!" Mom-mom fussed.

Bruce turned and ran out the porch door letting it slam and I sailed right behind him slamming it again. "Gimme it!"

Mom-Mom yelled from inside the house, "Children, quit bangin' that screen door!"

But once again we paid no attention. Pop-pop passed by on the way to the mailbox and just shook his head as I chased Bruce around one maple tree and then the other in pursuit of the kitten.

When I awoke the next morning, it didn't take me long to know what had roused me from my sleep. A profoundly rank smell was coming from the kitchen. In a few seconds I had yanked off my nightgown, pulled on my clothes and pushing hair back from my face, I ran into the kitchen pinching my nose. On the stove was a big pot simmering with onions bubbling to the top. Mom-mom sat at the table running syrup around her plate with a biscuit.

"What is that stench?" I blurted. She had not heard me enter the kitchen.

"Lord, child, you oughtn't to burst into a room like that!"

"Sorry, but what is that?" I pointed to the pot.

"Muskrat. Your grandfather checked his traps yesterde'."

"I didn't know he trapped them."

"Has for years. See, durin' the coldest months they's less for us to do, so coon huntin' and trappin' muskrat is different kinds of meat for the table. During the First World War, he made good money for the meat and hides, course we ate um too. He's trapped on and off since then. He don't stretch the hide no more, no call for the hides like they was years ago."

I opened the kitchen door and backed into the porch where a breeze was coming through the screens, then let go of my nose and shivered. Mom-mom seemed amused at my actions and I decided that she had no sense of smell at all or she would not be sitting there eating breakfast without retching.

"I guess I'm allergic to muskrat then."

She chuckled and it took her a minute to stop.

"Does raccoon smell like that too?"

"Not exactly."

That told me all I needed to know. "Well, I'm glad they didn't catch raccoon then, because both of them cooking at the same time would cause that stove to walk right out from underneath them."

"Well, you is just a sour puss this mornin'."

"I don't want any breakfast right now."

"Suit yourself, but you'll love that muskrat once it's cooked down and gravied."

"I'm not even going to try it!"

"You eat hog meat and you know the smell of the pig pen, and the smell of the renderin', the singin' hair and the innards. You know the smell of a chicken dunked in hot water to git the feathers off and then the singein' of the hair."

"That's different."

"Different cause you've eaten um all your life, and you got used to um."

"No, different cause the smell of that muskrat is worse than anything else I've ever smelled cooking on that stove. My stomach just turned up-side-down."

She chuckled again. "I guess the smell is bad, but it's good eatin' just the same. That smell'll go away in a while when I add more seasonin's."

After sitting on the porch for a while, the smell had ceased to be as strong, though I didn't want to admit it. By afternoon, just a hint of rank odor was left. *Probably clinging to the walls,* I thought. For dinner she had fixed mashed potatoes, and greens, and the stewed muskrat with gravy. I was skeptical. I tried a tablespoon of the gravy and then another, and then a piece of meat while Mom-mom just ate and watched. I couldn't admit it was good though, because I'd had too much to say, but Pop-pop gave his grunting approval and went out to check the hogs and the chicken house. But I decided that come the next coon hunt, *I am not going to spend the night. They might catch one!*

A typical scene of a country store during the 1800s into the 1900s where tall tales were told and checkers were played. No doubt some still exist with the potbellied stove, checkerboard on a barrel, and spittoons for the chewing tobacco that needed to be hurled somewhere. (Adkins Historical and Museum Complex, Inc., Mardela Springs, MD)

Thanksgiving

Hopping up the steps one at a time, I landed just inside the porch. A bushel basket of freshly picked cabbages sat on the porch floor. I'd heard that years ago farmers dug a hole into the ground and lined the hole with pine shats, put the cabbages in the hole, and covered them with dirt. But they left an opening to be chinked that was no larger than a cabbage could fit through. I stuck my head into the kitchen, "You going to mound these cabbages?"

"No child. I ain't done that for some years now," she answered while adding salt to a pan.

"Why not?" I asked.

"Winters was colder years back; vegetables keeped better." Changing the subject, she stuck her hand into a pan, and asked, "Just plucked and cut up these two chickens. You want to hand me each piece while I check um for pin feathers? I gotta put um in cold salt water to soak."

"Sure," I said, and entered the kitchen, although not convinced I wanted to do anything. With a few days off for Thanksgiving holiday, I didn't want any chores, but I stuck my hand in the pot and handed her the gizzard.

"They's nary a feather on a gizzard," She said lightheartedly, probably due to my less than eager attitude.

"I know," I giggled, accepting that she had made a joke.

We continued with the chicken until we heard the guineas screech and then go silent as if they had hailed the coming and going of something not belonging to the farm. Fred barked at their noisy intrusion and then quieted too.

"Where's your Pop-pop got his-self too?" She attempted an offhanded manner as she inspected the breast I had just handed her, but the undertones of frustration were clear. I couldn't tell if she was worried about him or the actions of the guineas and Fred.

I was not sure whether to tell her that I'd seen Pop-pop by the maples with his shotgun broken open and draped over one arm. He was wearing his knee high rubber boots with tops turned down, and corduroy pants held up by suspenders that kept his heavy flannel shirt neatly tucked. *No overalls today?* I questioned silently, *Cold weather is back.* Holding the brim, he had slapped his well-worn hat on his head and jerked it down over his forehead. One pocket bulged with shotgun shells.

"Only takes one to kill a turkey," I had teased.

"One for the turkey and five for them wild dogs, cain't be too careful. S'pect they's all gone now though, at least until some young'uns in town get puppies for Christmas and come spring they's out here starvin'," he had said with disgust.

"Maybe a shell for a squirrel or rabbit?" I had asked hopefully, not wanting to think about the wild dogs.

"Both is scarce just now. Anyway, your grandmother's got enough to do today without picking buckshot outta a squirrel."

"Oh heck!" Stewed squirrel was one of my favorites. But before I could say more, Pop-pop had turned and walked straight in back of the house toward the creek.

Pulling out of my daydream, I looked at Mom-mom and relented. I spoke just above a whisper with an air of revealed secrecy, "Saw him heading toward the back field with his shotgun. He's gone hunting for Thanksgiving dinner." Then I handed her the next piece of chicken, a leg that had just been walking around the smokehouse.

Inspecting the leg for un-plucked feathers and then plunging it in salt water to soak, she gave no reply. She took each piece handed her and performed the same action, inspecting and plunging, flicking any newly found feathers in a small sauce pan. Of course, it was no secret where he had gone. It was time for a Thanksgiving Turkey. But whatever she was concerned about was not voiced, so once all the pieces of chicken were soaking, she got a big pot filled it with water from the well and put it on the woodstove to boil. She dried her hands on a faded bouquets-of-roses apron and turned to get the buckets for gathering greens.

The turnips were easy to pull and took just a few minutes, so I did not really mind all that much. At least the chore was outside. The nutrients from manure had given the mustards a luscious deep dark green and the rain had caught them just right. She worked steadily, bent over at the waist just like she had done in the tomato fields.

Daydreaming on and off, I managed to produce my fair share of greens. It was a mild day for late November. *Probably in the upper 50s*, I decided, *but definitely sweater weather*. As sharp puffy clouds moved across a deep blue sky, I imagined all kinds of animals clothed in dresses, some with a bonnet or hat, and one uncovered head with long flowing hair. Seeming preoccupied, she simply gave an "Uh huh" with each description. When we finished, I didn't want to come inside, but she had to keep working on tomorrow's Thanksgiving dinner.

Using fresh water, she plunged and shook each large leaf and laid them in piles in a huge iron spider that was also used for a cutting board. She rocked a big butcher knife back and forth, put the chopped greens in already boiling water and threw in meaty chunks of fatback. She poured vinegar overtop and added baking soda. The water fizzed and nearly boiled over, but with constant stirring she kept the overflow under control. Not missing a beat, she peeled and cut the turnips into slices, dumped those slices in another pan of boiling water, and added chunks of fatback to them as well, but no soda or vinegar.

The greens only boiled for about fifteen minutes before she drained the luscious mound of bright green in her chipped agate colander—letting them drip into the empty fry-pan. Just a few minutes later, the turnips were dipped, fatback and all, into a huge bowl.

"I wish we could've stayed outside," I said wistfully, standing at the back kitchen door where the lilacs had bloomed in the spring.

She smiled in agreement, shown by the crinkles at the corners of her eyes, "Want to set on the porch while them chickens soak and greens drain? We'll fix ourselves biscuits with strawberry jam."

"Sure thing." I said and ran for the pantry closet under the stairs where she kept all her own canned goodies, but she called to me, "They's one already open in the Hoosier." She pushed up the Hoosier's sliding door, pulled out the jam, and then retrieved the biscuits from the shelf on the back of the stove.

The porch faced mostly south. The afternoon sun rayed through the bare branches of the maples and warmed the porch. In winter, the lay of the sun could warm a room even on a cold day. We rocked while consuming halved biscuits full of jam and feeling the sun and warm air. I plucked one half biscuit after another from the tin pan, licking my fingers in turn between each one shoved into my mouth.

"Saw you wash your hands after the chicken, but how about after the greens?" She asked.

"Nope."

She grinned.

"I wonder how much dirt we eat during our whole life."

"A right fair amount, I expect."

"Bruce says I eat too much dirt 'cause I don't wash the vegetables in the field, just wipe um on my shirt and eat. He says that one of these days I'm going to get all clogged up and you'll have to give me Caster Oil to get straightened out. Know what I told him? I said it was none of his business if I eat dirt, or worms, or bugs, but he just—" Stopping myself, I jumped up at seeing Pop-pop coming across the field. "He's got us a Tom turkey from the looks of it," I blurted, "and it looks like a big one! Those tail feathers are real pretty. You going to save 'um?"

She did not reply. There was no real expression on her face. She simply got up from her rocker, grabbed a tub from its post on a large nail, and stepped down the porch steps to begin the same routine she had just finished with the chickens. After gutting, she would save the giblets for stuffing, leave the turkey whole, and soak it in salt water.

Tomorrow, Thanksgiving Day, she will boil the giblets and make the stuffing "out and out," wash the salt out of the turkey and stuff it. Her recipes varied according to what she had available to put in them. Of course there were staples like sugar and flour, salt and pepper, vinegar, onions, lard, and eggs that went in her various recipes. So it was anybody's guess as to what seasonings might be in that dressing besides onions, bread, and giblets. All I knew was it would be delicious.

"Will you save me the neck and not put it in the stuffing? I love the neck after it's been cooked tender! The strips of meat just peal and I suck on the bone. Remember what Miss Stella said, that the marrow is good for you?"

She didn't answer. Pop-pop had reached the water pump, handed her the turkey by its feet. He turned the barrel toward the empty field and cocked open his shotgun to check for shells.

"Didn't hear the gun go off," I questioned.

"Prob'ly sounded on up the creek. I was a ways off."

"Did you see any wild dogs?" I asked tentatively.

"No."

"Any foxes?"

"No."

"Anything?"

Finding empty chambers, he snapped the barrel in place, "A coon out in the daytime."

"Did you kill it?"

"It shouldn't'a been out in daylight, not afraid'a me to boot." was the only answer he gave.

It must have had rabies, I thought.

I didn't know where he kept most of the guns in the house, but I never asked or looked. We knew there was a gun under his bed in case of any disturbance while we slept. Last winter, sounds had come from the kitchen in the dead of night. The first inkling that anything was wrong was the sound of a shell sliding into his single barrel 12-gauge, the unmistakable click of the lock, and that shotgun hit the top of the living room stove in the span of a waking breath. He leveled and aimed it directly through the dining room into the kitchen. In the moonlight pouring through the kitchen window, he saw the glowing eyes of a black cat that was standing on the kitchen table. "Dast a cat anyhow," we heard him say, but I decided that he had come downstairs on silent catlike feet. I slept soundly afterward convinced that Pop-pop was someone who not only saw everything, but heard every sound as well, even in his sleep—if in fact he slept at all.

We young girls were not taught how to shoot, not old enough, I guess. Somehow I knew that Mom-mom could shoot, but I never saw her actually pull a trigger. I knew of only twice she had carried a pistol, the time out at the clothesline, and while searching for the perfect oak. I understood one thing for sure though, *That raccoon is dead*. Suddenly I was standing by the pump alone. I realized that one of these days, daydreaming was going to get me in trouble. Alone, I ran off to find Fred.

Thanksgiving Day was mayhem, the same as in years before. Fifteen cousins, twelve Aunts and Uncles, and Mom-mom and Pop-pop were a houseful. It would seem that nothing was organized, but in its own way there was an order to be followed. I watched the women spread tablecloths and line the outside edge of the table with plates, forks and knives, and glasses. Not all the dishes matched; neither did the silverware, or the tablecloths either for that matter.

The food Mom-mom had cooked was placed in the middle of her table that held several added leaves to make it longer. Her stuffed turkey was in the center, surrounded by her fried chicken, greens and turnips, mashed potatoes and chunked sweet potatoes dripping with brown sugar and butter.

As Aunts filed in, they brought platters and bowls covered with tea-towels, food they had cooked at home. They brought, peas and dumplings, lima beans and corn, corn pudding, raisin pudding, stewed tomatoes, and numerous foods still covered that I could not see. Sweet potato and pumpkin pies lined the buffet and I wondered what Thanksgiving would be like without those pies.

After all the foods were on the table, the small vacant spots were filled with salt and pepper shakers, butter patties and homemade jelly still in canning jars, warmed bacon grease, and gravy. The simple unsaid rule was that if you don't see it, don't ask for it, because all she had was on the table.

The last foods Mom-mom placed on the table were a huge bowl of steaming biscuits and a pan of cornbread. The only thing left off the table was the jar of pickled-pigs-feet as some didn't care to look at them while eating. When she called out that dinner was ready, that did not mean the children. The grown-ups ate first, but not before some of us snuck a chicken leg, or a biscuit, or some food that could be easily snatched. I grabbed a chicken leg, ran down the porch steps yanking the skin off for the cats and tossed it under the house. Eating a couple healthy bites, I ran out into the yard calling Fred, determined that he should have the gristle at least, not that he wouldn't make out very well after dinner. Fred appreciated the morsel of chicken and sat waiting for the bone, but some people said that if it splintered and went down wrong, a dog could die. I debated the issue with myself, but figured that Mom-mom threw bones to the hogs and sometimes just out the back kitchen door and Fred had already survived many a chicken bone. So I pitched it in the air and he caught it, but instead of chewing the bone, he ran over to the side of the shed and dug a hole. *Saving it for later*, I thought.

"Looks to me like one of them chickens had only one leg!" Mom-mom had called after me, but it was half-hearted scolding because no one was allowed to be hungry in her house. Since we grandchildren had to wait to eat, she ignored our less than stealthy grab-and-run antics that were done when our parents weren't looking.

When we kids finally sat down to eat, the din of conversation saturated each room. The dining room was full of boisterous children ranging from ages five to seventeen all teasing and yelling at one another in between mouthfuls of the best food that ever graced a table. A couple younger cousins had catalogs for booster seats. Lyn had grown and was big enough not to need a catalog anymore.

The men had retired to the living room, quietly discussing what they didn't want us to hear, and smoking cigarettes and cigars that sent a gray haze floating into the dining room. Every now and then one of them sent a booming voice that seemed to shake our plates. The message was to quiet down.

The kitchen overflowed with women laughing, refilling bowls, and bringing them to the table. There were sounds of the kettle singing and then the splash of water being poured in the large basin time after time to wash the mountain of dishes that revolved from kitchen to table in front of us, back to the kitchen, and onto the table again. But, it was Mom-mom who fretted over us children, especially the younger ones.

She rounded the table checking the food, clucking like a mother hen first at one of us, and then the next, while using her pretty newly-made apron to wipe a nose or dab a chin. She figured an apron had its job to do whether it was old or new. "You best tuck that tea-towel into that little white collar and let me get that dribble on your chin or you'll ruin that brand new checkered skirt!—Look at them patent leather shoes, shiny as a new copper penny! You boys quit teasin' these little'uns!—Oh honey don't cry, he was just crossin' his eyes and if he don't quit they'll stick like that and that'll teach him! Here blow your nose.—Git that dog outta this dinin' room! Who let him in anyways?"

With my hand under the table, I had just slipped Fred a biscuit and out he went pushing the screen door open by himself, bread in his mouth and tail between his legs. Her worry continued until we flew from the table to chase each other through the kitchen and out onto the porch with our mother's yelling, "Don't you kids bang that screen door!" Which, of course, we did. And, "Don't get your clothes dirty!" That was really an understood occurrence, but our mothers knew the best they could hope for was that those best dress-clothes did not get torn.

The yard burst into chaos. A rooster got after one of the younger ones and before one of the older boys could get there, Fred jumped the rooster keeping it smashed to the ground with his paw. Finally, bored, he lifted his leg and that colorful little Banty took off strutting toward the long open front shed, fluffing his feathers and squawking as if thoroughly insulted. "Good boy, Fred," I yelled.

Someone was sitting in the corn shed window and had blocked the door so that others could not get inside. Boys were beating on the door yelling, "Open up." Walnuts were chunked and a game of chase began. Fred barked excitedly. The cats peaked out from under the house wary of coming out in plain view. Finally a kitchen window was raised with worried voices shouting the occasional order until the early darkness of late fall descended; the bedlam was over.

So shortly after sundown, another Thanksgiving ended as one-by-one cars left the yard for home. A stream of headlights moved up the road in single file, a pair of headlights wheeling in one home, and then another a little further, and so on until we reached our lane, our home being the furthest down that road, only a mile.

Harvesting turnips usually went rather quickly. The greens would be cut off and some dirt left on the roots for storage.

Some of the last frying pans Eva Townsend Pusey used; she still called them "spiders."

Wreath Making

The heavily misted forest loomed ahead of us like a vision one might dream. A thick frost from the previous evening had placed a shimmering coat atop the gum, pine and cypress trees, but only lightly dusting the shorter holly trees, and had not made its way to the forest's floor. That frost could have easily been mistaken for snow. The thin white cover on the lower trees added to the mystical effect of the surrounding fog. Shadows and shapes became trees and bushes. Through that silent beauty, Mom-mom and I made our way toward her favorite patch of crows-foot.

The path we traveled had been a dirt road beside Bounds One-room School and traversed by locals during the 1800's into the 1940's. The old school was long gone and the road had narrowed to a path that meandered through the forest to Dividing Creek where a small bridge had stood. That path started again at a bank across the creek into Somerset County. Areas near sections of the path were swampy. There had been many such roads throughout the wooded areas of the Pocomoke Forest that had lasted into the early '40's when rural schools and post offices began to close. Some have been kept open, but many narrowed with briars and brush due to nonuse, while others have been lost to history.

Sidestepping brambles, we continued alone as Pop-pop had stopped near a small group of lowland saplings he reasoned perfect for hoops. He was lost from sight as Mom-mom and I moved deeper into the woods. Again and again my pace slowed and then quickened during intervals of gawking at the forest, thus making Mom-mom disappear and then magically form once again. Walking behind her, all that could be seen was a gray woolen scarf tucked neatly at the nape of her neck beneath the collar of what was once a fine worsted-wool coat; that coat nearly touched the ground. Her hands would occasionally jerk backward as the four empty burlap sacks she carried would snag and loosen. Her unbuttoned galoshes made an occasional clicking sound as she plodded ahead of me like an imaginary image. As she moved in and out of vision, I sensed her as a figure belonging to the natural part of this forest in its virgin past.

Walking just a few yards off the trail, we landed in the middle of a huge thick patch of crows-foot. Dropping three of the sacks, she surveyed the surrounding abundance and nodded to herself as if in agreement with something unspoken and then bent over at the waist. Her hands began working swiftly. Following her lead, I picked up a sack and, after rolling the top down several inches, knelt and began to pull the tasseled crows-foot from the ground. Shortly, we produced a rhythmic ripping sound that mixed with an occasional bird call or rustling squirrel. We worked steadily and silently, no conversation between us.

Within half-an-hour Pop-pop took shape out of the mist. His tall lanky form, with slouched work hat and floppy rubber boots, clomped solidly toward us. Briars attempted to hold him, but he plowed those boots and suspendered corduroy pants through them instead of sidestepping. In the path, he dropped a bundle of saplings with rope wrapped around the middle and a loop protruding from one large knot. After gazing at us with his milky blue eyes, Mom-mom bent over at the waist and me sitting on my heels, he then turned away down the narrow path. Still bent at the waist, she simply glanced at him. I looked at her questioning his continuing. But, she just shook her head, keeping a steady pace at her task. As his footsteps and snagging of pants faded away, a hawk's voice resounded through the forest.

Practically sitting on my haunches, heels sinking in the soft ground, I ran my hand over the tops of the crows-foot, and marveled that each one looked like a miniature cedar tree, with the exception of tall yellow tassels protruding from the top. I thought, *The names of the plants, crows-foot and running-cedar, must have been switched over the years.* They both were connected through a root system, but the low-to-the-ground sprigs of running-cedar were shaped like crow's feet that when pulled, stayed connected by a vine. The crows-foot gave the appearance of a cedar tree and became an individual plant when pulled. Mom-mom had tied only a few running-cedar wreaths in the last few years since they were not as desirable because of the pale green color. The previous week we had picked only enough running-cedar to make a single wreath.

"No running-cedar today?" I questioned.

"They's no need," she answered, "I hung the one I made the other day on the porch-kitchen door."

"Saw it there. It's doesn't look as pale against the white paint," I replied.

"Years ago, I made some wreaths from cedar branches with the blue berries all over um, and no decorations of red berries or nothin', just the branches. They was some of prettiest you ever did see, but the berries will drop off pretty quick."

"I bet they were pretty," I said, as a picture of a large hoop of blue-berried cedar hanging on her kitchen door flashed through my mind, the scent filling the porch and kitchen.

"Some people decorate their crowsfoot wreaths with pinecones instead of berries."

I could see that too. "But probably not as pretty though," I said.

"That's a fact, they's something about them red berries."

"Yeah, sure is."

"I've seen wreaths of pine branches with the pinecones still holdin' on. Pine's pretty and smells good too, but I like my crowsfoot."

"Me too," I said, while soundly thrashing a handful crows-foot full of leaves against the side of my bag before pressing that bundle inside the burlap.

We did very little cleaning of the plants in the woods. That would have been a great waste of daylight and Mom-mom didn't waste time. Occasionally massaging her back, it was quite a while before she straightened. The misty fog was nearly gone, so she glanced toward the creek, "He'll get a few saplings along the crick-bank, still, I s'pect he's headed for Miss Prissy Pusey's old place, likely as not."

"But Mom-mom, that's across the creek."

"Yes child. But, the crick's narrower further up here where we is now than it is behind our house. Here they's a crossing, or was a crossing, a small bridge near Miss Prissy's place."

"But that bridge is probably gone by now and it's swampy too!"

"I s'pect he'll find something, even if it's just a log to cross. He'll cross it somehow."

"Couldn't he get there easier over on Denston's Dam Road?"

"He'd sooner cross his own land than someone else's, but you try to stop him if you've a mind to—may as well ask the mockingbird to quit chatterin'."

"Was Miss Prissy related to us?"

Mom-mom did not answer and there was no need to say more—she had bent back over her sack arranging her greenery in order to squeeze more inside an already bulging bag. I glanced at my own less than half-filled bag. How she managed to work so quickly was incredible to me, but there she was, bent at the waist, both hands busy, with coattail swaying side-to-side. She performed so many of her labors bent over at the waist. *I wonder how often I've watched the top of her head.*

In late summer and early spring, she had stood bent over at the waist, with only weathered arms, the top of her bonnet, and handmade dress visible as she had dropped seeds into each hole in her garden. She had used the same bent over stance while weeding and harvesting that garden, and when picking truck-crops in late summer. In winter, the only difference were her clothes; she appeared completely covered with thick woolen scarf and wool coat. With each task whether summer or winter, she swayed from one side to the other while bent over, planting this or picking that, even yanking greenery from the woods floor. I wondered, *What does she think about as she works, moving in a rhythm that is all her own? Surely her thoughts are peaceful. I can use some of that*, I thought. *Now that I know how to pay attention and really listen like I'd done on the creek, I should practice.*

I bent over at the waist, determined to make better headway. Looking over at her, I tried to mimic her movements while clearing my mind, and even attain a rhythm. After only a couple minutes, the blood had rushed to my head. As I stood up, her phrase, 'giddy-headed,' came to mind. I decided that staying bent at the waist must be gotten used to a little at a time, something else I needed to practice.

Back to sitting on my heels once again, I struggled to gain more of an even pace. But there was no rhythm to be had; when I moved my feet the result was a hobble, a jerking motion. *That was that*, I thought. Mom-mom had packed her bag with all it could possibly hold, so she came over to mine—offering help. Finishing my bag with a sigh, she straightened and pulled some squirrel nut candy from her pocket, handing me a few pieces. She popped one in her mouth and massaged her back again.

While we sucked and chewed the candy in order to soften it, I studied her standing there. Her scarf was more than big enough for her small head and shadowed her forehead. Turning toward the creek once more and trying not to show concern, she put her hand under the edge of her scarf and squinted, looking in the direction Pop-pop had gone. Her dress hem now hung below her coat revealing a muted black and white check, an older dress since she did not wear her newer ones while working in the woods. Not seeing him, she shook her head, gave a suck to the sweet caramel-like candy, and then took another bag. She began to pick in a new area of thick crowsfoot and even mentioned that this was the fastest picking she had ever done—clearly enough for a couple days of wreath making. I began to work with her. We were nearly finished with that bag in record time.

My stomach began to rumble. The candy had done little to relieve my hunger. Stepping out on the path, I noticed that the sun was lowering in the west. Must be three o'clock or maybe later. Days were getting shorter for sure and now the day's air was turning colder. The wind began to blow, even reaching below the treetops so I buttoned my coat tighter around my neck. I fingered the saplings Pop-pop had cut. They were about as big around as my thumb. These would make good hoops for the wreaths. He'd cut them about six feet long with triangle ends using Mom-mom's Barlow pocketknife, thus making what had been the thicker end easy to overlap when wired together with the smaller end—one step had been completed.

Suddenly, I heard something flying through the trees and hit the ground nearby, and then another thud. "What in the blue-blazes is that?"

Mom-mom didn't look up as she stuffed some last bunches into the bag, "Hickory nuts"

"Well, if they hit me on the head they'll knock me out."

"Not likely," she said, "but they do fall from so far up that they can raise a welt."

Brush rustling in the woods caught our attention. *That must be Pop-pop coming back from his mission*—and it was. Another bundle of saplings dangled from his right shoulder. He was soaked above his rubber boots. Mom-mom was settling the three bags in the path when she looked up surveying Pop-pop's condition. Nothing was said. Picking up the last bag, he began cutting berried holly branches from a nearby tree. Within a few minutes we were headed back to the county road. Pop-pop had a bundle of saplings slung over each shoulder with a bag of crows-foot in each hand. Behind him, Mom-mom was dragging a bag of crowsfoot. The two of them plodded ahead of me moving steadily forward while I struggled with the lighter bag of holly and was making enough noise to scare little creatures from their hiding place.

He was at least a foot taller than she was, even without his hat, both of them slim and fit and able to handle their load, his held well above the ground, her dragging hers. Even with old age creeping up on them, at that moment they appeared strong. I seemed to be the only one struggling, and glancing back down the path I saw that Mom-mom and I had swept a clean narrow swath along the old unused road. I saw something else, a shadow that moved so quickly off the road that I couldn't be sure I even saw it at all. I kept glancing back down the newly swept road, but didn't see that apparition again.

As soon as we were home, Mom-mom went in the house to start

supper while Pop-pop unloaded the bags and bundles. Immediately, Fred met us and nuzzled for food, so Mom-mom gave me a plate of scraps from breakfast and I tossed them to Fred. "I'll have to play with you tomorrow," I promised him.

I asked her where the cats were. Since they were still wild and sassy, my interest in them had not lasted for long.

She said that this week they had been walking all over the farm. She added, "Fred don't pay no attention to um now, got used to um. But cats is better at finding food for they-selves than dogs, mice mostly."

After settling their bags of greenery and saplings in the porch, Pop-pop sat at the table.

Mom-mom filled the cook stove to capacity and opened the draft up a bit to get a blazing fire. She filled the coffee pot with water and put coffee grounds in the round sieve at the top, and sat the pot on the stove to begin perking as soon as the stove heated enough to boil water. She said, "I may as well git down the big spider."

She fried potatoes, sliced some pork, and heated the morning's left over ham gravy. Pop-pop seemed tired. He did not talk, just sat waiting to eat. As soon as he finished eating, he left the table to build up the fire in the living room stove. When Mom-mom and I finished, she put the dishes in a pan to soak as she had done so often. She did not bother to clean the floor either. The process of wreath making would nearly require a shovel to clean up the mess.

She sat chairs back to the woodstove and handed me a dull paring knife, taking one for herself. After we sat down, she spread an old coverlet all the way across both our laps, explaining that the bedcovering was so worn it was well past saving. She placed an empty burlap bag in front of us. We began to clean the crows-foot. Placing a handful in my lap, I took half of them and shook what we called pine shats, but townspeople called shatters or needles, out of my half bunch. Then I began to pick the yellow tassels off the tops. Flipping that bunch to the other end, I ran the small wooden handled knife across the roots cutting off most of the runners, but leaving at least one long end on each. Roots and dirt, tassels, leaves, and shats lay on the quilt across our laps and spilled over onto the floor. As Mom-mom and I cleaned the crows-foot, we placed the trimmed bundles in the empty burlap bag at our feet. The bag began to fill quickly. Occasionally, she would sprinkle water over the plants to keep them from drying. Once that burlap bag was full of cleaned crowfoot, she drug it into her unheated sewing room and doused it with more water.

The stove in the dining room, as well as the living room, took either coal or wood. Pop-pop had chosen wood this year, probably because it was cheaper since he could cut it with little expense. He sat in a flat-plank, oak armchair next to the stove in the living room. There was an orderliness about his work. He had gathered all the material he would need, wire, wire-cutter, knife, and saplings. By whittling both ends of a sapling, he overlapped them six inches, and tightly bound them with wire. The result was a perfect circle of about twenty inches. If a sapling had been too long, he cut off one end to make his desired length. Those cut off pieces became spools for wire. He then trimmed the leftover pieces of sapling to eight inches and wound wire around them. The wire had come coiled in a large circle about sixteen inches across. When he wound it on his handmade spools, the coil sprang from the floor to his hands and looked like a large screen door spring. He wound a plenty wire as Mom-mom would be using the spools for attaching crowsfoot and holly onto the hoops.

Mom-mom and I were well seated and busy when he took two breaks, first, one just to see how we were doing. He glanced in the kitchen, grunted and returned to the living room. Later, he went to the Hoosier cupboard and cut a slice off the block of cheese sitting on the countertop and got a dipper of water from the reservoir, drinking from the dipper. I was pretty sure Miss Stella had made the cheese and I started to ask, but he went back to his hoop making and Mom-mom was quiet with her own thoughts. The only sounds inside the house were our scraping of roots and trashing of crowsfoot with the occasional crackle of the fire. Outside, Fred barked occasionally, letting us know we were well guarded.

As night wore on, a low fire of dying embers gave off less and less heat for our backs that were within inches of that Home Comfort. Well after midnight we were working on the last bag. We knew Pop-pop had finished the hoops and spools of wire since we heard him stoke the stove and then the creaking of floorboards upstairs. As we drug the last completed bag into the sewing room, she said, "My back is tired."

We washed our hands and faces, put on our nightgowns, and placed a glass of water on the marble-top stand. Then off to bed we went in her plump feather bed covered by two heavy quilts, bedroom unheated, on the northeast corner of the house. As usual, she said, "Turn your back to mine," and that is how we slept. We wore heavy flannel. She was a big believer in flannel nightgowns for us and flannel shirts for Pop-pop. I puffed my breath out, watching it rise illuminated by the moonlight coming through the far window.

I awoke to Pop-pop dropping wood into the living room stove and Mom-mom clattering pans in the kitchen. It was chilly. I jumped from the bed and into fresh clothes. She had swept the kitchen floor and all was ready for the wreath making to begin as soon as breakfast was eaten and cleared. Centered on her turquoise topped stainless steel table was a rose patterned tablecloth. It was one of her favorites for the kitchen, and although she rarely used a cloth for the kitchen table, I didn't question her. A platter of scrapple, fried eggs, and freshly made biscuits had been placed on top, with the lazy-susan in the middle. The table was beautiful. Pop-pop did not seem to notice. Mom-mom had even shelled corn for the chickens, so while we ate, we watched chickens peck the ground outside the kitchen window.

When we were finished, she put the dishes in a pan in the sink to soak, and said proudly, "Next week I'll git me a spigot and running water, makin' kitchen work a lot easier, 'specially around Christmas!"

Finally, was the only word that came to mind, but I didn't say it. I just finished brushing my teeth and spit down beside the pan, pouring water in afterward.

She let the leftover food stay on the table for something to munch throughout the morning. It took plenty of syrup for me to eat the scrapple. I expected to have jam on biscuits for my snack later, or maybe a hunk of cheese.

Mom-mom arranged her bag of holly berries on one side of her chair and a bag of crowsfoot between us. Then, she brought in a stack of the hoops Pop-pop had finished last night. She pulled on an old pair of brown cloth gloves with the fingertips cut out, picked up the first hoop, and began to wind a spool of wire around where Pop-pop had overlapped that hoop. She cinched the wire tightly and waited for me to hand her the first bunch of crowsfoot. Taking a big clean bundle from the bag, I laid it in my lap, and then separated out a small handful, handing her one little bunch at a time. She placed the first one on the hoop and wound wire around the brown roots, but close to the green foliage. I handed her another small bunch that she placed opposite the greenery already tightly affixed, and then wound those roots. She placed the next two inside the first two, but offset them and began staggering each small bunch down and around the hoop, except on the back of the hoop. At each one-fourth section, she reached into the bag at her right and pulled out a clump of holly berries and leaves. Breaking off little branches, she bunched the holly leaves and berries to her desired fullness and then wired that to the wreath as well. When she was done, the back of the wreath was flat and showed wire around the roots and then crowsfoot on the outer edges. The front was a mass of green and red beauty with no gaps or holes. The wreath looked as if she had placed each sprig individually with red berries growing from within.

Years ago, when her children were young, she would have her boys go get her clumps of red berries, what she called Bramble Berries or Hawthorn berries. They were clumps of red berries on bushes found along the Dividing Creek, many times near or around a fallen log overhanging the water. Those clumps were attached to a vine or branch by a half to two inch stem. The boys would break off that stem and collect those berry bunches for her. Using her wreath wire, she would then attach a couple of those bunches to a stick, and then attach that stick in the center of holly leaves in order to have enough red decoration. She kept some of those creek berries for her own use, but nobody knows why. I'd never heard of her using holly berries for anything other than wreaths.

With holly and berries tightly fastened to her hoop, she resumed taking the small bunches of crowsfoot I handed her, only stopping every quarter section to fix and place holly and berries. The spool of wire just spun in her hand as she finger-tipped the tightness on the back of the hoop and continued her work of art. We didn't talk very much. There was a feeling of ease, perhaps because of the quiet, or maybe because we were working with our hands and using the same motions over and over, no demands and no interruptions.

The wreaths stacked very well on top of each other. After eight or more had been made, she took four at a time into the sewing room and stacked them in her cleaned out corner lined with an old rug and burlap. She sprinkled water over the pile. On occasion, one or the other of us would stretch and take a break, usually by getting a dipper of water out of the reservoir, a biscuit or a slice of cheese, but there were few words spoken.

I asked her if she had something special in mind to buy with the money. She told me that one year she had bought a car from selling crowsfoot wreaths. Pop-pop had taken her wreaths to the auction in Fruitland. She also said that she and Pop-pop had made Holly Wreaths for a couple years and they were sold in Fruitland too. They had sold really well, but holly was harder to work with than crowsfoot, hard on the hands. She said all the wreaths sold so well because city people really liked Christmas wreaths on their windows and doors.

It was well past dinnertime when Mom-mom pulled her gloves off and said, "We worked enough this day. Let's clean this up and git supper—what would you like to eat?"

"Doesn't matter," I replied, "but maybe peaches. Haven't had any since canning season."

The garden Mom-mom and Pop-pop had planted in the spring and summer, had yielded plenty of vegetables as proven by her pantry under the stairs. The fruit trees had been just as productive. And so, after supper, we had her peaches—a real treat. Lima beans cooked in chicken juice with dumplings added were actually the main course. Where she found the energy to add the chore of making dumplings was a mystery.

The near silence of the last two days had seemed as if winter had brought it on naturally. The woods had been so chilly, quiet, and beautiful, that words could not equal the feeling. During the late nights with crackling fire at our backs, lengthy conversation would have been an intrusion. The steady and nearly mesmerizing movement of her hands winding and winding around the wreath had set private thoughts in motion, not conversation.

But, while we ate, I rattled on about how mice found their way inside the house, and the possibilities of how crowsfoot and running cedar got named, and wondered who had the gall to invent those potties with the small metal rim. "They hurt my behind if I sit there too long."

They listened and glanced at me once in a while, even Pop-pop who offered a sidewise grin. After a few minutes, he got up and went outside and Mom-mom put the coal-oil lamp on the kitchen table. I guessed she did that so that he could see the back of the house on his return, but once again I wondered, *Why doesn't she just turn on the electric lights*? Darkness had descended a couple hours ago. I was convinced that Pop-pop could see in the dark like a cat. I kneeled on a kitchen chair and looked out the window to see if I could see him, but it was dark. Clouds suddenly passed away from the moon and I saw the outlines of the smokehouse and shed. Mom-mom and I had gone to bed when he came inside blowing out one coal-oil lamp after the other. One of the glass globes rattled and the faint smell of coal-oil drifted our way.

The next morning, I took my time dressing. It was a school day and

Dad would be blowing the school bus horn soon. I had enjoyed the woods and rarely had I been given the opportunity to spend several hours working at a task within a setting where nothing demanded my attention. A place where all that could be seen was the simple beauty of trees and grasses, vines and bushes. I would rather go back there today. I imagine if school was not mandatory, I would stay home.

Mom-mom had breakfast ready and we sat quietly eating, my coat on the Hoosier ready for me to grab when I heard the horn. It was so quiet this morning that even the roosters had not done their usual cock-a-doodle-do. But one or two crows cawed and cawed just to be sure everyone was awake. I had just pushed aside a piece of sausage for Fred when Pop-pop came in from outside and stood in the doorway just looking at Mom-mom and she stared back at him. I knew that something had happened, but I had learned from the summer's tomato tragedy not to ask, just wait. The last couple days had been serene and a clear sign that winter was at hand, but the weekend was over. I knew that when Dad stopped the bus at Mom-mom's this morning, I'd have to get on and go to school.

She got up and went outside to Pop-pop and then came back inside. She sat down and folded her arms, resting them on the table. Rubbing one elbow and then the other, she finally looked at me.

"Things happen on a farm," she started. "Most times we don't know the reason for it, but it is farm life and you know the ways, near as much as I do."

I glanced out the kitchen window and saw Pop-pop walking across the yard with a shovel. A feeling hit the pit of my stomach.

"Now," she said, "Your Pop-pop's got his job to do, so we is gonna set here."

There was no animal I cared more about on this farm than Fred and I started to rise.

"Set," she ordered. Her words were not harsh, yet not sympathetic either. They were simple, but firmly made.

Suddenly, the bus horn sounded for me. Mom-mom got up and threw open the porch screen door and waved Dad on. I heard each shift of gears as the bus moved down the road. I heard her close the screen door and come back and sit down. I stared at the table.

"In the way'a things, it may be them cats come cause he was leavin,'" she said softly.

"Fred?" I asked

"Yes." She said.

I jumped and ran for the featherbed, slamming the bedroom door and burying my face in soft down. Mom-mom did not follow.

Crowsfoot in the Pocomoke Forest in its natural habitat, among cypress, hickory, pine, maple, and oak trees.

Close-up of a single crowsfoot plant with three tassels that turn yellow as it matures.

A handful of crowsfoot with roots cleaned and ready for tassels to be pulled.

Holly trees are striking in winter while holding onto their leaves and bright berries when many trees around them have lost their leaves. Hollyberries were beautiful against the green crowsfoot on wreaths.

Wreaths were made from branches of a cedar tree containing blue berries.

Christmas

Just like Thanksgiving, Christmas was a time when the family came together at Pop-pop and Mom-mom's, but first, Bruce, Lyn, and I opened presents at home. The gifts had been placed in separate piles under the tree. A cedar had been decorated with balls, tin figures of Jesus in a manger scene, an unfinished popcorn string, and lit with large multicolored electric bulbs, colors that danced with the movement of silver tinsel. A tree so beautiful the night before, but now had my first ever training bras hanging all over it. I snatched them down amid grins from Dad and Mom. With a furtive glance, I grinned at them, thankful Bruce hadn't made any comment. He was looking in the other direction as if he'd never seen them at all.

After eating breakfast and inspecting our toys a second time, we traveled the short mile to Pop-pop and Mom-mom's house. It had snowed on Christmas Eve as if it were the most natural thing to do on the day we desired it the most. When we got out of the car, we could smell a mixture of the foods that Mom-mom had been cooking the last couple days. Her handmade wreath of running cedar and holly berries—the wreath unwanted by city dwellers—hung on an unseen nail hammered into the kitchen door. That door needed touching up with white paint, yet it sharply accented her handiwork gleaned from the woods. The simplicity of the sight would even make the least sentimental person pause in thought.

Just for a moment, I had expected Fred to nuzzle my hand before entering the house. Pushing the thought from my mind, I opened the door and hot air rushed out into the porch. She had a window open on the opposite side of the kitchen to relieve some of the heat from cooking. She stood in front of the Home Comfort stove stirring a large pot. The bobby pins had been removed from her tightly curled salt-n-pepper hair, hair of which the salt had begun to outnumber the pepper during the past year. Her newly made apron was fresh and neat, very pretty and worn to keep her new, catalog ordered, J. C.

Penny 'frock' clean until dinner when she would remove her apron to sit and eat—that is, if she got the chance.

Removing my coat, I flounced over to her so she could admire my Robin-egg blue dress with patent leather belt and Peter Pan collar. The crinoline lined petticoat made the skirt of the dress standout, so the skirt flared and bounced when I walked. But she was too busy, nearly running from the electric stove to the woodstove, so I moved into the dining room checking the table to see if any morsel was there that might tide me over until dinner. The table had not been expanded and was empty.

Uncles stood outside talking as Aunts filed in; now Mom-mom had help with dinner. The kitchen had just been equipped with running water in the sink and I heard the spigot spewing water. I just had to see. Water came out so fast, the knob had to be turned back in order not to splash water. The large teakettle filled quickly. If only Pop-pop had run water and plumbing into the little washroom they could have a toilet, but he hadn't. The kitchen sink was the only place in the house where water flowed at the flick of a wrist. As she was putting the kettle on the woodstove, Pop-pop came in with an armload of firewood. His snow covered boots left puddles on each floor with every step all the way through to the living room stove. Mom-mom said nothing.

The Christmas tree was in front of the east window in the living room with presents piled beneath. Cousins, wearing brand-spanking-new clothes, barely gave the tree a glance. We all knew, or thought we knew, exactly what our presents were under that tree, the same things every year. We children began talking all at once about presents opened that morning, and the ones we brought with us. Besides a radio, the names for toys swirled around the room, sounding like single clipped words—swing, book sets, binoculars, play china, guitar, wagon, bicycle, records and players. Excited, my contribution was a camera. As the bedlam settled, the games were opened.

Soon dominos and checkers had been spread out on the floor and partners selected. A brand new, small transistor radio was pulled from a coat pocket and kept low so it would not be taken away. A discussion began among some of the boys about the small pen lite batteries inside that transistor. Some interests turned to BB guns and then a .22, a new one, not a hand-me-down, but neither gun had been allowed to be brought. Two bride dolls were placed side-by-side, one with a white gown and the other with pink. The dolls were too new to undress and redress. But while watching everything, my thought was that I couldn't wait to get back home tonight and play the phonograph that was under the tree, complete with red and yellow records. Too, the new set of Trixie Belden books would keep my head buried for weeks, and I would have to learn how to work my new camera. I brought my mother's old camera with me; I knew how to use that one. A sudden noise from the dining room turned our heads for a moment.

The men were grappling with the table, pulling it apart and installing all the leaves. They struggled with the fit until finally all the leaves had been pushed in place. Turning toward the living room, they had expected to wait for dinner there, but I guessed that they didn't make us move since we were quieter than usual with no arguing or yelling. We were absorbed in games. They lit cigarettes and stepped out onto the porch.

I stood in the doorway between the living room and dining room. Using my mother's camera, I flipped the metal lid up and held the camera box steady. Looking down into the glass I tried to center Lyn with the younger girls and their dolls lined up on the couch. After the flash, they rubbed their eyes complaining about seeing spots. After replacing the bulb, I turned the knob on the side of the camera; it was ready for the next shot. While waiting for my turn at dominoes, I rested my arm on the telephone stand and watched the dining room table come to life. One tablecloth painted with deep red poinsettias fluttered and landed on half the table; and then another with deep green holly and red berries fell in place to cover the other end—both the holly and flowers appeared to be neatly painted turned this way and that. No matter where I stood, I could find a perfect view.

The clatter of mismatched plates and silverware could be heard throughout the house as the table was being set. Various sets of chairs had been brought from every corner of the house. None of the mismatched items mattered a lick to anyone, except for maybe Mom-Mom, but I didn't really see any sign that it mattered, even to her. Bored, I then skipped from room to room. No one paid attention as I poked my head in the kitchen doorway. Mom-mom was talking about a Christmas card she had received from someone who lived in Canada and she had stuck it in the Bible. She came into the dining room and pulled the card from her Bible resting on the telephone stand.

As the women talked about the people from Canada, I could see the kitchen cupboard above the sink was bare and the doors left open. The skirt of my dress flared as I pirouetted in the kitchen doorway and back into the dining room where stood the now empty glass china cabinet. Every piece of dinnerware would be needed. I watched while Mom-mom made trip after trip to place cakes and pies on the sideboard opposite the china cabinet. The display of coconut cake and pies galore — pumpkin, sweet potato, apple, and mincemeat — was very colorful. There was a fruitcake which no one ate. Many businesses sent out fruitcake to their best customers. Mom-mom had two more in the sewing room which the cats would probably get to eat. Also two candy dishes sat on a small end-table where little hands could reach; one held chocolate drops and the other hard candy. But, I knew the reason for the display of those chocolate drops was so that the bags of drops in our Christmas presents would not have to be opened before going home.

"Love those sweet potato pies," I said to Mom-mom as she exited the dining room.

She patted me on the head, although she had to reach up to do so since I had reached her height this year. She said, "Go on and play now."

Studying the hard candy and drops, I decided on a piece of hard candy. Sucking and sucking, I finally bit it in half. It was called hard candy for a reason. When she came through with another cake, she saw me trying to work the hard candy around in my mouth.

"What's the matter?"

"I about broke a tooth."

"Well, just suck on it or spit it out," she said.

A voice from the living room called, "Who's next at dominos?"

"Me," I slobbered. "Me."

Bruce had been the latest winner. *This is a great chance,* I thought. *I've got to beat him at least once.* I was terrible at dominos and rarely won, but decided to give it a good go. "Take that," I said to him while pushing my pieces into place, and, "Got you on the run now." He just moved his pieces one by one. I lost.

We grandchildren could smell the food brought into the dining room, but we were so engrossed in our games that not one of us had attempted to grab anything to get us through until the grownups had finished. As they sat to eat, the smell of coffee filled the air, several conversations were happening all at the same time. Mom-mom hardly sat, refilling bowls and coffee cups. As soon as Pop-pop ate, he began to fill the woodstoves again, but we children just slid aside and hardly noticed since we were engrossed in our games.

Positions were traded from checkers to dominoes and back again. We slid backward for Pop-pop to put wood in the stove and then repositioned ourselves once he was gone—no puddle this time. When my turn came again, I won one game of checkers and then lost the next as the radio played on with plenty of static, which didn't matter to anyone. With the Christmas tree's scent of fresh cedar, candies to tide us over, and warmth of the woodstove we were content, yet when we were finally called to eat, we rushed the table.

A couple old Sears Roebuck catalogs had been placed in chair seats as boosters for the little ones and plates had been pulled close the edge of the table so they could reach. Tea-towels had been tucked under their chins since drips and spills were a sure thing. We girls flipped our long hair backwards so it would not fall into our plates. For all of us, care was given to our clothes which were mostly new;

we had been warned by our parents not to stain them, especially with cranberry sauce or Jell-O.

When choosing what to eat, we hardly knew where to start since our plate would be filled by simply taking a small sample of each dish—fried chicken, mashed potatoes, gravy made from chicken drippings containing crusty pieces of skin left after frying, Hayman sweet potatoes, stewed tomatoes sliced in squares, pans of wet cornbread, mashed turnips with chunks of fatback, pole beans, greens that were a mix of collards, turnip greens, and kale doused with apple cider vinegar, peas, a bowl of large slick dumplings—each one nearly the size of a saucer and when cut in the middle looked like bread—and a mountain of sliced ham. But the best of all was the huge bowl of thick dumplings with chicken gravy poured over them, the first food I piled on my plate. Mom-mom had done most of the cooking using both the electric cook stove and the Home-Comfort.

We took our time eating while the men moved into the living room, Mom-mom ran back and forth replenishing bowls and platters. The squeaking spigot could be heard turning on and turning off with the washing of dishes. There was not any hot running water since no water heater had been hooked up, so kettles were filled and put on the stoves, electric and wood, and heated for washing dishes. Mom-mom must have found running water in the kitchen a great relief.

The clattering of the hand-washing and drying of dishes seemed a constant din fading to the pop-pop-pop of the percolator coffeepot. Slowly the various sounds quieted. The dishes were finally done and had been placed back in cupboards and china cabinet. Everyone had eaten desert. The men held their desert plates while talking in the living room. We grandchildren carefully ate our deserts at the table and the women took theirs into the kitchen. But, when everyone had finished desert, coffee was carried into the dining room as we children were ushered back to the living room and the grown-ups seated themselves at the table once again.

Talk from the dining room was serious at times. Bombshelters were mentioned, a scare that had been going on for a few years, practically since the end of World War II and although little understood by the youngest children, we all knew it was a grim subject. Men from the forest had been killed in both world wars. Those wars came so closely together that it seemed to me the grown-ups had expectation of another war, but Bruce had said there was more to the situation than that. Drills at school had us sitting under our desks, head bent down, with our hands over our ears, and sometimes out in the hall, backs to the wall. Their talk finally moved away from war to farming and spring planting for next year, and finally, stories—ribbing one another followed by raucous laughter.

By five o'clock, everyone was full and quite satisfied. A couple of the older boys had gone outside, but not for long. They came in shivering from the cold. The sun had set and Mom-mom had lit some coal-oil lamps. We were told to put all the games away as the men retired in the big stuffed chairs and on the sofa. The time had come for presents. Pop-pop picked up each gift, called a name, and handed the present to Mom-mom. Although we grandchildren knew exactly what we were getting, we all sat obediently on the floor and received our packages from her. Watching him do that each Christmas never ceased to surprise me. Handing out presents at Christmas and taking us to the store during harvesting time were the only times he seemed to participate in any voluntary fun activity with us grandchildren. There was the afternoon I spent with him on the creek, and I wondered if that had been a lesson for me or enjoyment for him, maybe both. He seemed to enjoy tobacco between our toes, but to my mind, that didn't qualify.

We all opened our presents, and gave the proper thank you. Mine was different this year. There were chocolate drops as always, but instead of the white ruffled socks that the young girls got, I got a pair of hose with the dark seams up the back like the grown girls, a rite-of-passage. I had figured that the change to hose was coming, since one of my presents under the tree at home was a garter belt. I had mixed emotions, not sure I wanted to bother with that or the bras yet.

The boys got socks and chocolate drops as had been expected and the Aunts and Uncles brought presents for Mom-mom and Pop-pop, and in return, they received boxes of candy and some items we children paid no attention to.

When sleepy heads began to nod, that signaled that it was time to go home. A huge pile of coats lay across Mom-mom's bed and were brought out one heap at a time for us to claim. One family after the other said their goodbyes.

Lingering, I stood alone beside the Cedar Christmas tree that had been far from finished when I had to leave yesterday afternoon. Last night, Dad and Mom had taken Bruce, Lyn, and I to see a large manger scene set up in town. A big electric star hung above Mary and Joseph's head as they knelt beside a manger with straw in it. A baby-doll was in the manger and teenagers were dressed as Mary and Joseph, and the three wise men. Cardboard animals, a sheep and a donkey, had been placed off to the side—all under a wooden archway. It was quite a memorable scene since I had never seen one before. Snow had begun to fall as if by request since everyone wanted snow on Christmas Eve.

I pressed my nose to one of the living room windowpanes to see if the snow from last night had resumed. I couldn't tell, so I turned to the sedate tree, really looking at it fully decorated for the first time. Yesterday, on Christmas Eve, Mom-mom had gone shopping as was her tradition, to do all her Christmas shopping and decorate the tree on the Eve. I had tried to help decorate. I struggled and failed to lay the tinsel on the upper branches, so I had made attempts at throwing it as high as possible, but it had landed in bunches on the ends of those branches sagging the tips. Mom-mom had left it that way and finished decorating.

Various colored shiny balls, metal, and wooden ornaments hung on the inside of branches along with ornaments not found in recent years. A string of what looked like tiny glass beads of various colors rounded the tree with tinsel hung on that as well, creating a tree heavily laden with tinsel. Not the new kind that flies away when someone walks by, but the old heavy crinkled kind, almost like lead, that stayed in place and hung exactly where she had put each piece. There were no electric lights, but the sudden parting of clouds produced a moon that shone in the east window glorifying a snow covered ground and the shiny ornaments, beads, and tinsel. *Looks like someone just lit tiny candles on the tree*, I thought. The sight had an overwhelmingly sacred effect as did the sudden appearance of an eastern star which twinkled brightly as we all stepped outside to go home.

Similar to the record players children received as Christmas presents. Several had many speeds, 33, 45, and 78. In the 1960s, 45s were popular. Each record needed to be changed. (Adkins Historical and Museum Complex, Inc., Mardela Springs, MD)

Hog Rendering

Even though it was very cold upstairs, I had been allowed to sleep in the huge oak featherbed in an upstairs bedroom, a real treat. She had slept in her bedroom downstairs, and well before dawn she had lit the coal-oil lamp beside the bed where I was sleeping. I had not heard her come up or go back downstairs. I awoke to the lamp casting a shadow of the tall oak headboard across the ceiling. Why she continued to lite those lamps after the house had been wired with electric puzzled me, but maybe she preferred the soft light cast by the lamp rather than the stark overhead bulb, especially late at night or early morning.

The first hint of dawn had come as sounds from the backyard rang throughout the farm. From the clanging of iron kettles being readied for hog killing, to the banging of shed doors, from the clucking of riled chickens, to Roger whistling his way through the woods—sounds echoed in the January air along with freezing temperatures that signaled the season of hog rendering. I knew it was cold since I could see my breath in the bedroom, so it was sure to be a good day for cutting up fresh meat. In previous years I had not been asked to participate and could only watch, but I assumed that today would be different.

Everyone was outside when I entered the kitchen, so I looked out at the back of the farm where a huge, black iron, three-legged kettle had been placed over a fire, a fire of fast burning maple and long burning oak that had just been started. Lighter-wood had been used to start the fire. That heart from a rotten pine stump gave off a faint smell of turpentine that quickly dissolved in the air. Pop-pop had not wanted the scent of turpentine anywhere near the hog rendering, but had consented since the fire had been hard to start due to the heavy frost.

Yesterday, Pop-pop had dished out a place in the ground to build that fire and laid bricks under the pot. In the foggy faint dawn, the shadowy forms of men appeared and disappeared as they carried buckets of water over to that kettle, the fire outlining their silhouettes. They were preparing hot water for scraping hair from the hog. Beside the kettle were three cypress poles bound by a chain at one end of each pole, with a large hook fastened securely. A smaller, empty kettle sat beside the poles and a wooden barrel leaned against the smokehouse.

Though water could be had through the spigot at the kitchen sink, none of the kettles and only some of the pots would fit in that sink. Since in previous years men had pumped most of the water during the process of killing a hog, Mom-mom had told Pop-pop that she could fill the pots she needed in the kitchen for the rendering, "No need for them men to go traipsing through my kitchen to fill kettles and pots just 'cause there's a spigot in here," she'd added.

She had wanted running water installed in her kitchen by spring, but she was thankful that it had been completed before Christmas. Simply turning on a spigot relieved her from the constant burden of pumping water for every chore from baths, to cooking and canning. Watering the chickens by use of the kick-start pump had been a better setup than her chore of pumping water from the well outside the porch for her housework. *With running water in her kitchen, today's rendering will be easier for her than in past years*, I thought, *but still not easy*.

Mom-mom had her cook stove fired hot. Beside the reservoir side of the stove, she had stacked several pots and pans that had been put in the porch yesterday. All of the pans had a single long handle and fit neatly into each other. Most of the pots were larger than the pans, and had two short handles, one on each side at the top. Some of those handles swung and some were fast to rim. She had scrubbed them all. The kitchen door that opened into the screened porch was wide open, but with all her movements back and forth from outside to the kitchen, there was no need to close it. Besides, the stove was so hot the kitchen stayed warm with the heat rolling out onto the freezing porch.

I poked my head into the porch. In the far corner were several sacks of salt. Under a folding table, there were two huge lard pots which, when filled, held about four gallons each. Another pot, larger than the lard pots, sat off to the side. That table held a huge platter of last year's smoked ham and scrapple fried to a crispy brown, a mountain of biscuits, a small pot of boiled eggs, and a bowl of apples retrieved from the sewing room. Those who were hungry could step inside the porch and grab a bite to eat whenever they wanted; Mom-mom was going to be too busy to wait on anyone. I took an apple from the bowl, rubbed it on my pants, and took a bite.

I watched though the porch screens as Roger finished pumping and rounded the corner of the house to carry the last bucket of water to the now steaming kettle in the backyard. He had filled the old coffee can with water, but so much water would be pumped today that I doubted if the pump would need primed at all.

It was hog killing time and the entire day would require several hands right up until bedtime, and even into the following days. Grabbing my jacket off of a porch nail, the only garment left on the row of nails, I pulled a scarf from the pocket. Zipping up, I covered my head. Stepping outside, I immediately began to shiver.

A form emerged through the fog, coming from the garden toward the house. Mom-mom, slightly bent over, moved with a sauntering walk from side to side. As she neared, I could make out a woolen scarf tied under her chin, and a heavy sweater over her dress and apron. Her shoes were flat black shoes with shoelaces tied and could have passed for men's shoes. Those sensible large soled shoes seemed to help her move solidly across the ground. Her movements showed the weariness of hard work and age. Looking at her I considered what she had done during the past year, the strenuous jobs that never seemed to end. Looking beyond her, I saw that dawn had eked out a pale pink that was barely visible, not yet able to throw shadows.

"I'm up." I called through chattering teeth.

"Mornin', child!" she said, reaching the porch. "Will you see if you can find my cheesecloth? I've misplaced it som'mers. They's near 'bout a bolt," she said and then turned to look at me, "Got apple skin stuck between your teeth. Have you brushed um?"

Winking at her and ignoring my teeth, I went inside to look for the cheesecloth, starting in the most obvious place, the sewing room. Nearly becoming lost in the search, I finally found the bolt in the pantry closet on the top shelf behind canned goods. On tiptoes, I could just barely grasp the fabric. I was struck once again at the humble beauty in all the colors displayed by her fruits and vegetables, jellies, jams and juices, and golden honey in what was an otherwise drab closet behind a closed door. My eyes rested on the dried black-eyed peas and I wondered, *Did she eat black-eyed peas on January 1st for good luck, as is her belief? And, had she asked a tall dark haired man to be the first to come into the house?* No canned hog meats were left from last year's rendering, but no doubt, soon to be added were pickled pigs feet, neck bone segments, and maybe ears if Mom-Mom decided to can them—they held no superstition for her that I knew of.

Running outside to tell her I had found the cheesecloth, I was stopped by Pop-Pop standing beside her at the pump. Aiming his .22 toward an empty field in order to load, he shoved a bullet in the chamber, "You git back into the house now."

"Just wanted to tell Mom-Mom I'd found the bolt," I argued.

"She'll find it directly," he answered for her.

Mom-mom nodded her head toward the kitchen.

"Do like I told you. I'll holler when it's safe." With that said, he turned toward the pigpen.

Glancing just beyond the well, I could see that Bruce had arrived and would be allowed to stay outside with the men, their outlines just barely visible. But before I could say anything to him, Mom-mom held the screen door open, ushering me inside. I settled myself at the kitchen window looking out back at the buildings. I wanted to see everything that was happening, but the fact that I was not allowed to stay outside when the hog was shot did not escape my understanding. Stories had been told of a shot that had not killed the hog immediately and the animal had gone momentarily mad, running everyone around the yard. Any hog could be dangerous, but a crazed hog was a far more serious threat.

Mom-mom untied the scarf from her head and tucked it in her sweater pocket. Taking a sideways look at me sporting a downcast expression, she said, "Even I come inside. In case'a some commotion, I won't be in the way if another shot is needed, not that such a thing has ever happened with your Pop-Pop." Changing the subject, she added, "I see you found them wrappings."

"Under the stairs on the top pantry shelf, it was nearly hidden behind the jars."

"I should'a remembered that," she replied, as she placed a huge pot of water and coffee grounds on the stove to perk, and then began rummaging through the drawers of the Hoosier cupboard for her knives.

Pop-Pop had sharpened the butcher knife he would need and left the old worn whetstone on the table. Mom-mom placed her wooden handled kitchen knives beside that sharpener in an order from smallest to largest. After squirting oil on the stone, she began to slide the blade of each knife, one side and then other, over the oiled stone. Rhythms of farm life sounded in the kitchen, the persistent pop-pop-pop of the percolator and the constant rasp-rasp, rasp-rasp, of knives on stone. She did not lose a stroke when the gun went off.

The scent of a bonfire had now saturated the air inside the house. Looking outside at the poles, I tried to remember the first time I had seen them. In my limited 11 years, they had been a part of hog rendering for as long as I could remember. Those poles were far older than me.

The previous afternoon Dad had dropped me off to see what Mom-mom was doing in preparation for the hog rendering. Flying into the house to find her, I nearly ran into stacks of cooking pots and pans she had retrieved from the sewing room and from the smokehouse as well. Dusty and dirty, they all had been stacked in the porch, but she was nowhere to be seen. Looking out the kitchen window, I saw dust sailing out the open smokehouse door. She was whisking every nook and cranny of that ten by ten foot space.

Once outside, I had poked my head in that door, saying good morning. She had smiled and stepped down on the short wooden block used for a step, her apron held onto the dark sooty dust. The shelves on each side of the door inside had been cleaned and a stack of new burlap bags was piled in a corner, bags for chinking holes to prevent smoke from escaping. A small black, two handled, cast iron kettle with three legs and no wider than two feet across or tall, sat under a shelf. In years past, green hickory and oak had been used to smoke the meat, but this year the kettle contained a large chuck of what Mom-mom called 'green apple wood' with more blocks piled off to the side. Mom-mom answered my questions, explaining that the smokehouse was ready for meat to be smoked, but first that meat would be salted and shelved for a few days and then smoked. This would be the first hog rendering where I could help and see everything that would happen—or so I thought.

"All clear," Pop-pop bellowed from somewhere beyond my eyesight. We knew the bullet had hit its mark; the hog had fallen dead with one shot. He came from the pigpen to look into the massive kettle of boiling water and stuck his long butcher knife into the steaming water. No doubt, he had quickly slit the hog's throat to bleed it as much as possible. The men stood around for a while and appeared to be telling jokes to one another, and laughing.

I had not seen the hog killed, and stuck my face to the windowpane seeing the steaming black kettle lit by the fire, the tripod laying on the ground, and the small kettle off to the side. Then through the fog of barely dawn, I watched as the men carried boiling water from that big black kettle to a round wooden barrel leaning against the south side of the smokehouse in case a north wind would begin to blow while they worked. They filled that barrel with boiling water. Then four men brought the hog from the pen over to the barrel and dunked it headfirst into the boiling water. Leaving it there for just three or four minutes, they then pulled it out and dunked it tail first into the water.

While they worked Bruce had scattered straw onto the ground and when the men finished scalding the hog, they took it out of the barrel and laid it on the straw. Immediately, they began to scrape the hair and then turn the hog over and scrape some more. The scratching sound the scrapers made on the hog's skin reminded me of Pop-pop shaving his beard, only louder. They continually rinsed the hog with hot water from the kettle between scrapings. They worked until the hog's skin looked squeaky clean and gave the hog a final rinse.

Mom-mom got her largest pot from the porch and placed it beside the sink. "You want to get a pan and half-fill that big pot for me. It's gonna stay settin' right here and I'll go find a box of salt."

I left the spigot running full blast and holding onto the handle of the pan, I stuck it into the running water until it was full and dumped it in the pot, performing the same action over and over. It was fun to see how fast I could finish the job. When she came back in the kitchen, I had splashed water all over sides of the sink and in the floor.

"Now, want to clean up that mess?" She said. It wasn't really a question.

"Yep," I answered, "What's this pot of water for anyhow?"

"The hog's head."

"Oh," was all I could think to say. I'd been silenced by just the raw facts before.

She put the boxed salt on the table, "Dump that salt in the water and mix it around." She turned to the stove where she slid the coffee pot to a cooler side. She then pulled out her longest shallow cake pan from the bottom doors of the Hoosier, and placed coffee cups inside the pan. She poured coffee in the cups, heavily sugaring some cups and pouring cream in a couple.

I mopped up the floor and sink. Dumping salt, I used my arm as a paddle, swirling it around in the deep, cold, salty water. While drying my arm with a tea-towel, I looked out the window again. The men had already raised the poles to a tripod position, a sight I had seen before. After the hog was hung, they lit a coal-oil soaked rag wrapped on the end of a broken axe handle, and singed whatever fine hair was left.

A thick mist from Dividing Creek had risen above and beyond the trees serving as a backdrop to the hog which was now hanging, attached to the hook by a rod run through tendons and bones of its back legs. The men stood next to the hanging hog. Since the frost had not yet melted, the temperature was probably right at the freezing mark. A vapor swirled around each man's head from exhaling breath and steaming coffee, even steam from the hog's body rose. Some of the men lit cigarettes which sent up white clouds that hovered overhead with the various vapors. There was not so-much-as a breath of wind. Set against the dawn they appeared as silhouettes with strangely misshapen heads. I desperately wanted my Christmas camera for a picture of the entire scene, but there was no time to bicycle the mile down the road and back before the spectacle would be gone.

Hungry, I fixed a plate of boiled eggs and ham and seated myself at the kitchen window. While eating, I watched the men stamp out cigarettes as the real work was about to begin.

The broken axe handle, cast aside on the ground, reminded me of how nothing ever went to waste. Broken items were saved to be used for unforeseen needs. A trashcan in a corner of the porch served little purpose, as nearly anything that was burnable went into the Home Comfort, and too, cans, such as coffee were used to hold nuts and bolts or some of Mom-mom's worn out sewing items, broken needles, buttons cut from old clothing, anything that might come in handy. In huge boxes she saved every scrap of material, even some small salvaged scraps were cut into slim strips, same sized squares, or suitable shapes to be sewn seamlessly into her shabby quilts—then quilted.

Not realizing how much time had passed, I looked up and did not see Mom-mom but heard her clanging pots on the porch. Back from serving coffee, she brought the lard pots into the kitchen and set them on the wood-box beside the stove. The three big pots were now in the kitchen. She then chose a pot from beside the stove. She had cleaned all the pots and pans, so whatever size might be needed would be ready, but not all of them would be used.

A stench that would turn anyone's stomach filled the air. The smell of burning hair had seeped into the kitchen. I wrinkled my nose, "That singed hair stinks to high heaven."

"That it does," she said, while wrestling a pot under the spigot, "and that hog weighs a plenty." She put the pot of water on the stove to heat.

"How much?"

"Better'n 200 pound, I expect, and that is a lot'a lard,"

"Wow, that's as heavy as you and me put together."

The phone rang, ending our conversation. She went to the dining room stand and lifted the receiver; she answered with her usual, "Hey-O," and after a pause she said, "We don't need none."

"That was the ice man," she said, adding, "Well, I gotta git outside in a minute and wash the hog's head. Now, if you's squeamish, don't watch!" She kept talking about how it was the perfect day, cold enough for keeping the meat from spoiling and not needing ice. She said that even though there was a lot of work involved, hog meat was worth the effort since there were so many kinds of meat that come from a hog.

When Pop-pop yelled, "Evie," I realized she had been talking to keep me from looking out the kitchen window until the deed had been done. The men had placed the empty four-legged kettle underneath the hog, so that as soon as the head had been severed, it dropped in the kettle.

She picked up a medium sized pot from the kitchen floor and a well-sharpened knife from the table, then an old towel from the washroom and laid it on her rocker in the porch. She went outside with pot and knife. I followed as far as the porch. Pop-pop and Bruce placed the kettle near the well, but not so close that she couldn't rinse the head and tip the kettle letting the red tinged water run down the little gully that had been dug long ago to drain her sink. That gully angled out the side yard and ran water into the field across the top of the ground. Mom-mom pumped water into the pot, filling the kettle one pot-full at time. She scraped and scrubbed, and tipping the kettle, poured the water out. She did the same thing again and again until she was satisfied that all possible blood had run from the head. With the last rinsing, she rubbed her hands all over the head producing squeaky clean skin. She asked me to hand her the towel, and she wrapped it around the head and then called, "Harvey." Pop-Pop brought the bundle inside, and removing the towel, lowered the head into huge pot of salted water beside the sink. The head would soak in that salted water and would be cooked later today or tomorrow after the salt had been thoroughly rinsed away.

I had seen various sequences of a hog killing before, but the hog's head being put in a pot of water was a sight to behold. The snout was clearly visible under water and the ears stuck up out of the water. Mom-mom would cook the head for hours, long enough for the meat to fall off the skull. With that meat, she would make scrapple. In years past, souse had been made and I had always refused to eat it because the taste was sour and the texture was like mushy meat.

She came inside, washed her hands and rinsed the butcher knife leaving it in the sink. With the hair removed and the head now soaking, the fire outside under the huge kettle had not been stoked and only dying embers could be seen. That kettle would be left there until the fire was out and kettle was cool.

Their next move was to gut the hog. The same small kettle that had been used to catch the hog's head, was now placed to receive the guts. Pop-Pop cut, splaying open the hog from the neck, down the belly, and continued cutting until the innards fell into that empty black kettle.

Watching, I spoke of Fred. "Fred would have probably been hard to handle if he was here during all of this, smelling the guts and all. He would have tried to grab them and run."

"I expect so," Mom-mom said mildly and retrieved one small and one large pot from the porch. "I'll put the vitals in this one and I'll set the larger one at the pump and put the intestines in it," with that said, she grabbed another butcher knife from the table, a box of salt, and two pots, carrying it all outside. "Keep an eye on them cats, so's they don't git into one'a these pots out here."

I sat on the porch steps watching her out by the maple near the garden where two men had carried the kettles full of innards. Cutting some of the organs away from the guts, she put those 'vitals' in the small pot. She was careful with the liver, while cutting away the gall bladder. When she had all the parts she wanted, except the intestines, which were still in the kettle, she came over to the well and filled the pot of vitals with water. She rinsed and rinsed those organs, pouring the water down the gully, and lastly added fresh water and salt. Then she picked up the larger pot and went back out to the maple to clean the intestines.

Pop-pop came to the porch asking for two of the biggest pots left. I hauled them from the kitchen out onto the porch, and over to the steps. He took them and went back to the hog. While I watched Mom-mom work, I missed some of Pop-pops steps in getting the meat ready for his final cuts.

A couple of cats poked their heads out from under the house. I yelled "Git" and they ran back under the porch. As far as I was concerned, they had not replaced Fred. They had never become friendly, no matter how hard I'd tried. I had not named a single one.

Mom-mom turned her head when I yelled, but went back to squeezing out the large intestines into the kettle. Then, she turned them inside-out, put them in a clean pot, and came to the well to wash those sausage casings. Once again, she washed, rubbed, and rinsed, over and over, using the same efforts as with the vitals. Finally she covered the intestines with water and salted heavily.

The smell of those guts rival the burning hair, I thought, but I didn't say that out loud. She was stirring the pot with vitals and then the pot of intestines in an attempt to dissolve the salt when I went in the house feigning to check on the pot of water on the stove and to get a dipper of water. The smell had not seemed to bother her in the least.

She brought the small pot of organs inside and placed it beside the hog's head. Before coming inside with the large pot of clean intestines, she yelled to Pop-pop, "Them guts is ready to be dumped—som'mers far from the house."

Roger volunteered, saying, "How do, Miss Ebba?"

Long ago, several of the neighbors and even family called Mom-mom 'Ebba,' and those people outside the family added the 'Miss' out of respect. Ebba was just a nickname, I supposed.

She nodded to him and climbed the porch steps carrying the intestines; he held the door for her to go inside. His whistling could be heard all the way to the back woods, as he and Bruce carried that kettle, and again when they were on their way back.

I watched from the table as Pop-pop cut out the fat that had held the intestines in place and dropped the fatty sections into one of the large pots; that fat would be cooked into lard. When the long lengths next to the fat had been cut out, I asked Mom-mom what they were and she said "Tenderloins, and under that is the fatback." That fatback, mostly fat containing just a little meat, was not turned into lard. It would be salted and used to cook her greens and turnips, some of which were still in the garden. When the men cut that fatback, the backbone and ribs could be seen. The tenderloins had been put in the other large pot with the fatback. Roger knocked on the screen door and came in with the fat for lard, and then the pot of loins and fatback, lining them up beside the hog's head, organs, and intestines. Mom-mom's work was piling up.

Before now, Roger had not come in the house. Times were changing and I thought of one neighbor's response to my questions in the tomato fields, "Them changes is comin'; you can count on that!"

Watching the process once more, I marveled at the clean ribs and backbone. They looked just like the packages of ribs in the grocery store. Just before cutting the hog into sections, Pop-pop retrieved some fresh pine boards he just had cut at a nearby sawmill. He laid the clean boards out flat, and the men took the hog down from the tripod, and laid it out on those clean boards. Pop-Pop used an axe to cut out the entire length of the backbone leaving two identical sections of meat and one long length of backbone segments. The two sections were ready to cut into pork shoulders, ribs, fatty and lean bacon, hams, and feet.

Mom-mom asked me to help her carry the sacks of salt stored in a corner of the porch outside. We carried two each. Pop-pop had built a box made from freshly milled pine nearly three feet by three feet with a thick solid bottom. He was ready for us to dump salt in the box. As soon as we finished, he dropped the first slab of meat down into the salt, turning and rolling every inch of meat until it was heavily covered by the granules, but he did not cover the skin. The men brought out more fresh pine boards and he cut and salted each section of meat and placed them one at a time on the boards. He then took a freshly sharpened, white oak spike and drove it beside the bone into the middle of each ham and shoulder. Dropping salt into each hole, he pushed with the spike until the salt was well inside.

One by one, the men carried the meat laden boards into the smokehouse and put them on the shelves where the salted meat would dribble juice on the floor for a few days, before being hung and smoked.

When passing the food table, Mom-mom and I nibbled from morning until afternoon. Occasionally, the screen door would open as one man or the other would get an egg, biscuit, or whatever could be retrieved with fingers and promptly go out again. But like Mom-mom, they never really stopped to sit and eat.

Finally, she was able to get started on the lard in the kitchen. She wrapped those chunks in cheesecloth and then put them in a pot on a part of the stove where the heat was not so intense, just hot enough to melt the fat. I was asked to stir that fat with a long wooden paddle so it would not burn. Those chunks were heated until the fat melted through the cheesecloth while the membranes or the crackles remained in the cloth. Mom-Mom lifted the cheesecloth with crackles out of the fat. That lard was removed from the stove and left to harden in the same pot. Lids were put in place and the pots of lard were stored in the sewing room, the coldest part of the downstairs.

Putting the rest of the sharpened knives on the Hoosier countertop, she spread wax paper on the table, poured the salt on it, and then rolled each piece of fatback in the salt. Then she rolled the fatback up in the wax, ready to be taken out and spread on a board. It was now late afternoon. The sun was fading and the guineas began to make quite a racket, unusually loud. In getting themselves perched for sleeping at night, they always seemed in a turmoil, but it wasn't sundown yet. She raised her head to the ruckus, but went on washing her hands at the sink.

She must think that having running water is a blessing. I could see how water flowing from the spigot would become an absolute treasure in cooking the hog's head and organs, and in the making of sausage, scrapple, and souse too. I was glad she was going to make scrapple this year, since I considered it just one step better than souse, and because she would add tenderloin to the mix taking away some of the mushiness. But, some events would have to wait until tomorrow. As well, certain steps in rendering would continue for days. She simply looked at the pot of water that had been boiling away on the woodstove and said, "Not today." She was tired.

I heard one of men come to porch door and call. When Mom-mom went to answer, I heard her fuss, "Of all things to happen right now!"

"What?" I ran into the porch.

She held a cardboard box of baby chicks. "Was, most likely, the smell'a blood from the hog that caused a fox to work its way up to the back'a the shed and snatch the mother hen. The men weren'ent quick enough to shoot that thief before it disappeared into the woods with one of my best hens. Now they's chicks to raise."

"Oh goody!" I exclaimed. "I wish I had my camera here; they are so cute."

She moaned and shoved the box in back of the cook stove. "Git um a bowl'a water. Cats to feed and now chicks! Off all things, baby chicks in winter. Bet that's what them guineas was carryin' on about."

"If Fred had been here, he would have run that fox clean to the woods," I said.

"I expect he would have. Well, since Christmas has come and gone, another one will come along. We know city people will get rid of some dogs and one is sure to find us."

"It won't be Fred, though," I said.

"No, no it won't," she agreed.

It is now 1963, I thought, and considered how the beginning of the year had brought such hard work. I knew in the days that followed, that hard labor would continue. *The iron S hooks in the smokehouse will be used to hang the meat from the rafters. Pop-pop will move the kettle to the middle of the smokehouse floor and chink burlap in between all the boards, from the ceiling down level with the top of the kettle, leaving the lower boards open without burlap so the fire can get air. He will start his unseasoned apple-wood fire in that kettle which is held just inches off the ground by three legs. Then air, drawn inside from the gaps between the lower boards, will send smoke hovering in the rafters—that smoke, not able to escape, will smoke and flavor the meat. They will have fresh cured meat soon, and the meat left hanging in the spring will not get wrapped until the flies come out. After wrapping the meats in brown paper bags, each packaged meat will be put in a pull string sack and stored in the house, the balance to be eaten summer through early winter until it is hog rendering time again.*

Meanwhile, Mom-mom will be in the kitchen making sausage and scrapple; probably canning feet and perhaps ears. She will be scrubbing and rinsing pots and pans, even those used today will be cleaned and used again. The combination of all tasks involved in hog rendering rivals the height of tomato picking season, although the strenuous part of hog rendering will be completed in far less time.

But, while the hog rendering process was being finished, Bruce and I would be shivering on the cold school bus in morning, and back in warm classrooms during the day, only to get a cold bus ride home in the afternoon. The middle-school heat had been fixed for good it seemed, but the long buses had not been equipped to stay warm. Although the bus windows had been open on the hot days with the wind blowing our hair, we girls suffered by having to wear dresses in winter. I wondered, *will they ever change that rule? They should, at least, let the girls in Primary School wear pants to keep their legs warm. Lyn starts 1st grade next year and she's still little—she'll freeze. I wonder who I can talk to about that!*

The soft light of a coal-oil lamp casting shadows across a wall. These lamps were used before and during the transition to electric lights.

**Cypress hog rendering poles, tripod with chain and kettle.
(Flea Market 13 Antiques & Used Furniture, Pocomoke, MD)**

Hog rendering kettle used for boiling water.

Top of hog rendering poles with hooks.

Quilts

Late January brought freezing weather and heavy snow. When the sun went down, the cold seeped into every nook and cranny of Mom-mom's unheated bedroom. Shadows flickered and died as she blew out her coal-oil lamp and new images emerged from the moon finding its way through ice-patched windowpanes. She said to me once again, "Now turn your back to mine," like we always slept, but this time with quilting on our minds. "Stretch your feet out and you'll find the warm flatiron. Don't know whatever happened to the handle." She had heated that old flatiron on top of the woodstove, wrapped a towel around it, and put it between the covers at the foot of the bed. So with the bottom of her feet up against one side and mine against the other side, we slept soundly.

The next morning the sun shone through the ice covered windowpanes casting yellow glittered figures on the faded wallpaper. The raised pull shades at the upper window held only shadows of those figures. While leaving the comfort of my flannel nightgown, I delighted in the changing silhouetted shapes. Folding the still warm flannel, I placed it on the organ stool. After putting on my training bra, a contraption that seemed to serve no purpose whatsoever, I buttoned my cotton blouse, pulled on my wool sweater, and then my corduroy pants, socks, and shoes. Mom-mom had already dressed and built a fire in the Home Comfort cook stove. This I knew, since the distinct smell of homemade bacon and her fresh fixed biscuits wafted through the rooms pulling me past the stairs toward the kitchen.

Anyone entering her kitchen on a cold winter's morning could not help but become invigorated by the warm fire, the aroma of breakfast, and the white wallpaper splashed with turquoise, red, and yellow in the individual displays of coffee grinders, chickens sitting on their nests, spinning wheels, and flowers galore.

Mom-mom smiled as I entered. Still sleepy-eyed, I grinned back at her and ogled the bacon sizzling in the spider. "They's a basin'a fresh water and a cloth in yonder." She motioned to the washroom. "Wash up, breakfast is near ready. Let me add some hot water." She leaned inside the washroom doorway and poured some scalding water from the kettle into the agate basin sitting on the washstand. "There," she said, "but come on out to the kitchen zinc and brush your teeth first."

I grabbed a cup from the drain-board, filled it with water from the spigot, and then swished my toothbrush and dumped baking soda on it, scrubbing teeth and spitting into the sink. Rinsing the cup and brush, I put them back on the drain-board.

"Has Pop-pop shaved yet?" I asked while snitching a small piece of bacon that had broken away from one crispy fried slice.

"You is gonna to ruin your breakfast," and she added, "and no, he ain't."

"Alright, then," I said, giving her waist a hug and scooting into the washroom.

After taking survey of his shaving gear, I grasped his hairbrush and reconstructed my ponytail while looking in the corroded mirror. Scrubbing my face, I rinsed and squeezed the cloth and placed it on the arm of the washstand. We understood that I would leave the water for Pop-pop's morning shave as more hot water would be added later.

While our breakfast was cooking, I sat in the chair by the window looking out at the farm buildings as I had done so many times. I studied each one in turn and then focused my attention on the chickens pecking corn from the ground. I considered searching for eggs in the half-bushel baskets settled here and there in each open building. My hesitation was based on the fact that I had been attacked a couple times by simply coming near the nests of setting hens, especially last spring, when the hen attacked me after I'd messed with her chicks. That mishap was still fresh in my mind.

My attention turned suddenly to an urgent need. "Mom-mom, where is the toilet paper?"

"They's some in the washroom. Didn't you use the slop-jar in the bedroom this morning?"

"No! I don't like having to empty it."

"They's one in the washroom."

"I'd just as soon be done with it. I'm going outside."

Pop-pop was nowhere in sight when I squatted behind the implement shed. They had refused to have a modern bathroom in the house, but why they hadn't put an outhouse outside was beyond my understanding. At home we had an outhouse until I was five years old and I considered that far better than squatting on the ground or cleaning out potties. By the time I returned to the kitchen, my fingers felt frozen.

"Should'a got your coat, as cold a morning as this is," Mom-mom scolded.

"Couldn't wait," I said.

Holding my hands above the stove, I stood, watching as she pulled a pan of biscuits out of the oven and placed them on the woodstove's shelf. Her bobby-pinned spit-curls had been set tight against her head. An apron was tied at her waist around her well-tailored feedbag dress that hung midway between her knees and ankles where thick seamed hose rolled with garter bands clung just below her knees. There was comfort in all that I saw.

I ate quickly, gobbling the bacon and eggs with the exception of tidbits for the cats. I finished the spiced pears, and biscuits dipped in syrup. Strands from my ponytail had already loosened, so I pushed them back and swiped my pink flowered plate clean using the last crumb of my biscuit—a biscuit made 'out n' out' as Mom-mom was so fond of saying.

She took her time eating and sipped her coffee for several more minutes, just holding the cup and sipping. I waited and began to do what she called 'twiddling.' Seeing dribbled egg yolk on the table beside my plate, I swiped it and then sucked it off my finger. My skin began to itch where wool touched my wrists, so I pushed the sweater sleeves up past the blouse's cuffs. My attention wandered to the stove where the percolator made a popping sound each time hot coffee reached the glass bubble at the top, and I wondered why she didn't warm her coffee. Fingering the lazy-susan in the middle of the table, I gave it a spin sending the salt and pepper flying. I gingerly reached out to stop the spinning and put the salt back; she replaced the pepper and continued to sip her coffee, which I was sure must be cold by now.

To fill the time, I chatted about how well my record-player worked, the one I got for Christmas, and how the lid closed right up and clipped on the front, and how it had a handle, and I could carry it like a suitcase. I told her about the yellow and red records and how I had been fussed with for playing my favorite song, over and over again. I told her about some of the scary parts in my new mystery books, but how I loved the ones about the horses. Listening, she nodded now and then.

Finally, she got up and put the dishes in a pan of cold water, and wiped the spider with a cloth retrieved from a nail on the wall and then rehung the soiled cloth. Next, she sat a plate on the table, filled it with bacon and two cold sunny-side-up eggs and added a large helping of pears, then sat the biscuit pan and King Syrup tin beside the plate—all for Pop-pop when he finished his morning chores. I placed his Melmac turquoise coffee cup and a sugar bowl side-by-side. Whenever he finished drinking his coffee one of two things were left, either unstirred sugar or cheese stuck to the bottom. Mom-mom closed the damper on the cook-stove. Finishing her cleanup just as the stove had heated the kitchen to a tolerable warmth, we left to set up sewing in her large unheated bedroom.

She picked up two pieces of wood from her wood-box and dropped them in the living room stove, a fire that had been rekindled by Pop-pop before he went outside. She left the living room door open to the hallway so that her room would get warm. Once in the bedroom, heat from the living room stove began to warm both rooms.

While she gathered sewing necessities, scissors and pins, needles and thread, various cardboard patterns and pencils, a yardstick, and an array of thimbles, I studied the two quilts covering her feather mattress that had kept us warm just hours ago. One was a combination of different kinds of materials, all done in a variation of log cabin design. And the quilt under it had no real pattern design, simply a wool blanket as backing tied to a top piece made of six inch squares of dull-colored wool—blues, grays, tans, and greens—stitched together, tacked at each corner, with thick red string tied on top in a visible knot.

She noticed me inspecting the quilt's wool squares, "That wool is like military uniforms. I've wanted to do one of brown squares from the World War II uniform and dark blue squares of the Navy coat, coats my boys wore while in the service. Many women has sewed pieces'a war uniforms into their quilts and some has braided um into rugs so as family would remember they had people who has served. Your Pop-pop and I married in April 1916. Two and a half years later, just a month before the Great War ended in November 1918, a real bad flu hit the forest. They was lots of people who died all over the world from that flu and war wounds. I know lots of prayers must'a been said over the makin' of them war uniform quilts."

When sleeping the previous night, I had been sandwiched between the sheet covering the down ticking and those two coverings—a combination of feathers, muslin, cotton, wool and flannel together with Mom-mom's warm back and my sock covered feet hugging a warm flatiron. I felt as if I had slept within a soft warm cloud in a freezing room. But now, the room was still cold even though it was quickly warming from the living room stove, but the warmth from the sun could not be felt as the ice covered windows had not fully melted.

In an attempt to change the somber conversation, I brought up the snow that had just melted. "When it snowed last week, I saw a bluebird sitting on one of our rock garden stones in front of the sheds. It had snow on its beak and hardly moved when I got close. That snow was so pretty!"

"I guess, but it covered up the wood so's Harvey couldn't chop that maple into firewood. Snowed so hard we was hard pressed for the longer split lengths." she said.

"Bruce and I sledded that rise where the sandy road runs uphill just past our house."

"We finally got some wood up to the house and made out alright though."

"Well, Bruce and I pulled the sled up to the top and slid down the road, fast too! He was up front steering the wooden handles. When we reached the bottom of the hill, we'd just drag it back up and do it all over again. It was fun!"

"It was a good thing we was able to keep the kitchen stove goin'. Don't like ice on them kitchen windows—chills me to the bone just to look at it."

"That sled nearly flipped us one time, but it probably wouldn't have hurt us deep as that snow was," I said, still shivering.

She dropped the quilting utensils at the foot of the bed. "It'll be toasty warm in here directly," and with that said, she took a sweater from a small chest and draped it around my already wool covered shoulders. Since her room contained a window to the east, the sun streamed in until past noon. On cloudy winter days, the cold of the bedroom would nearly freeze the fingers.

For us, or others, to carry on two different conversations at the same time is not unusual. I heard what she said about the trouble the snow had caused her and Pop-pop, and I am sure that she heard about my sleigh ride; she might even mention it later. She never seems to be in favor of snow, I thought. *I guess it had been hard for Pop-pop to pull wood from the frozen ground and too much snow for her to wade through when she had gone outside to feed the chickens or hang clothes.*

"I'll get you started lookin'," she offered while pulling the first huge box out from under her bed, "then I'll go through the mending pile—need to fix a pair of your Pop-pop's britches."

Her quilts were not made from fancy materials. They contained scraps left from making home-sewn clothes, salvageable parts of worn-out clothing, feedbag material saved from hog and chicken feed, drawstring salt sacks, and even the better parts of damaged quilts were saved. A wholly damaged quilt would be used as the center batting of a new quilt. Sometimes faded coats were taken apart and the inside turned out showing the original unfaded color and then made into a coat again, but, if too badly worn, the best parts would be saved until enough was gathered to sew a bed covering. All good material, whether from garments, quilts and sheets, or curtains, had been cut away from the worn out sections and saved along with feedbags. All buttons were clipped off of the worn-out clothing and put in wooden cigar boxes, boxes saved from Pop-pop's father's store that had stood at the crossroads in the Pocomoke Forest in the 1930's.

"This cardboard box has the best parts from some'a your Pop-pop's britches and shirts, parts that weren'ent worn out," she said, "and this is what's left'a feedbag curtains used the fall and winter'a '32. I remember because it was my favorite pattern and was made the year Doris was born."

Mom-mom had five sons plus two who died, one premature boy died in 1916 and another in 1925. The first healthy son was born in 1918. Finally, in 1932, her last child was a girl. She had babies in diapers for many years, and from 1918 until nearly 1950 she was raising children, and by then, she had grandchildren. Bending over the bed, Mom-mom held that material out to me as if it were a precious offering. It was feedbag as one could tell by the weave of the fabric. The background was a cream splashed with bright red petaled flowers and larger blue flowers with green leaves and deep dark purple leaves, unmistakably vibrant Christmas material.

"Lyn would love this purple!" I said. "Purple is her favorite color."

"Well, they's plenty of purple here. And look, here's couple'a red cotton yard goods I couldn't resist orderin' from The Sears Catalog in the spring."

So, I thought, *that's what the postman delivered during planting season, the day she went straight back to her bedroom. I wonder when she got her Christmas dress in the mail.*

"Too, here's one I traded for eggs better'n forty year ago at Shockley's store at Whitesburg—the store in the forest before your great-granddaddy opened his'n a few miles north. So you can see pieces'a goods from many different places that's been used in my quilts over the years. But here, you rummage through and pick some'a your favorites to use." She added, "They's a couple more boxes under the bed, most materials is mixed together, the muslin, fine cotton, feedbag, and wool."

Mom-mom set aside two dresses she had begun, both bodices were finished and made from the same pattern, but of different colors, one green and the other a pink and white check. The skirts that went with each bodice were pinned at the seams, yet to be sewn. The opening at the waist was on one side where she placed snaps; that made the waist wide enough to pull over her head. As with all her dresses, she made her own belts. "I started these frocks last year," she explained.

Next, she pulled out a finished bonnet and a few others in various stages of sewing. They were a marvel to me, but seeing both the cut pieces and the finished bonnet together told the story. It was two-pieced, a rim and a hat. The hat section had a gathered tail, and was also gathered around the edge of a wide rim. That rim was double faced, and stitched every quarter inch with a full five inches at its widest, from the top of the forehead to down over the eyes. The genius of her bonnet was—the brim shaded the eyes and the tail protected the neck from becoming sunburnt. The practical design of the bonnet became clear to me now. My fussing about having had to wear one while picking crops came to mind.

As I crawled up on the bed and began to inspect the first box, she grasped the pile of clothes in need of mending and placed it beside her oak National Two Spool sewing machine. She picked up her Bible off the top of the machine and put it on her walnut washstand. She swung open the hinged wooden top of the sewing machine. It lay flat, providing a working space. She then swung the machine upward and outward while laying the hinged braces down, and eased the machine into the grooves. She opened one drawer and fiddled with the wooden spools wound with thread. She pulled open the metal bobbin cover and changed the spool of white used for a bobbin, to a spool of tan thread, and grasped the spool on the top of the machine, replacing it with tan too. Poked into the corner of the pull shade above her head were several threaded needles, each needle with a different color thread.

Glancing at her once in a while as she readied her machine, I plunged deeper and deeper into the box of scrap materials. There were no satins, no frills or lace. The first one was a mustard yellow muslin plastered with white rabbits hopping, playing, and hiding behind flowers, and older rabbits dressed in vests. The next piece had a bright red background boasting what appeared to be a church with two people dancing out front, the woman's coal black hair flowed behind her and the man wore knickers with suspenders and a plume in his hat. Another one contained rows of blue and gold stick figures of a dog, a man and woman, birds, and trees. One bundle was tied with a string and appeared to be scrap pieces, none of which matched.

Several yards of the feedbag material had stripes, checks, and some had backgrounds of bright red, purple, and blue that had been boldly splashed with flower prints. The color combination would compete with anyone's imagination. The patterns seemed endless. One sassy mishmash was a white background splashed with red roses, and another, the figure of a girl who was right side-up and up-side down with roses for hair, red legs, and roses on her skirt. There were yards of feedbag with bright red poinsettias that must have been popular. But I promptly decided my favorites were the white flower vine designs, one having an all red background and the other blue. I tossed some other flower designs next to each other, the contrast confusing my eyes. I dove back into the box again, rummaging.

Also, she had fashioned a feedbag bodice for a dress, or 'frock' as she was so fond of calling her dresses. I mused that no large piece of yard goods was needed for her clothes as she was so short and slender. Today the dress she wore was a cream color with yellow and blue flowers accented by green leaves, other flowers had a creamy background with a narrow burgundy border. When I rolled the colors around in my mind they sounded awfully boring, but the combination was a pleasing mellow blend. She stood inspecting clothes with her back toward me while I studied her dress.

Noticing how still I had become, she turned around questioningly and I replied, "I was just studying the design on your dress." I could tell she was pleased. Her smile sent the wrinkles on her face in several directions at once and then she turned back to her work.

The next box was much smaller. I dug down and pulled out several pieces, fingering the material before I realized what I held. They were doll clothes—dresses of high-laced collars, fitted bodice, and ankle length hems, and double breasted coats with hoods, but mostly little muslin and feedbag dresses. I had given up playing with dolls just a few months ago. Something about wearing a bra and playing with dolls didn't seem to go together, but sucking in my breath, I clutched a particularly colorful dress to my chest.

Mom-mom was laughing now, her deep throated laugh with head tilted toward the ceiling, a laugh rarely seen, but used when she was truly amused.

"Jeez-e-whiz, Mom-mom." I oozed, "Did you make these?" She nodded.

Seized by an urge to create, I retrieved the last box and struggled to lift it onto the bed. On top were some already hand-stitched blocks for her next quilt top. Those blocks were made of small squares and some long narrow pieces forming a square of log cabin design strips. Large pieces of what appeared to be store-bought material, sections of sheets, and a quantity of more feedbag with plenty of shades of reds filled the box. I was intrigued by some stitched blocks that looked like older material, yellowed but still holding color and of a design that did not look like hers. I wanted to know more and held it up, glancing at Mom-mom.

She looked at the old, coarse, yellowed muslin stitched to faded black and mustard colored material. Holding a pair of Pop-pop's pants, she turned to stand in front of the east window. The sunlit panes cast her shadow across the flowered linoleum tacked to the wooden floor. She had left the room as surely as if she had glided out the door. Even the guineas piercing voices did not shake her from her trance. How long she stood there still holding Pop-pop's pants, I'm sure neither of us knew, but the sun had shifted enough to fall on my corduroy pants drawing my attention. I brushed my hand across the corduroy one way and then the other taking note of the change in the green color from shiny to dull and then from dull to shiny while struggling to recall grown-up conversations.

Finally, Mom-mom said quietly, "It might have been hers."

"Who her?" I whispered back, suddenly feeling as if no one should hear.

She pointed her finger to the wall above the pump organ, and on dull, aged, pink and yellow wallpaper, hung the grayed-brown and white picture of a very old woman wearing a dress that hung to the ground with a half apron around her middle. Clearly all her teeth appeared to be missing and her thick white hair was parted off center in either a bun, braid, or ponytail. I fingered my hair pulled straight back from my face into a ponytail at the back of my head, but not straight down and parted in the center like hers. *Nope*, I decided—s*he has a braid, not a bun.* Her long nose shadowed her upper lip and large ears with long earlobes protruded out from her hair. Piercing eyes probed mine from behind a wrinkled, heavily eye-browed face.

I knew that when Pop-pop's parents had passed away, he had cleaned out their attic and brought many things with him, storing them in his own attic. I glanced at the ceiling as if I could see two stories above where I was sitting. I had only been in the attic a couple times, but had seen scattered items of old receipts, of which many were paperwork from his father's country store, stored pictures, and boxes full of things unknown to me. There was clothing rolled up in balls, and broken sugar bowls and dishes kept for sentimental reasons, I had supposed. There were pictures and tintypes. I had seen small beads and Mom-mom did not wear jewelry, only her gold wedding band. I had seen things that defied current use such as button hooks for the shoes she had worn as a young woman. I had wondered if her and Pop-pop's Indian ancestors had worn or used some of the unexplainable things. I looked from the ceiling to the picture on the wall, "Well, is that your Mom-mom, your grandmother, or Pop-pop's grandmother?" Mom-mom eyed me again. Was she Indian? I was wondering what…."

Mom-mom interrupted, "Her name was 'Mary.' Your Pop-pop's brother and sisters all got the same framed picture'a her, and some'a my family did too. They's a reason that the money was spent to take her picture and buy the large frames—it's cause she was cared for and we wanted to always remember her. Long as we remember, she still lives."

I was not sure, but I expected that this woman's blood ran through both of my grandparents.

"Her Ancestors were here before the big sailing boats ever came across the Atlantic Ocean, right? Tell me more!"

There was no studying me this time. Mom-mom simply turned from me again; her shoulders slumped. I knew there was no use in probing further. She laid Pop-pop's pants over the machine's open top and then sat, attempting to thread the needle time after time, battling her failing eyes, squinting through heavy black framed eyeglasses. Just as I offered to help she was successful and began testing the tension on a scrap piece of material similar to Pop-pop's pants. Some of the black paint had been worn off the wheel from her pulling on it, sewing for over thirty-five years on that machine. The sun shone on the top of her head like an aura glinting off the bobby-pins.

She said, "Slide that back under the bed when you is done lookin'."

I wondered, *When is she or Pop-pop going to tell me about Mary or Eleanor? Apparently it isn't going to be today.* So, as she sewed Pop-pop's pants, rocking the treadle with her foot, I placed the pieces back inside the big box. I gently pushed it back under the bed and ran my hand over the quilt upon which I sat, once again studying stitches. The stitching was so tiny and close and the fabrics had been sewn so evenly, that the corners met perfectly. Two triangles had been sewn together to make a small square and then two larger triangles sewn to make a larger square. Once small and larger squares had been stitched together, the smaller squares looked like a ladder. I attempted to arrange my choice pieces while eyeing the cardboard patterns. Mom-mom had asked me to pick colors and a particular cardboard design for cutting shapes.

"They clash!" I blurted.

"Then, they can make a splendid quilt! You know, many a colorful bedcover was made at Olivet Church. When your Pop-pop and I lived up at the home-place, I used to quilt with my family and neighbor women on Saturday's, when we could spare the time. Sometimes we went to the church and then other times to someone's house. The women would work together on one quilt for a special occasion. We'd bag a lunch or git ourselves a good dinner. We all enjoyed that. Sometimes a quilt was made for a weddin' couple or someone in need, and we would sing, hymns mostly. I taught Sunday School at that church for a while, till we come here."

"I guess there's lots of the older people that were there that have passed on now. Do you ever think about them?"

"My land, yes! I can still see their faces and hear the way each of um talked—the tilt of their head, the tone of each voice. I can try to speak it for you, but it wouldn't be the same and you'd still not know um. You'd only know um by what I tell you. Then, you'd only see um through my eyes and not your'n. But they should be remembered."

I got the idea that she was talking more to herself than to me, but I offered my own remembrance, "I remember the old man that walked everywhere he went and lived in a little house between here and 'The Home Place.' He'd always be carrying something, sometimes just sticks of wood."

"Well, he whittled some of that wood and people would buy his carvings to set up on their mantel. I cain't remember his real name. He knowed this forest backwards and forwards like many of the Old Ones did. I don't know all that they knowed; wish I did. So much has been lost—the homemade medicines, the old names for plants in the woods, the fine weavings, and so on. Makes me sad sometimes just to think about that part of it, but when I recall seeing the Old

Ones—that's the good part." Then, turning her eyes in the direction of the landing at the bottom of the stairs, it seemed she anticipated something.

Sounds that had been coming from the kitchen telling us that Pop-pop was eating breakfast had long since ceased, but he had probably been shaving since without warning, he yelled, "Evie." That meant, 'come here', which she promptly did and I was left alone to ponder my design. At nearly twelve years old, I was not seasoned to interactions between many grownups, but I knew theirs was one of few words and predictable behavior.

"Lemonade," I heard Pop-pop say.

The previous day Pop-pop had driven the five miles to Hickman's market beside the Pocomoke River so he could buy fresh fruit and he had taken me with him for a bag of penny candy and an orange Nehi. During January, fresh lemons could be found if Mr. Hickman had brought them back from Florida with his Christmas order of grapefruit and oranges—and he had. I heard Mom-mom stirring and stirring the ton of sugar it took for Pop-pop to tolerate lemons, but he saw them as a cure for many things—a cure-all.

While she was gone I thought about the quilts the Old Ones might have made: log cabin, drunkard's path, wedding ring, or some of the more difficult kinds of quilts. I had seen such patterns in books like the stained glass quilts and patchwork quilts where each square was a different design. The crazy quilts were made of many different shaped pieces crossing other seams and designs. There was no pattern to be followed making a crazy quilt, but the different stitches of thick thread made that finished quilt one of great study. There were perfectly plain quilts of one color such as cream colored muslin on the front and back; the quilting was the artwork. Most often, there was a quilted circle in the center with surrounding designs.

When she returned with lemonade for us, we sat on the edge of the bed quietly sipping our drink. Mom-mom and I fingered material and we smiled at each other once in a while as sunlight flooded the room. We heard a car coming—the first one of the day. Not being a heavily traveled road, but one in which all people were related except Stella and Filip, we naturally glanced through air bubbled glass to see who was passing. We missed the car and looked at each other again, smiling in comfortable silence. I spilled lemonade on my white blouse and down her sweater. There was no fussing, no frown; she just retrieved a cloth from her apron and dabbed at my spill. One of the first things she did every morning while getting dressed was to fill her apron pocket with tissues or a cloth to wipe up whatever mishaps would occur. It was a well-used cloth that she used to dab at my bodice. Then, wiping her mouth, she placed it back in her apron for the next need. Her reused cloths carried with them no inhibitions about their previous uses.

Mom-mom's eyes traveled to a chifforobe that stood in the corner. She rose, handed me her glass, and swung the doors wide. Then she removed two worn out quilts. Placing our lemonade on the marble-top nightstand, I sat on the bed while she spread one of the quilts over our laps. She said, "I wasn't told who quilted this one, but I always thought it might have been Mary. She never wore eyeglasses. Her eyes were sharp until the day she died. I can remember just as well as if it were yesterde', her sittin' in the rocker quiltin' at my mother and father's home. And she rarely talked, and would answer a question with only a few words."

"Well, was she Mary or Eleanor? I can see that even in old age she had very thick hair and long earlobes. Some say that is a sign. What do you think?"

She did not answer my blatant questions directly. Instead she sidestepped the question, "See, in the early 30's your Pop-pop and I and his parents traveled to Delaware, to the Nanticoke pow-wows. We met some'a 'The People' who traveled there from Oklahoma." She had used the term before, 'The People,' which referred to Indians, Native Americans, who had traveled a long way to be at that pow-wow. "Many things was traded at that gatherin'."

"What year was she born?"

"She was borned in the mid 1830's."

"Who were her parents?"

Mom-mom's eyes clouded, eyelids nearly shut. I felt as if I had pulled a curtain in front of the sun once again. Silence ensued once more, giving respect to the few words she had shared about our ancestors. I had heard some call the woman Mary, but according to family history, some had said she was Eleanor. I decided on Mary.

I did not doubt that they had traveled to the Nanticoke Pow-wows and met people from Oklahoma. So many of the family members had said so, and I did not doubt that I have Native American blood running through my veins. What wasn't clear to me is why Mom-mom and Pop-pop would not talk about it. I had asked them so many times. *Maybe I'm just not old enough yet.* Deciding to let it go once again, my concentration switched to the other quilt she had pulled out of the chifforobe.

Looking at Mom-mom, I raised my eyebrows, questioning. I gently lifted the quilt that could no longer be used because the stuffing was coming out. The bright colors seemed to jump from the quilt and it was clear to me that Mom-mom and her women ancestors liked red.

"My sisters and I worked on that one before I ever married your Pop-pop," she said, lifting her lemonade. While she sipped, I created a vision. I pictured Mom-mom and her sisters Vera, Susie, Zenia, and Betty dressed in long handmade dresses, sitting around a huge quilting frame on a winter afternoon such as this one, having picked whatever room might be the warmest, perhaps a bright fire in an old fireplace with a popcorn strung Christmas tree still in one corner of the room after the New Year had come. Also, I pictured their mother, Alice, coming and going looking over their work while offering advice and compliments as she baked for them—six women chatting and quilting and, perhaps, solving each other's problems and telling stories over a span of several cozy winter days.

That vision was mine alone and I didn't know if it was correct or not, but refusing to have my image squashed, I didn't ask her to explain. I just folded that quilt and then moved to pick up another, a very colorful one from the shelf inside the chifforobe. I observed, "This isn't in too bad a shape, just the edges are worn."

She said, "That one was made in '33—the year'a the great storm. Your Pop-pop was selling watermelons in Pennsylvania durin' the last'a August and he like to never made it home. The water was so high everywhere, even in the forest. We lived at The Home Place then. He struggled for a few days to git back to us and fell just inside the front door from exhaustion. So I covered him right where he landed and let him sleep for a spell. The next day he told me to go look on the front seat'a the truck where I found bright red, store-bought yard-goods."

"And the next quilt, well, it's made from the only feed sacks that I got one winter. I had plenty'a cotton battin' set aside, but them chickens the company brought me that year got so sick we had to destroy um all. Cause of disease, we had to lay out for a couple months. So, with no chickens we got no more feed, and, with no feed we got no more feed sacks. That was a hard year anyhow. It was in the 40's. I don't remember the exact year. Don't want to, I expect."

Setting aside the feedbag quilt, I lifted the last worn quilt from the shelf. "What about this one? It's, well, it's different."

"The lesson here is that you use what material you got. This is an early one I made from leftovers. I picked out scraps, all made'a the same thickness'a material, see, you can tell. That is the scrap I had on hand. Notice, they's no store-bought fillin'. In order to make do with what I had—I used those pieces quilted together for the top, and for the bottom an old muslin sheet, see," she said flipping a corner over. "And for battin' in the middle, I put frayed and badly faded material that couldn't hardly be used for anything else. Still, it is one'a the few I ever made from a single old design with no changes made to it. It's well-worn now, but take notice how the darks and lights was used to make the pattern, nearly like flyin' geese, but not quite. That bein' a good idea for many different colored scraps. As I recollect, Christmas and the New Year come and went with me workin' on this quilt."

"Oh well, as you can see, all them quilts is badly worn and quiltin' ain't done now like it was then, so they may never be repaired or even reused as battin'—beddin's got too easy to come by now. Throwin' um away was hardly ever done then, but I cain't bring myself to pitch um out now. My good quilts is on the beds, the three upstairs and mine down here."

Her stitching was streamlined to suit her straight plain patterns, patterns which were easy to piece together, easier than the ones with sharp points or rounded curves. No doubt, she liked to quilt, but she quilted out of necessity and had to work quickly. As she had said, quilts covered the many beds in her house. I realized that while some women found great pleasure in intricate pattern designs and complicated stitching, Mom-mom found her satisfaction in the colors and prints of her material rather than time consuming patterns. Using what she had, she arranged the various materials so that the color in each piece enhanced the next and so on. The result was pure genius. I had already thought of her as talented while watching her make crowsfoot and holly wreaths for Christmas, but now I was sure—*Mom-mom is a gifted artist!*

She placed the quilts back into the chifforobe and I supposed that we were ready to begin, but she was simply getting me started again. She had me choose a pattern. I considered many designs and really liked the star pattern, but realized that piecing the points of the stars exactly right might be too difficult for a first quilt and a wedding ring quilt was also tricky, so I chose the flying geese pattern and decided it would represent her and her sisters all grownup and leaving their parent's home for homes of their own.

She began to instruct me with the basics by first separating the dark and light colored fabrics. "Flying geese is made from two triangled pieces sewn together to make up a square and then them squares is sewn together for to make the geese pattern." So she had me fold some pieces into triangles and form one large square containing four squares of flying geese. "Keep in mind that the geese is the darkest material." She added, "That'll give you a fair likeness to what your finished quilt'll look like. They is many a quilt where shades make the pattern." Then, she held out a callused, farm-weary hand and patted the top of my head as she moved off the bed to finish mending Pop-pop's pants.

So, I romanced the folding while making the geese, surrounding some geese with blue for the sky, and surrounding some with green for the earth. Loving birds anyhow, I was pleased with the selection. I sat cross-legged on the bed setting aside certain cardboard pieces and began rearranging my disarrayed material into shades, turning some this way, and then that way. I became engrossed in constructing my own pattern. My quilt had begun by sitting on my Grandmother's bed, using scraps that had come from my ancestors, and had been started with Mom-mom's guidance, and under Mary's intent gaze. Suddenly I realized—my quilt already has a history and I haven't needled the first stitch. And then I understood—*Every quilt made by hand has a story:*

> *Each quilt is a tapestry of events—Where the material had come from, whether given, or ancestor's scraps; What pattern had been chosen, whether flying geese, log cabin, Jacob's ladder, or a new creation; The reason it had been made, for wedding, birth, or need; Whose hands had helped design and sew the stiches, family or friends; Which songs had been sung, popular tunes or hymns, war songs or ballads; Who told stories and which ones, the harvesting for the year or maybe tales about the men out coon hunting; Where the quilt was made, in Church, one home, or separate homes to be pieced later; Who had slept under each quilt, or bore children, or were born, or lay in sickness and lived or died; Who had cleaned and repaired the heirloom—a string of events that create a history for every quilt.*

Now, I could see that she had planned for me to examine the old quilts and go through materials and pattern pieces in order to imagine one of my own choosing. I also knew that I was just as interested in deciding my own quilt as she was in seeing what my choice would reveal. Maybe later she will help me cut my first few pieces and lay her mending aside once again.

Finished with the sequence of colors, I began to ponder a new arrangement of geese, at least one I had not seen. *Maybe for a first try, I'll send the geese flying around the edges of the quilt in straight lines. A circle of flying geese will be better, but,* I mused, *that might not even be possible. I'll make my own new pattern that, in a few years, will become an heirloom itself. Perhaps by spring, when the weather gets warm enough to bicycle up and down the road again, I will have a quilt of my own design well under way. I know my ancestors must have made changes to some of the oldest quilts. So for the next couple months, before the planting of crops, before that first season of the year begins again, I have weekends and snow days to stitch, listen to records, and stitch some more.* Suddenly, I knew the excitement I had felt during the couple hours of going over quilts with Mom-mom, would last. I decided that quilting was one art that I would practice, even into old age and hoped that my sight would stay with me. This time, when I raised my eyes to Mary—I winked. I'm sure she winked back!

Alligator skin pattern on tin covering Eva Townsend Pusey's humpback trunk that was her grandmother's. Eva kept the history book of the McGrath family inside. That book was compiled by Minnie Murrell McGrath, January 1950. Mary McGrath who married James Edward Denston in 1870 were Eva's grandparents and parents of her mother Alice Edward Denston who married Harvey W. Townsend.

Ancestor Mary (A photo copy by author of a framed portrait of Ancestor Mary believed to have been taken in 1909.)

Eva Pusey's National Two Spool Treadle Sewing Machine was bought on August 16, 1927. The machine is unique in that a spool of thread like the one atop the machine is used for the bobbin as well - two spools. When the spool atop the machine ran out of thread, so did the spool used for a bobbin. No winding of a bobbin was necessary. It was on this machine that she began to piece quilts together (those quilts not hand pieced) and sew her dresses and some clothing for the family as well.

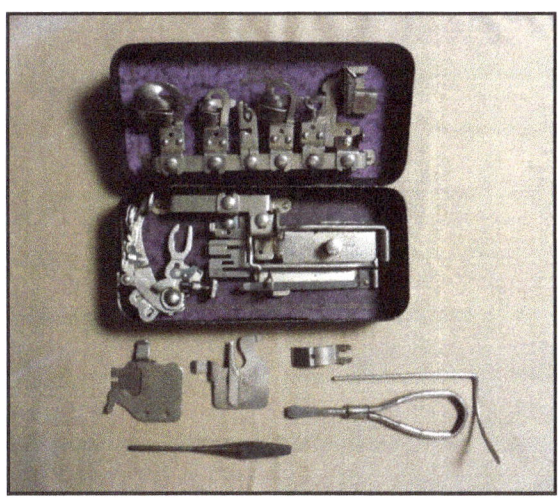

Greist Attachments she bought after purchasing her National Two Spool sewing machine.

Sierra Bloom standing in front of a persimmon tree and wearing a feedbag dress and bonnet made by Eva Townsend Pusey, Sierra's great-great-grandmother.

Bodice (showing scalloped neckline) of Feedbag dress made by Eva Pusey. The dress had a side opening where snaps or a zipper would be sewn, but she had not placed them due to the fraying of the material at the waistline.

Squares of Eva Pusey's Feedbag and dress materials from 1930s.

Worn quilts with edges gone made by Eva Pusey or one of her ancestors. When making quilts, she used the scraps she had saved and occasionally added new material in the design. The design above is Log Cabin and the one below is the Nine Patch.

Quilts designed, cut, and pieced by the author displayed along a lattice fence. Wild violets are in the foreground.

Log Cabin corners, striped quilt designed, cut, and pieced by the author and hand quilted by the late Mary Hostetler, Snow Hill, MD.

A variation of a Lone Star quilt designed, cut, and pieced together by author with a bold center in the circle within the star, and the four-directions in mind at the corners. Hand quilted by the late Mary Hostetler from Snow Hill, MD.

Left: Lone Star quilt outer edge design. Right: Star design used on the four squares made of green and tan triangles. In the spaces where the Lone Star and the half stars are absent, Mary Hostetler hand quilted a star. She even quilted a half-star in some other places. The border is the only place on the quilt that does not have a star in either the pattern or the quilting, but shows bows on the outer dark green and flying geese on the inner.

Made of triangles, small squares, and strips, this quilt contains Eva Pusey's feedbag material and one of her dresses, one of the author's dresses and one of her daughter's dresses, and odd pieces from Eva Pusey's scrap cardboard boxes. Square and triangle shapes are cut and placed in the Monkey Wrench pattern, but the colors are not. This quilt was designed, cut, pieced, and hand quilted in part by the author, but most of the hand quilting was stitched by the late Mary Hostetler of Snow Hill, MD.

A slight variation of Grandmother's Flower Garden Pattern, Yo-yo quilt, cut and sewn by author.

A Log-cabin with sunrise center, wall hanging, designed, cut, pieced, and hand quilted by author.

An old mustard-colored background, double wedding-ring quilt-top that is pieced, but not yet quilted. (Owned by the author).

In this pieced quilt-top made from satin-like materials of squares and triangles, many different designs can be seen largely by paying attention to color. The two main patterns are Broken Dishes and Nine Patch. (Owned by the author.)

This pale pink and white quilt-top, badly stained, appears to be the Honey Bee patern with a block center, some quilters use the Nine Patch pattern in the center. (Owned by the author.)

Quilted hanging, Shadowbox Design, cut, pieced, and quilted by author.

Hen Gladdie is inspecting an old Crazy quilt with various types of heavyweight materials and stitches. Many quilters have and will continue to use the older named stiches, but some quilters also add a tack, a variation to those classic stitches. As well, many will design their own stitches that may never be named. (Owned by the author)

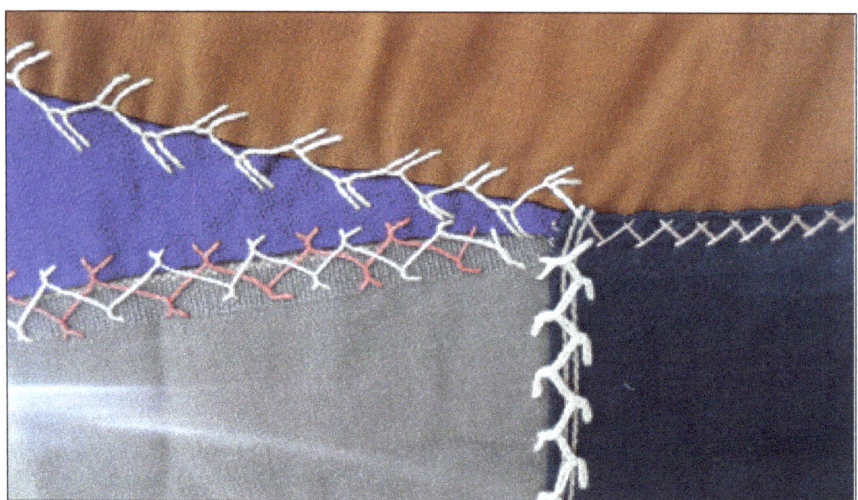

From left to right at the top is a double Feather Stitch and below is a double Herringbone using two colors. In the middle, vertically, is a single Feather Stitch using a Chain Stitch over a parallel row of either a Chain Stitch or a Darning Stitch. On the right is a single Herringbone.

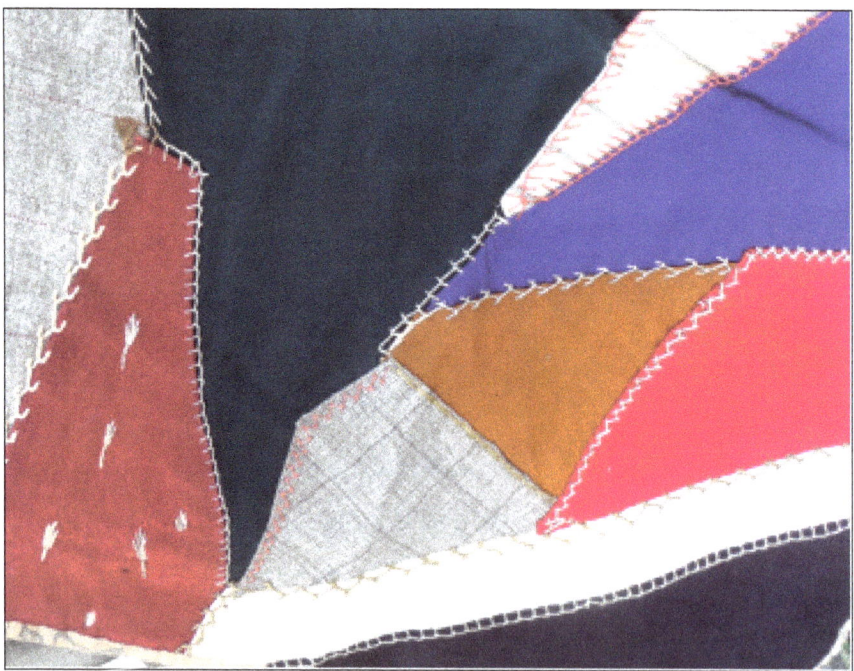

Besides the Feather and the Herringbone Stitches, the Buttonhole Stitch was used along the bottom and middle.

On the top left is a Buttonhole Stitch, then a single Herringbone; the middle has a single Feather Stitch, and on right is what some call Turkey Tracks on each side of a triple Feather Stitch.

On left top is a Lazy-Daisy Stitch with extended tack, below is double Herringbone using two colors and then a double using one color. On right side are a single and double Feather Stitch, and double Herringbone using two colors.

Once again, shown here are the Lazy-Daisy, Feather and Herringbone Stitches, neatly done.

The large Lazy-Daisy Stitches seem to be holding the purple, black and gray material together and are accented by Herringbone and Chain Stitches with a double Buttonhole Stitch on bottom left. On top right, the dots are Satin Stitches.

Here, using white on purple, the triple Feather Stitch shows just how expressive stitching can become when using the right colors.

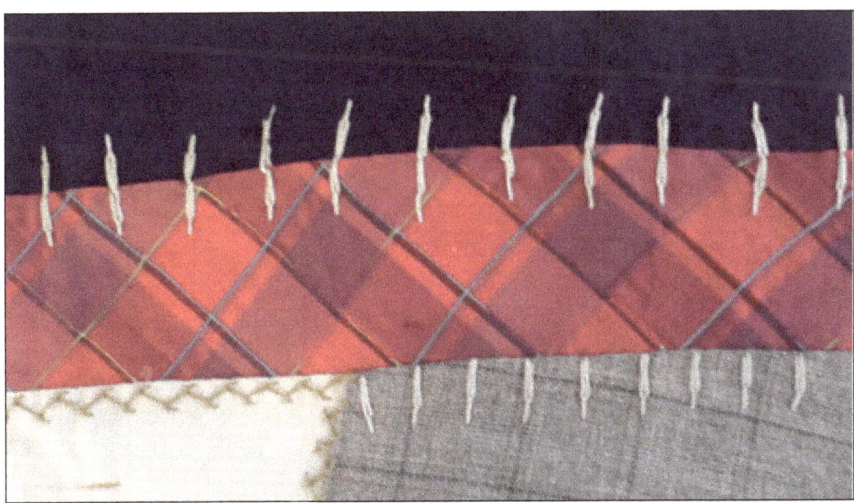

In this close-up of the single and double Lazy-Daisy Stitch, one appears to hold the material together while the other seems to appear out of the seam.

A snow storm with wood yet to be split.

Un-chopped wood frozen to the ground in winter.

Bluebird in winter.

Family portrait taken about 1922. Eva Townsend Pusey, Harvey T. Pusey, and their children to date, Welton Pusey and older child Orville Pusey.

Epilogue

Looking back at my grandparents, Harvey T. and Eva Townsend Pusey, it seems that their time was eked out, measured by the demands of essential daily tasks and the more laborious seasonal work, which meant food on their table and the tables of others. Witnessing their work year after year, a set pattern could be found—an enmeshing, an overlapping of seasonal work intermixed with chosen events and daily chores. They could not afford to become emotional every time a mishap occurred, but took each calamity in stride through six children and fifteen grandchildren—loving each child in their own special manner. They seemed absolutely methodical, even when they dealt with unexpected events. They were not cold; they were realistic, having worked and persevered through 20th Century diseases, world wars, and economic collapses—some of the most challenging periods ever endured in American History. Unwavering, they remained steadfast in their way of life by holding onto the survival techniques of their ancestors. Should anyone want to write an epitaph for Harvey and Eva Pusey, it might read: "They worked and then they worked. They epitomize an era of self-sufficient living that began to end with the 20th Century Industrial Revolution."

Glossary

Quotes by Bruce and I use correct English.
Quotes by Grandparents and Neighbors are as follows:
Correct English is replaced by their dialect.

- An = A
- Any = None or No
- Are = Is
- Aren't = Ain't
- By the way = By the by
- Can't = Cain't
- Because = 'cause
- Creek = Crick
- Did = Done
- Expect = S'pect (except when using "I expect...")
- Going to = Gonna
- Got to = Gotta
- Get = Git
- Have = Got, has, git, ain't
- ...ing = ...in'
- Isn't = Ain't
- Knew = Knowed
- Kept = Keeped
- Of = ...'a
- Off Of = Off'a
- Out Of = Outta
- Pretty near = Pert-near
- Saw = Seen
- Sit = Set
- Somewhere = Som'mers
- Suppose = S'pose
- Them = um (them used when necessary)
- There = They
- There are = They's (They is)
- The other = t'other
- Those = Them or um
- Were = Was
- Were not = Weren'ent (used occassionally)
- Yesterday = Yesterde'
- Young one = Young'un (occasionally "Child" is used)
- Young ones = Young'uns
- Youngest ones = Little'uns

About The Author

Ann Pusey Bloom was born and raised on the Lower Eastern Shore of MD. Armed with a camera and endless questions, Ann at the age of 11, began recording local and world history which became her passion. Those passions led to her Associate of Arts Degree in General Studies from Wor-Wic Community College, Salisbury, MD in 2001. In 2003, she was inducted into the National History Honor Society of Phi Alpha Theta, and completed a Bachelor of Arts Degree with a major in History and minor in English, Magna Cum Laude, from Salisbury University, Salisbury, MD. While obtaining her degrees, her short stories, poetry, and photographs were published in Wor-Wic's *Echoes and Visions* and her short stories were published in Salisbury University's *Mid-Atlantic Review*. Some of those published historical fictions were about 1960's rural Eastern Shore life.

While pursuing her studies, Ann researched, organized, and videoed class reunions for people who had been students in one-room schoolhouses in the Pocomoke Forest during the 1930's. She wrote articles about two of those reunions which were published in local newspapers. She also expanded her collection of audio taped interviews begun in 1979. Those subsequent interviews of the eldest residents of the Pocomoke Forest, as-well-as centenarians, included their remembrances about a variety of subjects. Those interviews are a wealth of information that will undoubtedly be used in future publications.

However, in the historical literature, *Seven Seasons*, Ann focuses on her grandparent's hard work and livelihood through her eyes as a child, seeing her Grandparents struggle to hang onto a way-of-life that was rapidly changing. As a resident of the Pocomoke Forest, she and her brother witnessed and performed various tasks on both her parents' and grandparents' farms. Ann lives near Pocomoke, MD on a small farm with her husband, Bob, and has a daughter, Elizabeth, and granddaughter, Sierra.

The author at age 12

www.ingramcontent.com/pod-product-compliance
Lightning Source LLC
Chambersburg PA
CBHW061249230426
43663CB00022B/2952